JESUS
GOSPEL

INTRODUCING ... NEW TESTAMENT

Author Acknowledgments

I offer my sincere thanks and gratitude to the faculty and staff of Cardinal Stritch University who allowed me the time and space for the writing of this project. Two other individuals warrant special thanks. This book would not have come to completion without the keen editorial eye of Jerry Ruff at Saint Mary's Press; his constant attention to detail was invaluable. Also, the assistance of Dr. James A. Kelhoffer proved invaluable. Dr. Kelhoffer spent countless hours combing through my manuscript, offering his biblical knowledge and insights to help shape the final product. Finally, and most especially, I thank my wife, Bonnie, for the patience, guidance, and wisdom she has provided for me throughout the process of writing this book.

Acknowledgments

The publisher owes a special debt of gratitude to James A. Kelhoffer, PhD, who advised throughout this project. Dr. Kelhoffer's expertise and passion both as teacher and scholar contributed immeasurably to this work. Dr. Kelhoffer holds a PhD in New Testament and Early Christian Literature from the University of Chicago and is associate professor of New Testament and Early Christian Literature at Saint Louis University.

The publisher also wishes to thank the following individuals who advised the publishing team or reviewed this work in progress:

Catriona M. K. MacLeod, PhD, College of Notre Dame of Maryland

Sheila E. McGinn, PhD, John Carroll University, Cleveland

Judith Schubert, RSM, PhD, Georgian Court University, New Jersey

Jeffrey S. Siker, PhD, Loyola Marymount University, California

JESUS IN THE GOSPELS AND ACTS

INTRODUCING THE NEW TESTAMENT

DANIEL J. SCHOLZ

SAINT MARY'S PRESS®

The publishing team included Leslie M. Ortiz, acquiring editor; John Vitek, director of college publishing; Jerry Ruff, editorial director; and James Kelhoffer, consulting editor; prepress and manufacturing coordinated by the production departments of Saint Mary's Press.

Cover image royalty free from Shutterstock

Printed in the United States of America

7008

ISBN 978-0-88489-955-6

Library of Congress Cataloging-in-Publication Data

Scholz, Daniel J.
  Introducing the New Testament : Jesus in the Gospels and Acts / Daniel J. Scholz.
    p. cm.
  ISBN 978-0-88489-955-6 (pbk)
1. Bible. N.T. Gospels—Textbooks. 2. Bible. N.T. Acts—Textbooks. I. Title.
  BS2556.S36 2009
  226'.061—dc22

2008042318

Contents

Instructor's Preface

Teaching about Jesus and the Gospels presents a variety of challenges for today's college professor. Typically, classes are religiously diverse: student profiles include the biblically literate and illiterate, the "churched" and "unchurched." Classes as a whole are neither historically minded nor easily impressed. Some students are budding religious studies or theology majors, whereas others are simply fulfilling a degree requirement. Our challenge is to get this motley mix to make sense of Jesus and the New Testament Gospels.

Introducing the New Testament: Jesus in the Gospels and Acts is intended for the "average" student attending a college or university today. It assumes that Jesus and the Gospels can engage readers' curiosity and inform their worldview.

This book also assumes that you, as professor, have one term to cover the New Testament Gospels, Acts, and a handful of other early Christian gospels, as well as the historical Jesus. For this reason, chapters are modest in length and information is organized for ease of readability and review. As an instructor, you will find this book affords ample time to focus on primary sources—the Scriptures and other texts—and to assess as you proceed. There is also breathing room for other materials you may wish to use to supplement the core text.

Introducing the New Testament does not supplant the Gospels but complements them, offering literary, historical, and theological insights that can help readers make sense of the biblical text under study.

In addition to the organization of the text, the charts, maps, sidebars, and summaries offer the visual variety and graphic support essential to visual learners. The layout conveys the hierarchy and types of information, calling out core concepts and supplemental information.

Each chapter concludes with questions for review and theological reflection. An annotated bibliography at the end of each chapter provides recommendations for further reading or a starting point for writing a class paper. Recommendations include a range of authors who represent some of the best in biblical scholarship.

For instructors, chapter notes are provided with information about the academic approach used and sources consulted in compiling each chapter. More advanced students may also be interested in these notes.

You will not agree with everything I present in each chapter. This is both unavoidable and preferred. Such areas of disagreement can be teachable moments for students. Students should be exposed to the complexity of current biblical studies, the intricacies of our competing positions, and the collegiality of our discipline.

Furthermore, Jesus and Gospel studies have become increasingly compartmentalized. That is to say, most of us tend to specialize in one area of New Testament studies (such as the historical Jesus, Luke-Acts, extracanonical gospels, and so on). Within each of these specialized areas of study, new and exciting insights are being developed at a remarkable pace. When and where appropriate, the latest research and some of the more significant breakthroughs are presented.

This book concludes with a chapter on the early Christian gospels outside of the canonized Christian Scriptures. Many students are aware of these extracanonical gospels (for example, the gospels of *Thomas* and *Judas*), and so it is appropriate to consider them here in their proper historical and theological contexts.

Introduction

Studying Jesus and the Gospels

This book focuses on the central figure of the Christian Scriptures: Jesus. Arguably, no other figure in history has had more influence in shaping many of the religious and cultural norms in the world today. Whether you belong to a specific faith tradition or none at all, possessing a working knowledge of Jesus and the Gospels is important for religious, historical, and cultural literacy. In the Christian Scriptures, the four Gospels of Matthew, Mark, Luke, and John are the primary sources that inform us about Jesus. Other sources close to these Gospels (for example, the Acts of the Apostles, writings of the early Church fathers, and second-century extracanonical gospels) augment them.

Before we begin our study, three points must be stressed about Jesus and the Gospels. First, Jesus of Nazareth was a first-century *Jew* of the ancient Mediterranean world; therefore, any understanding of the historical Jesus must be grounded in situating him within his Jewish social, political, and religious environment. Second, the Hebrew Scriptures, especially the prophetic books, heavily influenced the authors of the four Gospels and Acts; thus, a working knowledge of the entire Bible, as well as of the types of Judaism that existed in Jesus' time, will help make sense of Jesus and the Gospels. Third, the Gospels and Acts were written by first-century authors who believed that Jesus was the Jewish Messiah and Son of God. The four Gospels and Acts are, in fact, a complex interweaving of history, literature, and theology that is not easily disentangled. Separate books could be written on each of these areas. They are highlighted here because much of the content and structure of this book reflects these realities.

For Christians, the Bible divides into two parts: the first testament, also called the Hebrew Scriptures or Old Testament; and the second testament, also called the Christian Scriptures or New Testament. We will use the New Testament in our discussion here. The writers of the New Testament had both a literary and a theological dependency on the Hebrew Scriptures, as they proclaimed their belief in Jesus as the Jewish Messiah and the Son of God. Nowhere is this more evident than in the four Gospels of Matthew, Mark, Luke, and John, which narrate the life of Jesus. Jesus is the central figure in the Christian Scriptures, but the Gospel evangelists relied heavily on the Hebrew Scriptures as they shaped and framed the story of Jesus.

While the New Testament authors relied on the texts and theology of the Hebrew Scriptures to support their faith-claims about Jesus, they also employed a new literary form (that is, the gospel form) to tell the story of Jesus. There are no gospels in the Hebrew Scriptures.

What then are these four Gospels on a literary level? Three of the four Gospels (Matthew, Mark, and John) tell us about the life and death of Jesus. In this sense, the Gospels can be broadly described as ancient biographies, because they essentially provide a written account of a person's life. Many scholars argue that the Gospels are in fact a subtype of an ancient Greco-Roman biography, with a unique focus on Jesus. Yet the claim of the Gospels (for example, Jesus as Son of God and Jewish Messiah) and the mixing of various subgenres (for example, miracle stories, parables, genealogies, and passion narratives) into an overarching genre (biography), likely pushed the Gospels beyond the typical ancient Greco-Roman biographies, which neither made such claims nor mixed genres.

The word *ancient* is stressed with the Gospels because unlike modern biographies that rely heavily on reporting objective facts and offer a context for the information presented, the Gospels provide modest objectivity and selective contextualization. The authors of the Gospels have an agenda: they are trying to convince their audience of what they *believe* about the life and death of Jesus. Often, the Gospel writers assume the audience has the necessary background and information to make sense of the details they offer. At times, this assumption includes knowledge of and familiarity with the Hebrew Scriptures, as well as certain other sources, both oral and written.

Again, this is not to suggest that the Gospels and Acts are utterly subjective or that they provide no context at all. It is an objective fact, for example, that Jesus was a Jew and that he was executed by crucifixion. And the Gospel writers do provide some context for the life of Jesus, including events and figures of his day (see Luke 2:1–2; 3:1–2), as well as events and figures from the Hebrew Scriptures (see the genealogies of Matt 1:1–18 and Luke 3:23–38). However, most of the work involved in sorting through issues of objectivity and contextualization belongs to the modern reader of the Gospels and contemporary and evolving scholarship.

What else do the Christian Scriptures contain in addition to the four Gospels? There are twenty-seven "books" in the Christian Scriptures. Twenty of these books are actually letters; these are attributed to the earliest followers of Jesus: Paul, James, Peter, John, and Jude. There are also the Letter to Hebrews, which is actually a sermon by an anonymous author; the Acts of the Apostles (part 2 of the Gospel of Luke); and the book of Revelation.

The order of the twenty-seven books in the Christian Scriptures follows the sequence of events beginning with the life of Jesus and ending with the *eschaton* (the end of the age). The chart on page 6 shows the order of the books and the events they narrate.

Just as the four Gospels are a type of ancient biography, the remaining books of the Christian Scriptures are ancient forms of letters, sermons (Hebrews), history (Acts), and apocalyptic writing (book of Revelation). The subject of Jesus and the beliefs of his earliest followers are evident throughout each of these books. Like the Gospels, all of them are complex tapestries woven from the beliefs of the authors, the theology of the Hebrew Scriptures, and the literary forms of the ancient Mediterranean world.

Introducing the New Testament: Jesus in the Gospels and Acts addresses some of the contextual and background information needed to make sense of Jesus of Nazareth and the four Gospels. Chapter 1, "Understanding the World of Jesus and Interpreting the Gospels," bridges the span between the ancient Mediterranean and the twenty-first-century Western (U.S.) world. A distance not only of time (two thousand years) but also of culture (social, political, and

Sequence of events	Order of the 27 books
The life of Jesus	Matthew Mark Luke John
The story of the early Church	Acts of the Apostles
The letters of Paul, the Apostle to the Gentiles (from longest to shortest)	Romans 1 Corinthians 2 Corinthians Galatians Ephesians Philippians Colossians 1 Thessalonians 2 Thessalonians 1 Timothy 2 Timothy Titus Philemon
A sermon	Hebrews (anonymous author)
The letters of other apostolic figures	James 1 Peter 2 Peter 1 John 2 John 3 John Jude
The story of the age to come	Book of Revelation

religious) must be overcome if we are to understand Jesus and the Gospels. Chapter 1 provides a lens through which to view Jesus and read the Gospel narratives. It also introduces some modern methods for interpreting the Gospels. Chapters 2–6 take up the Gospels of

Mark, Matthew, Luke, John, and Acts. The Gospel of Luke and the Acts of the Apostles are included as back-to-back chapters because nearly all scholars are convinced that Luke and Acts were written by the same author and that these two books have a coherent, consistent literary and theological design that is best understood when read as one narrative. These chapters focus on the relevant historical, theological, and literary issues at play in each of the Gospels and Acts.

The order of the chapters, beginning with Mark and ending with John, follows what most scholars think is the chronological order in which the Gospels were written:

Mark:	about 65–70 CE
Matthew:	about 80–85 CE
Luke-Acts:	about 85–90 CE
John:	about 90–100 CE

We use the term *about* above because scholars are not certain as to the exact dates the Gospels were written. It is, however, their near-unanimous opinion that Mark was written first and that both Matthew and Luke relied heavily on Mark in producing their own Gospels. To begin with Mark, then, makes sense.

Chapter 7, "The Historical Jesus," has a twofold aim: to discuss scholarly attempts to discover the historical Jesus and to offer a sketch of the historical Jesus based on contemporary research. Chapter 8, "The Other Early Christian Gospels," is included because these writings reflect a developing tradition that reached back to the era of the Christian Scriptures. Gospels such as Thomas, Mary, and Philip warrant our attention because these writings give us a bigger picture of the Christian beliefs and understandings of Jesus well into the second and third centuries. Having some background on these extracanonical gospels can also help us better understand the canonical Gospels of Matthew, Mark, Luke, John, and Acts.

Understanding the World of Jesus and Interpreting the Gospels

Introduction

The aim of this chapter is twofold: to provide a lens through which to view the world of Jesus and to introduce some of the methods scholars use to interpret the New Testament Gospels. This dual focus will create a fuller picture of the Gospel narratives as they were read at the time of Jesus and as we understand them today.

Anachronism and Ethnocentrism

As we enter the world of Jesus and consider various methods for interpreting the Gospels, we should be wary of two pitfalls: *anachronism* and *ethnocentrism*.[1] Anachronism literally means a chronological misplacing of a person or thing. With respect to Jesus and the Gospels, anachronism occurs when we project our twenty-first-century time and culture onto the Mediterranean world of Jesus and the Gospel authors. Ethnocentrism means perceiving something with the attitude that one's own group is superior. Relative to the Gospels, we are guilty of ethnocentrism when we impose our cultural norms and values onto the cultural norms and values of Jesus and his contemporaries. Anachronism and ethnocentrism skew and distort understanding.[2]

Overcoming the Distance between Us and Them

To be aware of anachronism and ethnocentrism is to recognize that a tremendous distance must be traveled to understand Jesus and the Gospels. The distance is not simply one of time but also of culture: a social, political, and religious distance.[3] The ancient Mediterranean world in which the Gospel authors lived bears little resemblance to our world in the twenty-first century. We have to conceive of these authors on their terms, because in creating the Gospels, they were not thinking of us on our terms.[4] Jesus' call of Levi illustrates the distance we need to travel.

The call of Levi is preserved by three Gospel writers: Matthew 9:9–14, Mark 2:14–17, and Luke 5:27–32 (see sidebar). To answer our twenty-first-century question, "Why did the Gospel writers consider the call of Levi significant?" we must understand the perspective of first-century Jewish culture.

The Jewish social norms of Jesus' day left the call of Levi nothing short of scandalous. As a tax collector, Levi belonged to a profession despised by most Jews, who saw tax collectors as collaborators in their oppression by the Romans and the Jewish ruling elites. The scandal centers on Jesus' eating and drinking with Levi and his friends, sharing table fellowship with them. In Jewish culture, who you reclined at table with was directly tied to your identity and to the identity of your kinship group. Respectable Jews would have avoided table fellowship with a tax collector. In this story, Jesus not only eats with Levi he also invites him to "follow" him, to join the kinship group that Jesus is forming with his public ministry. Many Jews would have been appalled by such a deliberate

The Call of Levi

After this [Jesus] went out and saw a tax collector named Levi sitting at the customs post. He said to him, "Follow me." And leaving everything behind, he got up and followed him. Then Levi gave a great banquet for him in his house, and a large crowd of tax collectors and others were at the table with them. The Pharisees and their scribes complained to his disciples, saying, "Why do you eat and drink with the tax collectors and sinners?" Jesus said to them in reply, "Those who are healthy do not need a physician, but the sick do. I have not come to call the righteous to repentance but sinners." —Luke 5:27–32 invitation from Jesus. This is a likely explanation for why the call of Levi was remembered and preserved by Jesus' followers. Knowing the social stigma associated with tax collectors, the social norm of sharing meals with your kin, and the personal identification with your kinship group helps modern readers of the Gospels better appreciate the radically inclusive nature of Jesus' invitation to discipleship—a core meaning of this story whenever and from whatever perspective a reader might encounter it.

Part 1: Understanding the World of Jesus

So what kind of world did Jesus live in? The Hebrew Scriptures that predate Jesus provide us with some valuable clues. But before we consider the development of Israel as told in the Hebrew Bible, let us first consider a few precautions.

The Hebrew Scriptures and the World of Jesus

We must be careful when speaking of Jewish *biblical history*, because much of that "history" is unverifiable by evidence outside the pages of the Hebrew Scriptures. Although there is a general consensus on many of the events reported in the Hebrew Scriptures (for example, the united monarchy began about 1020 BCE), the cycle of stories found in Genesis 1–11 (creation, Adam and Eve, Noah and the ark, the Tower of Babel) comprise a notable exception. Historians do not attempt to date these stories, which begin the Hebrew Scriptures; Genesis 1–11 remain a "prehistory" due to the mythological nature of the texts.

House of David

In 1993 and 1994, biblical archeologists discovered fragments of a stele (a stone slab) at Tel Dan, a mound in northern Israel where a city once stood. The fragments appear to contain the Hebrew letters for "house of David."

As is often the case with finds such as these, questions have been raised about whether the inscription is authentic or a forgery. If authentic, the discovery of the Tel Dan stele is significant because it offers evidence of a figure recorded in biblical history.

According to the Hebrew Scriptures, David ruled as the King of Israel for about forty years. Most historians date King David's reign from about 1000 to 961 BCE.

Archeological discoveries have helped verify some events narrated in the Hebrew Scriptures. Even though evidence exists that supports the existence of King David (see sidebar page 11, "House of David"), this is not to say that beginning with King David and the monarchy (about 1000 BCE) all of the events and people in the Hebrew Scriptures are verifiable by external evidence. In fact, most of the people and events in the narrative before and after 1000 BCE await external confirmation. Furthermore, not everything presented in the Hebrew Scriptures can be externally confirmed. For example, the story of the Nephilim (Genesis 6:1–4) is more literary in nature than factually real.

Questions regarding how the Hebrew Scriptures shaped Jesus and the world of first-century Jews can be addressed independently of questions regarding the Scriptures' historical accuracy. What is more certain than the historicity of the people and events of the Hebrew Scriptures is the influence of the *storyline* of the Hebrew Scriptures, the narration of Jewish biblical history, on Jesus, his fellow Jews, and the Gospel writers. What follows, then, is a brief overview of certain narratives and themes in the Hebrew Scriptures.

Abraham and Moses

Taken together, the Hebrew Bible presents a nearly two-thousand-year narrative history prior to the time of Jesus and the Gospels. According to the story-line of the Hebrew Scriptures, the

Changing Names: The Hebrews, the Israelites, and the Jews

HEBREWS: The Semitic tribal people who originated about four thousand years ago and followed the leadership of patriarchs including Abraham, Isaac, and Jacob were first known as the Hebrews.

ISRAELITES: After the Hebrews were freed from Egyptian slavery under the leadership of Moses, they founded the nation of Israel. With a newfound national identity, the Hebrews became known as the Israelites.

JEWS: After the Israelites' release from exile in Babylon (587–538 BCE), it is said that only the descendents of the tribe of Judah (that is, the Judeans, or Jews) survived. Thus, the postexilic Israelites became commonly referred to as Jews.

The people of the first-century Jewish world would have understood any of these three names as a legitimate reference to themselves. See, for example, how Paul describes himself in Philippians 3:5–6.

Jewish people transitioned from a tribal people known as the Hebrews to founders and citizens of a nation called Israel to, after a period of exile in Babylon, a people called the Jews. The politics and religion described in these three periods differ dramatically. What is consistent in the storyline of the Hebrew Scriptures, however, is the Israelites' understanding of themselves—historically and culturally—as a people defined by their relationship with God. This relationship formed Israel's identity as a people and as a nation.

From their origins as a nomadic tribal people (families or clans grouped and traveling together), the Hebrews were *elected* by God to be God's people. According to the book of Genesis, Abraham, a chieftain from a tribe of people in Babylonia, entered into a covenant with YHWH. YHWH offered to bless Abraham with land and descendents if Abraham agreed that his tribe would be God's people. This covenant was sealed by a "mark in the flesh" (circumcision of males). It was the mark of

> ## God's Name
>
> Out of respect for Jews who do not pronounce the name of God (*Yahweh*), it is common to use the tetragrammation (YHWH) or the alternative vocalization of the name (*Adonai*).

circumcision that confirmed this tribe's identity as YHWH's people. Under Abraham and the mark of circumcision, the tribal members came to be known as the Hebrew people. In the book of Genesis, it is clear that YHWH's election of Abraham and the mark of circumcision had political and religious ramifications. Circumcision was both an outward religious sign of fidelity and a statement of political allegiance to YHWH.

The book of Exodus tells of YHWH's call of Moses to lead his people out of Egyptian slavery and form them into the nation of Israel. With Moses, YHWH established a new covenant, a binding relationship, not just with one man (Abraham) but with an entire nation (Israel), centered on the Law (the Torah, or "teaching," "instruction") that Moses received from YHWH on Mount Sinai (see Exodus 20–23). While other cultures at that time lived by similar codes, Israel's understanding and practice of the Law helped Israel define itself. For Israel, the Law was more than a code of conduct, the Torah (Genesis, Exodus, Leviticus, Numbers, and Deuteronomy) also recounted the stories of Israel's ancestors such as Abraham and Sarah, Joseph and his brothers, and the Israelites' forty years of wandering in the desert. Also integral to living the Law for Israel was the practice of offering sacrifice to God, including animal sacrifice, as a means of maintaining a covenantal relationship with YHWH. Following the Law would become the founding doctrine that defined Israel's national identity.

Saul, David, and Solomon

Israel indeed became a nation in the ancient Near East, building itself over time into a united monarchy under the leadership of three kings: Saul, David, and Solomon. The books of 1 and 2 Samuel, 1 and 2 Kings, and 1 and 2 Chronicles narrate the events leading to the creation, successes, and failures of this monarchy. These six books are by no means "objective" history in the modern sense of the word. Their final written form came together centuries after the events they are reporting, with historical hindsight and often with an agenda— sometimes favorable, other times not—regarding the monarchy.

Subsequent generations of Jews would look back to the period of David's kingship as Israel's "golden age." During the monarchy period, Israel was enjoying the fruits of the covenantal promises God made with Abraham (the Promised Land and descendents) and Moses (Israel had become a great and purportedly holy nation). Subsequently, David established Jerusalem as the capital of Israel, and David's son Solomon built Israel's Temple, the central place of worship for the nation, in Jerusalem. God also established a new covenant with David: "Your house and your kingdom shall endure forever before me; your throne shall stand firm forever" (2 Samuel 7:16).

Jesus as "Son of David"

Matthew, Mark, and Luke all tell of the story of Jesus' healing of the blind man (men): see Matthew 20:29–34, Mark 10:46–52, and Luke 18:35–43. Although many of the details differ in each Gospel, the reference to Jesus as "Son of David" is consistent. The Davidic covenant from 2 Samuel 7:8–16 tied Jesus' identity as the messiah to the house and lineage of David. The reference to Jesus as "Son of David" was the blind man's confession of faith in Jesus as the long-awaited messiah.

This covenant planted the seed for Israel's later anticipation of the messiah. Together, the city of Jerusalem, the Temple, and the Davidic covenant formed the defining characteristics of Israel's religious and political identity.

Solomon reigned as the third and last king of the united monarchy. Known for his wisdom, Solomon secured Israel as an important nation in the Near East of the tenth century BCE. After Solomon's death, the monarchy was divided between Solomon's sons, Jeroboam and Rehoboam.

A People Divided

As powerful and formative as the united monarchy was, under Solomon's sons the monarchy was unable to maintain a united vision and leadership. Consequently, Israel entered a new phase as a divided nation living under two kingdoms. The Northern Kingdom of Israel consisted of nine and one-half of the original twelve tribes, while the Southern Kingdom of Judah had the remaining two and one-half tribes. No longer a united monarchy, Israel now lived in separate "houses," the house of Israel and the house of Judah.

Roughly coinciding with the development of the nation of Israel was the rise of the prophets. In times of crisis, the prophets attempted to awaken in Israel a sense of social justice and radical monotheism, the belief that YHWH was the Lord of history

The Prophets of Israel

The Hebrew Scriptures depict the rise of prophets in response to three major crises in Israel's history: the Assyrian crisis, the Babylonian crisis, and the Persian crisis.

- The eighth-century Assyrian destruction of the Northern Kingdom of Israel led to the prophets Isaiah, Micah, Amos, and Hosea.

- The sixth-century Babylonian capture and exile of the Southern Kingdom of Judah led to the prophets Zephaniah, Habakkuk, Nahum, Obadiah, Jeremiah, Ezekiel, and Second Isaiah.

- The fifth-century Persian release and restoration of Israel led to the prophets Third Isaiah, Haggai, Zechariah, Joel, Malachi, and Jonah.

and the universe. The prophets taught Israel that YHWH alone is their God (see Deuteronomy 6:4–9, later embraced as the heart of the Mosaic Law). The prophets envisioned an Israelite people whose strong sense of social justice should be combined with its belief in monotheism.

At the time of the first crisis, the house of Israel and the house of Judah were unwilling to live by the standards set by the Torah, according to the Hebrew Scriptures. The people of Israel lost sight of their singular allegiance to their God of history and the universe and did not heed the prophetic warnings of impending exile. Consequently, the Northern Kingdom of Israel was captured, destroyed, and exiled by the Assyrian Empire. Roughly two hundred years later, beginning in 597 BCE, the Babylonian Empire captured and destroyed the Southern Kingdom of Judah. The exile in Babylon (597–538 BCE) marked some of the darkest days in Israel's history. Stripped of the Promised Land, with Jerusalem and the Temple in ruins, what little remained of the united monarchy of the twelve tribes of Israel was now forced into exile.

It was not until the rise of the Persian Empire in the sixth century BCE that the captive and exiled Israelites in Babylon saw hope for a new day. King Cyrus of Persia destroyed the Babylonian Empire and released the Israelites from captivity and exile. This, along with the prophetic visions in Ezekiel and Isaiah, breathed new life into the exiled Israelites. With the Babylonians destroyed and the Persians now in power, King Cyrus of Persia allowed the exiles to return to their Promised Land and begin rebuilding their city of Jerusalem and their Temple. Some of the exiles went back to the Promised Land (Judea), while others dispersed outside the regions of the Promised Land. The latter became known as the *Diaspora*, literally, the "scattering" of Jewish communities throughout the Greco-Roman world.

Period of Rebuilding

Israel now entered another phase of its history, a period of rebuilding. The process of restoring the ravaged ancestral land and rebuilding the destroyed Temple was instrumental in the formation of the political and religious identity of the community of Israel, now called the Jews. Ezra and Nehemiah led the small postexilic community in the restoration of Israel. The priest Ezra refocused the community on fidelity to the Torah, which most likely reached its final written form during this period. With the support of the prophets Haggai and Zechariah, Ezra led the community in religious reform. Nehemiah oversaw the rebuilding of the walls of Jerusalem and the instituting of administrative reforms that assured the post-exilic community its political and economic survival. The rebuilding of Jerusalem's Temple in 515 BCE proved crucial, as it once again became the center of the religious life of the Jews in Judea and surrounding lands.

According to the Hebrew Scriptures, it was a history of election and covenant combined with a growing awareness of God's fidelity to his chosen people in Israel that preceded and shaped the world of Jesus and the Gospel writers. The awareness of God's fidelity, however, was matched by a growing recognition of Israel's infidelity and failure to keep God's covenant. We turn next to the social, political, and religious realities of Jesus' day.

Overcoming Our Social Distance

In order to grasp the New Testament, we need to travel a considerable social, political, and religious distance and examine the ancient Mediterranean world from which it emerged. We begin with the social distance.

In recent decades, scholars studying the New Testament from a social science perspective have found intriguing contrasts between our modern Western social norms, values, and perceptions and those of the ancient Mediterranean.[5]

Honor and Shame

All cultures have social norms and values that shape and regulate life among their members. These norms and values apply to individuals and groups and help define appropriate and inappropriate behaviors. At the time of the New Testament, people followed social norms and values different from ours. For the ancients, honor and shame were pivotal values that set the standard for all social interaction. Furthermore, God was viewed as the source and arbiter of social values and norms. Honor was both ascribed (set by one's birth) and acquired (gained through social interactions). Upholding and defending the honor of one's immediate family and larger kinship group, as well as protecting them from shame, was paramount.

Collective Identity

Closely connected to the importance of honor and shame was the ancient Mediterranean's emphasis on collective identity. For the ancients, a person's kinship group, or immediate and extended family members, formed the basis for one's sense of self. The honor and reputation of one's kinship group provided the basis for self-understanding, or identity. For modern Western people, freedom, independence, and individuality are arguably the pivotal norms and values of social interactions. For people of the ancient Mediterranean, honor, shame, and group identity were the pivotal norms and values of social interaction.

Limited Goods

The perception of resources presents another social disconnect between the people of the New Testament and us. People in the United States and many other modern Western countries enjoy unprecedented wealth and access to resources such as food, water, and land. That sense of abundance also applies to our human resources such as love, honor, and reputation. For people living in the New Testament world, however, all resources, material and human, were seen as limited. To a large degree, the ancients' perception of limited resources was based on the reality of their world: by modern standards, the vast majority of ancient people were extremely poor, with restricted access to natural resources such as land. They carried this perception of limits to human resources as well. In a social network of neighbors and kin, honor and reputation were, like land and food, carefully distributed and never hoarded. This is one reason that Jesus' call to leave family behind and follow him had enormous social, economic, and religious implications and powerfully affected one's relations with neighbors and kin.

Human resources such as honor and shame were exchanged in more informal, less easily measured ways than were material resources such as food and land. For example, the system of patron-client relationships, common in the ancient world, included both human- and material-resource exchanges: a patron could offer a client access to material resources otherwise unavailable to him or her; in exchange, the client could provide the patron with an honorable reputation in the arena of public opinion.

Purity Laws

In the tightly controlled social world of the ancient Mediterranean, purity laws, many with their roots in Old Testament Scripture, were central to the rituals that defined the Jewish sense of collective identity. Keeping the Law was considered key to keeping Jews clean (pure) in the presence of each other and in the presence of God. Jewish purity laws were intended to separate the clean from the unclean and, ultimately, the sacred from the profane, in religious ritual observances. The purity laws kept unclean Jews (such as menstruating wives and men with seminal emissions) separated from clean Jews; for example, husbands might be separated from wives until both were ritually clean. These Jewish purity laws were deeply rooted historically and psychologically in the desire to be clean in God's holy presence. At the time of Jesus, however, not all Jews agreed on how to interpret and practice the principles of purity. Such debates among Jesus' followers and critics provide an essential background for the story of Jesus' cleansing of the leper (see sidebar).

Jesus' cleansing of the leper illustrates the actual and symbolic value of purity at the time of Jesus, as well as Jesus' allegiance to and respect for his Hebrew ancestry. According to Jewish purity laws in the first century, lepers had to be separated from the community because their contagious disease made them unclean. Notice that upon healing this man of leprosy, making him "clean," Jesus tells the man to go to the priest, for it is the priest alone who determines whether the man can return to the community. When Jesus tells the man to "offer the gift prescribed by Moses," he is referring to the Hebrew Scriptures, the book of Leviticus, 14:1–9, which prescribes the procedure for "purification

> ### Jesus Cleanses a Leper
>
> When Jesus came down from the mountain, great crowds followed him. And then a leper approached, did him homage, and said, "Lord, if you wish, you can make me clean." He stretched out his hand, touched him, and said, "I will do it. Be made clean." His leprosy was cleansed immediately. Then Jesus said to him, "See that you tell no one, but go show yourself to the priest, and offer the gift that Moses prescribed; that will be proof for them."　　—Matt 8:1–4

after leprosy." In his healing ministry, Jesus clearly works within the context of Jewish purity laws.

Not only purity laws are at play in the story of Jesus cleansing a leper; principles of honor and shame are also important. The leper paid Jesus "homage" in front of the "great crowds," and the crowds bore witness to this healing (cleansing) event, thus increasing Jesus' honor and reputation. Additionally, the leper's shame and separation from the community were removed as he was made clean. The former leper could now identify himself with the "clean" collective community that he had belonged to prior to contracting this disease.

Understanding basic ancient Mediterranean social norms and values such as honor and shame, collective identity, limited goods, and purity laws gives valuable insight into the meaning and impact of Jesus' words and actions, as well as the intent of the Gospel writers. But we must also travel a great political and religious distance to appreciate the ancient Mediterranean world. To do so, let's examine some of the religious and political institutions of Jesus' time, how they evolved, and what they meant to Jesus and his contemporaries.

Overcoming Our Political and Religious Distance

The political and religious institutions and groups that Jesus encountered in his lifetime had roots reaching back centuries. Together, these institutions and groups formed the world in which Jesus lived.

The Greco-Roman and Jewish Political and Religious Landscape

Jesus lived in a territory known as Palestine, a strip of land on the eastern side of the massive Roman Empire. During Jesus' lifetime, Palestine stretched about one hundred fifty miles from north to south and sixty miles from east to west. The Mediterranean Sea formed its western shoreline, while farther inland were two smaller bodies of water, the Sea of Galilee in northern Palestine and the Dead Sea in southern Palestine. The Jordan River connected these two seas. Jesus grew up in the northern region of Palestine known as Galilee, in the small village of Nazareth.

The ancient territory of Palestine, which included Galilee, Samaria, and Judea, has a special place in Jewish history and religion. Palestine was Israel's historic Promised Land and was the territory

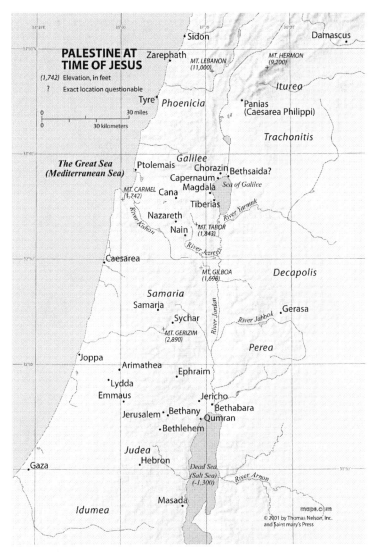

held and ruled by the great King David (beginning about 1000 BCE). While many first-century Jews lived and practiced their religion in Palestine, the territory was nonetheless under foreign control. (See table 1 for a time line of events within Judaism from the rebuilding of the Temple in Jerusalem following the Babylonian exile to its destruction by the Roman Empire.)

TABLE 1: Time Line of Events within Second Temple Judaism

Second Temple Judaism covers the years 520–515 BCE to 70 CE, from the rebuilding of the Temple in Jerusalem after the return from the Babylonian exile to the destruction of the Temple in Jerusalem by the Roman Empire.

539–332 BCE	The Persian Empire dominates
520–515 BCE	Jews return from Babylon and rebuild the Temple
336–323 BCE	Alexander the Great conquers the Persian Empire; "Hellenization" begins
circa 300–200 BCE	Ptolemaic rule of Palestine
197–168 BCE	Seleucid rule of Palestine
168–164 BCE	Maccabean Revolt
142–63 BCE	Hasmonean dynasty
63 BCE	Pompey enters Jerusalem
40–4 BCE	Herod the Great rules Palestine
20–19 BCE	The Temple renovated
circa 6 BCE	Birth of Jesus
4 BCE	Death of Herod
4 BCE–39 CE	Herod Antipas rules over Galilee
26–36 CE	Roman Prefect Pontius Pilate governs Palestine
28–30 CE	Public ministry of Jesus
66–73 CE	First Jewish Revolt against Rome
70 CE	Destruction of Jerusalem and its Temple
132–135 CE	Second Jewish Revolt against Rome

In fact, as table 1 demonstrates, foreign domination characterized the Jewish state of Palestine during the Second Temple period (515 BCE–70 CE) and beyond. But numerically speaking, at the time of Jesus most Jews lived outside of Palestine in what is called the Diaspora (or "scattering"). Jewish identity in the Diaspora remained strong, because most Jews had been living in their locations outside Palestine for generations and consequently had not experienced foreign domination.

Alexander the Great, His Successors, and the Rise of Hellenization

Alexander the Great, king of Macedonia, ruled for a relatively short time, from 336–323 BCE. However, in that time, Alexander and his armies were able to overthrow the Persian Empire that had stood for nearly two centuries and establish the Empire of Alexander the Great as the dominant force from Greece all the way east to India. The widespread dissemination of Greek language, ideas, and customs beyond Greece and Macedonia to other peoples and regions is called *Hellenization*. Even after the Roman Empire had conquered the Greeks, Hellenization remained a major influence in the eastern portions of the empire, including Palestine.

As brilliant a military and political leader as Alexander was, the united force of his empire did not last long after his untimely death (possibly from fever) at age thirty-two. The vast territory that Alexander controlled during his life splintered after his death. Large sections of Alexander's empire, however, did remain intact and under the control of his successors. Two of Alexander's successors, Ptolemy and Seleucus, emerged and established their own dynasties beginning approximately 300 BCE. Ptolemy took control of Egypt and Palestine, while Seleucus took control of Syria. For nearly a century (about 300–200 BCE), the Jews in Palestine lived peaceably under the Ptolemaic dynasty. Jewish fortunes in Palestine began to change, however, when the Seleucid kings of Syria took control of Palestine and forced out the Ptolemaic presence. The Seleucid dynasty ruled Palestine from 197–168 BCE. These were difficult years for

The Second Temple Period

The years between the rebuilding of the Temple under the Persians (515 BCE) and the destruction of the Temple by Romans during the Jewish Revolt (70 CE) are referred to as the Second Temple period. This was an important time in Jewish history. Indeed, most of the Hebrew Scriptures came together in their final form during this time.

The First Temple period was the time between Solomon's original building of the Temple in Jerusalem (about 1000 BCE) and the Babylonian destruction of the Temple in 587 BCE.

Palestinian Jews, especially when Hellenization was forced upon them under the rule of Antiochus IV Epiphanes, 175–163 BCE.

Whereas many Palestinian Jews welcomed Hellenization, others fiercely fought for their Jewish ancestral traditions and practices. Jewish resistance to Antiochus and his Hellenization policies was led by the *Hasidim* ("pious ones"). Many Hasidim, refusing to succumb to Antiochus, died for their faith. The Pharisees of Jesus' day counted themselves as descendents of the Hasidim.

Led by Mattathias and his sons, some Jews banned together to fight Antiochus and his Hellenistic Greek army in Syria. Although Mattathias died, his son, Judas Maccabeus, continued the revolt. Beginning in 168 BCE, in what was known as the Maccabean Revolt, Judas Maccabeus and his band of fighters ultimately defeated the Syrian army. In 164 BCE, Judas Maccabeus reclaimed the Temple in Jerusalem, used for some two years prior for the religious services of the occupying Seleucid soldiers, and purified it of the "abomination" of the presence of foreign gods (that is, Zeus). By 142 BCE, the Syrians had no other choice but to grant independence to the Jews. Although by no means popular with all Palestinian Jews, the Hasmonean (Maccabean) dynasty was established.

Palestinian Jews maintained their independence until 63 BCE, when the Roman general Pompey occupied Palestine and seized control of Jerusalem, later placing Syrio-Palestine under Roman control.

Jewish Revolts

During foreign occupations of Palestine, the Jewish people marshaled three major revolts, one against the Greek Seleucids and two against the Roman Empire.

Maccabean Revolt
against the Seleucids: 168–164 BCE

First Jewish Revolt
against Rome: 66–73 CE

Second Jewish Revolt
against Rome: 132–135 CE

Only the Maccabean Revolt succeeded. The two revolts against the Roman Empire resulted in the destruction of Jerusalem in 70 CE and again in 135 CE. After the second Jewish Revolt (the Bar Kokhba Revolt of 132–135 CE), Romans prohibited Jews (and Judaic Christians) from living in Palestine.

The Roman Empire and Emperors

The Roman Empire was the foreign power occupying Palestine during the life of Jesus. In the empire's early decades several men (Julius Caesar, Pompey, and Crassus) shared rule, overseen by the Roman Senate. In 40 BCE, the Senate appointed Herod the Great as king of Judea. Strong Jewish resistance to the appointment required Herod to take control of Jerusalem by force. It was not until 27 BCE that the Roman Empire had but one ruler, Octavian, named "Augustus" by the Senate. Augustus served as Rome's first emperor, 27 BCE–14 CE; he was succeeded by his stepson, Tiberius, 14–37 CE. Both Augustus and Tiberius reigned as emperors of Rome during the life of Jesus. In fact, it was Tiberius who appointed Pontius Pilate to govern Judea, 26–36 CE. It was Pilate who would eventually hand over Jesus to be crucified.

The Gospel of Luke and Acts of the Apostles mention three Roman emperors by name. Luke tells us that Caesar Augustus was emperor at the time of Jesus' birth (Luke 2:1) and that Tiberius was emperor during the public preaching of John the Baptist and the ministry of Jesus (Luke 3:1). Luke also tells us that Claudius expelled Jews from Rome because of riots (Acts 11:28–30).

Roman Emperors in the Time of Jesus and the New Testament

Augustus (Octavian)	27 BCE–14 CE
Tiberius	14–37 CE
Gaius (Caligula)	37–41 CE
Claudius	41–54 CE
Nero	54–68 CE
Galba, Ortho, and Vitellius	68–69 CE
Vespasian	69–79 CE
Titus	79–81 CE
Domitian	81–96 CE
Nerva	96–98 CE
Trajan	98–117 CE
Hadrian	117–138 CE

Only three of the emperors are mentioned by name in the New Testament (Augustus, Tiberius, and Claudius). Some scholars suspect that the two "beasts" of the land and sea from the book of Revelation 13:1–8 is a reference to the emperors Nero and Domitian.

The Herod Family

More so than the emperors of Rome, the family of Herod the Great had a direct impact on Jews in Palestine. Herod the Great ruled Palestine for nearly four decades, 40–4 BCE. After Herod's death in 4 BCE, his kingdom was divided among his three sons: Antipas, Philip, and Archelaus. It was Herod Antipas, ruler of Galilee and Perea (4 BCE–39 CE), who beheaded John the Baptist (Mark 6:14–29, Matt 14:1–12) and who, during Jesus' ministry, purportedly sought to kill Jesus (Luke 13:31–33). According to Luke, Jesus is put on trial in front of Herod Antipas (Luke 23:6–16).

Greco-Roman Cult Religion: Roman and Mystery

Jews were distinct in their belief in, and worship of, one God (monotheism). The vast majority of people living in the Roman Empire were polytheistic, worshipping many gods. Cities within the Roman Empire had their own gods and sanctuaries, where devotions to the gods took place, and cultic activity within Rome was diverse as well. Worshipping the gods of the Roman Empire did not involve a profession of creeds (a statement of beliefs) but rather a practice of rites (ceremonial acts), which were performed by those specifically trained for the tasks.

There was also the practice of the emperor cult, which held that some of the Roman emperors possessed divine qualities and were, in fact, gods themselves. How widespread this belief was among the people is not known, but it was expressed by assigning titles such as "Lord" or "Son of God" to the emperors, especially after their deaths, in recognition of their accomplishments.

Mystery cults were also integral to religious practices in the Roman Empire. Members of these mystery cults vowed to keep secret the practice of the rites performed to their god. The sharing of meals with the god and other members of the mystery cult was a common practice. In turn, the god you worshipped would offer its protection, special knowledge, and even the promise of "salvation" (life after death). The most popular mystery cults were those of Dionysus, Mithras, and Isis. Each of these gods had its own myths and rituals. Some of the rites and beliefs about these gods of the mystery cult may have influenced Christian beliefs about Jesus.

Greek Philosophy: Epicureanism, Stoicism, Cynicism

The numerous Greek philosophies, or systems of thought, formed a major feature of Hellenism. Epicureanism, stoicism, and cynicism were three of the more popular philosophies in the Roman Empire. Epicureanism, founded by Epicurus (341–270 BCE), stressed the material nature of all things, including the body and soul; thus, it held that immortality was only an illusion. According to Epicureanism, which stressed inner peace and harmony in this life, the gods of the other world have no need for a relationship with mere mortal humans. Stoicism, founded by Zeno (336–263 BCE), stressed the divine spark present in each human. Stoics believed that the universe was held together by a controlling principle called the *logos* ("word") and a vital spirit or soul called the *pneuma*. Stoics emphasized harmony between oneself and the universe and held the practice of virtue as the highest ideal. Cynicism, founded by Diogenes (404–325 BCE), emphasized living simply, according to nature. Cynics believed that a lack of possessions and a life of poverty would bring true freedom. Each of these diverse philosophical systems influenced the philosophy that underpinned the beliefs of Christians in the first-century world.

Jewish Apocalypticism

During the Hellenistic period, some Jews adopted the worldview of apocalypticism. This view was in response to the desperation and crisis experienced during this period by many Jews. Apocalypticism is rooted in the belief that reality is dualistic (fundamentally good and evil) and that everything is aligned with either good (God) or evil (sometimes identified as the Devil). When Jews applied this worldview to their history, they began to see their own age as corrupted by evil. Over time, some Jews began to hope for an age to come in which God would again control the earthly realm. Jewish apocalypticism is evident in writings emerging from the Hellenistic period, some of which are part of the Hebrew Scriptures (for example, the books of Daniel 7–12 and Zechariah 9–14), and others of which are not (for example, 1 Enoch and the Ascension of Moses). Much of what Jesus says about the coming Son of Man (for example, Mark 13:24–27, Matt 25:31–46) as well as the coming kingdom of God (for example,

Matt 13:44−50) was influenced by apocalypticism and should be read in that light. The apocalyptic worldview is fundamental to a correct understanding of the Gospels.

Jewish Groups

Although most Jews were simply "people of the land," first-century Judaism, like first-century Greco-Roman religion and philosophy, was diverse and encompassed many different groups. These various groups point to a relatively small number of educated Jews who disagreed, sometimes vehemently, with each other on matters ranging from biblical interpretation to relations with the Romans. While these groups were largely united in their monotheistic belief in YHWH as the Lord of history and the universe, a reverence and adherence to the Mosaic Law, and a devotion to the Temple in their capital city of Jerusalem, they differed over many religious and political issues that affected the practical daily living of their Jewish faith. In this sense, we can speak of diverse forms of Judaism in the ancient Mediterranean.

The vast majority of first-century Palestinian Jews belonged to the *'Am ha-'aretz* (in Hebrew, the "people of the land"), Jewish men and women who lived in the countryside of Palestine. It was to this group Jesus directed his message and public ministry.

First-Century Palestinian Jewish Groups

'Am ha-'aretz	"people of the land"
Pharisees	interpreters of the written and oral Mosaic Law
Sadducees	conservative aristocracy
Scribes	trained scholars
Essenes	isolated community
Zealots and Sicarii	revolutionaries against Roman occupiers

The Jewish groups most commonly mentioned by the Gospel writers are the Pharisees, the scribes, and to a lesser extent, the Sadducees. The Pharisees thought of themselves as the descendents of the Hasidim, a resistant movement that originated in response to the oppressive rule of Antiochus IV Epiphanes (175–163 BCE), as mentioned earlier. In the Gospels, the Pharisees are most frequently depicted in opposition to Jesus. In fact, the New Testament depiction of the Pharisees is highly stylized, stereotyped, and caricatured. What little we do know of the Pharisees is that they were primarily an organization centered on social reform through fairly strict observance and enforcement of the Mosaic Law and the oral law that evolved from its interpretation. The Pharisees survived as a group into the second century CE, growing in power and influence especially after the first Roman–Jewish War (66–73 CE). In the centuries following the second Roman–Jewish War (132–135 CE), the Pharisees evolved into rabbinic Judaism, which survives today.

The scribes were the professional copyists and secretaries for the Pharisees and other civil and religious groups. Trained in reading and writing, the Jewish scribes were from the educated class and considered scholars of the Law. Like the Pharisees, scribes are often portrayed in opposition to Jesus.

The Sadducees, like the Pharisees, were a religious sect within Judaism. Beyond that, the Sadducees shared little in common with the Pharisees. Originating in the first century BCE, the Sadducees were fewer in number than the Pharisees. The Sadducees rejected the Pharisees' "oral law," the ongoing and evolving interpretation of the written Law. In fact, the Sadducees followed only the written Torah and did not believe in a future resurrection as did the Pharisees. The Sadducees were made up largely of wealthy aristocrats, landowners who worked in cooperation with the Roman rule of Palestine and exercised extensive control over the priesthood and the Temple in Jerusalem. With the destruction of Jerusalem and the Temple in 70 CE by the Romans, the Sadducees quickly faded in influence and power. With the structures that empowered them destroyed, they did not survive beyond the first century CE.

The Essenes are not mentioned directly by Jesus or the Gospel writers; however, they were an identifiable group in first-century Palestinian Judaism. This group consisted mainly of celibate Jewish males who lived in community, where they shared a life of fasting and meditation. In anticipation of the coming messianic age, this Jewish sect separated themselves from the purity regulations and rituals practiced in the Jerusalem Temple. The Essenes originated about 140 BCE, in the period of the Maccabean Revolt, and were dispersed (or more likely slaughtered by the Romans) as a result of the first Jewish Revolt against Rome in 70 CE.

The Zealots and the Sicarii were two Jewish groups who actively, and violently, opposed Roman occupation of Palestine. The Gospel of Luke and Acts state that Simon, one of Jesus' original apostles, was a Zealot (Luke 6:15, Acts 1:13). The Zealots rallied around their "zeal" for the coming reign of God. Although present as a loose group

The Dead Sea Scrolls

The discovery of the Dead Sea Scrolls in 1947 is widely regarded as the greatest archeological find of the twentieth century. The "scrolls" of the Dead Sea were discovered in a series of 11 caves at Qumran located on the northwestern shore of the Dead Sea. Led by the "Teacher of Righteousness," the Essenes produced many writings, including the oldest copies of the Hebrew Scriptures, commentaries on the Scriptures, and their own community documents (e.g., *The Manual of Discipline*). The discovery of the Dead Sea Scrolls tells us much about this sect and its views toward other first-century Palestinian Jews.

Caves at Qumran in the West Bank, Middle East. It was in this area the Dead Sea Scrolls were found. *Inset:* Dead Sea Scroll, part of Isaiah Scroll (Isa 57:17 – 59:9).

throughout much of the first century, the Zealots cohered in response to the Jewish Revolt of 66–73 CE. The Sicarii, never directly mentioned in the Gospels, were even more radically violent than the Zealots, resorting to assassinations of Roman officials and even killing Jews who collaborated with the Romans. The Sicarii were known to kidnap officials to secure the release of fellow Sicarii from prison. Like the Zealots, the Sicarii used bloodshed to help facilitate the coming reign of God.

Jewish Institutions

First-century Palestinian Judaism was united around identifiable institutions: the city of Jerusalem, the Temple, the synagogues, and the Sanhedrin.

First-Century Palenstinian Jewish Institutions	
Jerusalem	traditionally the holiest city and spirtitual center of the Jewish people
Temple	the location of YHWH's abiding presence
Synagogue	a gathering place to read, study, and instruct in the Torah, as well as a community center for Jewish life
Sanhedrin	the supreme judicial council of the Jews

Jerusalem was the holiest city as well as the spiritual center for all Jews living in the Roman Empire, whether in Palestine or outside Palestine in the Diaspora. As Israel's capital city, Jerusalem held historical and theological significance. King David himself established Jerusalem as the capital city, and the Temple was housed there. Jerusalem and the Temple symbolized God's historic and covenantal relationship with Israel.

The Temple in Jerusalem was the center of the Jewish people's religious and political identity. It was Israel's center for sacrifice to YHWH, and sacrifice was fundamental to the Jewish worship of YHWH. Jews believed that God's holy Presence resided in the

Temple. In the Temple, the priests offered sacrifice at the altar of burnt offerings and incense at the golden altar. Numerous Palestinian and Diasporic Jews would pilgrimage to the Temple to celebrate the great annual festivals (for example, the feasts of Passover and of Unleavened Bread). Jews living in the Diaspora would try to pilgrimage to Jerusalem at least once in their lifetime. The First Temple dated back to the days of King Solomon in tenth century BCE and was destroyed by the Babylonians in sixth century BCE, only to be rebuilt and dedicated as the Second Temple in 515 BCE upon the Jews' return from Babylonian exile. Herod the Great began a massive renovation of the Temple in Jerusalem in 20–19 BCE, which was completed in 26–27 CE within the lifetime of Jesus. The Temple in Jerusalem not only provided greater financial stability for Jews (via the Temple tax) but also served as a symbol for Jews of their religious and political identity.

The synagogues (meaning "assembly" or "gathering") were part of the landscape in Palestine as well as in the Diaspora. The synagogues probably originated in the Babylonian exile (587–538 BCE) when the Israelites no longer had Jerusalem and the Temple as their center of worship and faith. The reading and teaching of the Torah took place in these gatherings. The synagogues kept the transmission and practice of the Jewish faith institutionally alive for Jews inside and outside their Palestinian homeland. Synagogues survived the Babylonian exile and became the local places of worship and faith instruction as well as the centers for the administration of daily affairs in first-century Jewish life.

Little is known about the Sanhedrin ("council"). Instituted in the third century BCE, the Sanhedrin is thought to have had the authority to rule on both religious and civil matters for the Jewish people. During his trial, Jesus is brought before the Sanhedrin in Jerusalem and condemned for blasphemy. In the Gospel narratives, we see that the Sanhedrin is composed of the Jewish religious leadership (for example, Sadducees, priests, scribes, and so on), with the High Priest of Jerusalem in charge of its deliberations.

With a better sense of the social, political, and religious realities of Second Temple Judaism, we are now prepared to take a closer look at the time of Jesus and the New Testament Gospels.

The Time of Jesus and the Gospels

The writings in the New Testament were contributed over a time span of about one hundred years. The contemporaries of Jesus himself—the Mediterranean people (mostly Jews) who saw, heard, and bore witness to Jesus of Nazareth—left us no written record of their experiences with Jesus. But this is not to suggest that their impact is not present in parts of the New Testament. In this regard it is important to realize that the ancient Mediterranean was an oral world. Very few people (perhaps 5 percent) had any practical need or ability to read and write.[6] People interacted almost exclusively with the spoken word. Thus Jesus' contemporaries passed on their experiences with Jesus orally, by word-of-mouth. This oral tradition was a major source of the written Gospels and the driving force behind the New Testament letters, including Paul and the later New Testament letter writers. The oral tradition that preceded the Gospels will be discussed in greater detail in chapter 7, "The Historical Jesus."

The first generation of Christians emerged after the death of Jesus. Most prominent among this first generation were the original disciples of Jesus. During his public ministry, Jesus amassed many disciples. Disciples were anyone who followed Jesus and accepted him as their teacher (rabbi). The terms *rabbi* and *disciple* mean "teacher" and "learner" (student), respectively. We are not certain of exactly how many disciples Jesus had. It may have been in the hundreds, perhaps even the thousands. The numbers could have easily fluctuated at various times in Jesus' ministry. Unfortunately, the vast majority of Jesus' disciples are unknown to us. The "apostles" were disciples selected and sent by Jesus to preach and cast out demons. The Gospel writers list the apostles by name, often referring to them as "the Twelve." The names of the Twelve vary from list to list (compare, for example, Mark 3:13–19 with Luke 6:14–16). Many scholars suspect that the specific number twelve refers to the twelve tribes of Israel, symbolically brought together in Jesus' public ministry. Additionally, the number twelve may have been a part of the oral tradition, with particular names filled in differently by different Gospel authors. Consequently, scholars often understand "the twelve apostles" more as a literary image than a literal number. Furthermore, other New Testament writers include Paul, Barnabas, Junia, and others as apostles beyond the Twelve.

The First Christians

Jesus' contemporaries: Scholars debate the exact dates of Jesus' birth and death. But most agree that Jesus was born during the end of the reign of Herod the Great, 40–4 BCE. We also know that Herod began restoration of the Temple in Jerusalem in 20–19 BCE, which took forty-six years to complete (John 2:20). This would place Jesus' public ministry beginning about 27–28 CE and ending 30 CE, given John's report of a three-year public ministry for Jesus. The dates of 6 BCE and 30 CE are therefore commonly associated with the birth and death of Jesus.

First generation: The death of Jesus around 30 CE and the Jewish Revolt of 66–73 CE, with the destruction of the Jewish Temple in Jerusalem in 70 CE and the fall of the Jewish city of Masada in 73 CE, are the events setting the parameters of the first generation, between 30 and 70 CE.

Second generation: The destruction of the Temple (70 CE) and the final piece of written literature in the New Testament (2 Peter, commonly dated around 125 CE) set the parameters of the second generation, approximately 70–125 CE.

It was this first generation of Christians that began the written record we know today as the New Testament. Paul's First Letter to the Thessalonians is thought to have been written about 50 CE. The thirteen letters attributed to Paul make up nearly half of the New Testament writings. Most scholars believe Paul actually wrote only seven of the thirteen letters, with the additional six attributed to the next generation of Christian letter writers. Paul's letters bear strong witness to the written record left behind by the first generation.

The majority of the books in the New Testament are written by the second generation, 70–125 CE. Here we have the four Gospels and Acts, the other New Testament letters (in addition to Paul's letters), the Letter to Hebrews, and the book of Revelation. The four Gospels and Acts were produced between 70 and 100 CE. The later letters of the New Testament (Hebrews; James; Jude; 1, 2, and 3 John; 1 and 2 Peter) were produced between the years 80 and 125 CE. And the book of Revelation was written in the final years of the first century.

The second generation found itself at a social, political, and religious crossroads. The first generation had passed. The city of Jerusalem and the Temple had been destroyed by the Roman Empire. In the generations to come, Christianity would become more and more a Gentile phenomenon. And what began with Jesus as a Jewish messianic movement would in time evolve into a separate religion.

As you can see, the New Testament writings bear witness to a span of more than one hundred years. The experiences and circumstances within this time span differed significantly. Even within the same generation, there were differences in not only circumstances but also perspectives. We better understand Jesus and the Gospels when we take into account the circumstances of those who told and composed the New Testament witness that survives to this day.

Thus far we have presented the basic narrative of the Hebrew Scriptures, as well as some of the social, political, and religious realities of the ancient Mediterranean world. We have also taken a brief look at the times of Jesus and the Gospels. In order to better understand the New Testament, we need this historical and cultural context. Next, we'll examine the methods scholars use to further discern who Jesus was and what the Gospel writers intended in telling his story and the story of the early Christian Church.

Summary of Understanding the World of Jesus

Core Concepts

- The narrative of the Hebrew Scriptures helped shape the world and viewpoint of Jesus and the Gospel writers.
- We have a vast social, political, and religious distance to travel in order to understand the world of Jesus and the Gospel writers.
- The formation of the Gospels took nearly one hundred years.

Supplemental Information

- Anachronism and ethnocentrism are two common pitfalls when reading the Gospels.
- Election, circumcision, covenant, law, and monotheism defined Jewish identity.
- Shame, honor, purity, and collective identity were important in Jesus' day.
- The widespread dissemination of Greek language, ideas, and customs is known as Hellenism.
- Jewish apocalypticism informed Jesus and the Gospel writers.

Part 2: Interpreting the Gospels

Since the nineteenth century, scholars have used a variety of methods to study Jesus and the Gospels. Before we examine several of these methods, let's look at some assumptions scholars make about the formation of the Gospels in the first century, particularly about the literary relationship among Matthew, Mark, Luke, and John.

Stages in the Formation of the Gospels

Although the chart below implies clear-cut stages in the formation of the Gospels, scholars acknowledge that these stages overlap in numerous, complex ways (for example, the oral traditions about Jesus continued well past the writing of the Gospels). Nonetheless, one of the first major assumptions scholars make about the Gospels is that they passed through stages of development. The written Gospels of 70–100 CE are heavily dependent upon the early oral teaching and preaching of the words and deeds of Jesus (the *kerygma*), 30–70 CE. And these oral traditions are rooted in, and grew from, the public ministry of Jesus from 28–30 CE.

From Oral *Kerygma* to Written Gospel

Stage 1: 28–30 CE	Begins with the public ministry (words and deeds) of Jesus
Stage 2: 30–70 CE	Begins with the formation of the oral traditions (*kerygma*) about Jesus
Stage 3: 70–100 CE	Begins with the formation of the written traditions (Gospels) about Jesus

It may seem strange that the ancient Mediterranean, driven almost entirely by oral modes of communication, would have produced any written Gospels at all. Two factors played a key role in the decision to put the oral tradition of Jesus in written form. First, the Jewish Revolt of 66–73 CE likely had a major influence on the decision to write the story of Jesus. With Jerusalem and the Temple destroyed — two of the pillars of Judaism — there was concern for the long-term stability of Judaism and by extension Christianity. Thus, the Jewish Revolt was one of the major motivations for committing the developing oral traditions about Jesus to writing. Second, with the deaths of the original disciples and eyewitnesses of Jesus and his public ministry, there would have been a desire to preserve the story of Jesus in written form, especially because Judaism was a religion already grounded in the written word of the Hebrew Scriptures.

Each of the Gospel writers wrote in Koine Greek, the common language of the people in the eastern portions of the Roman Empire in the formative years of the New Testament period. The decision to write the Gospels in Koine Greek and not, for example, in Aramaic, the native language of Jesus, or in Hebrew, the ancestral language of the Jews, reflects the setting of these authors in the Eastern Mediterranean, where Koine Greek had been the common language since the conquests of Alexander the Great. The rise of Hellenism (about 300 BCE) brought about the development of Koine Greek, although many Hellenistic philosophers continued to write in classical Greek.

The Synoptic Problem

A second major assumption about the Gospels has to do with their shared literary relationship. When the Gospel narratives are laid out side by side, the Gospels of Matthew, Mark, and Luke share much material in common. Because of this, Matthew, Mark, and Luke are often termed the *Synoptic Gospels* (*syn-optic* meaning "seen together with the same eye"). This has naturally led to the question of the literary relationship among these three Gospels, commonly called the "Synoptic Problem." The "problem" is to account for the many similarities and differences among the three Gospels.

The overlapping materials in the Synoptic Gospels fall into various categories. There is material shared by all three Gospels (*Triple Tradition*), such as the story of the call of Levi (Mark 2:13–17, Matt 9:9–13, Luke 5:27–32). There is material shared between only Matthew and Luke (*Double Tradition*), for example, the Lord's Prayer (Matt 6:9–13, Luke 11:2–4). Then there is material found only in Matthew (*Special Matthew, M*), such as the visit of the magi (Matt

2:1–12). There also is material found only in Luke (*Special Luke, L*), such as the story of the resurrected Christ appearing to two disciples on the road to Emmaus (Luke 24:13–35). The Gospel of John, finally, shares little material with the Synoptics, implying little or no literary relationship between John and the Synoptics and creating its own set of questions regarding sources.

Competing Theories, Markan Priority, and Q

Three basic "solutions" are offered to account for the literary relationship among Matthew, Mark, and Luke: the Two-Source theory, the Farrer theory, and the Griesbach theory. Central to each theory are two questions: (1) which Gospel was written first? and (2) what written sources were available to each of the Synoptic Gospel writers?

Two-Source Theory

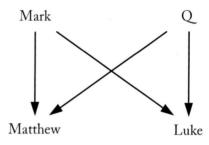

The most commonly accepted solution among scholars for solving the Synoptic Problem is called the Two-Source theory.

The Two-Source theory argues that Mark was the first written Gospel ("Markan priority") and that Matthew and Luke used Mark as one of their written sources. Furthermore, Matthew and Luke had access to another source, Q (from the German word, *quelle*, meaning "source") for the writing of their Gospels. Thus Mark and Q are the theoretical "two sources" for Matthew and Luke. Postulating Mark and Q as sources for Matthew and Luke is attractive because together these two sources could account for all the material that Matthew and Luke share in common, much of it coming from Mark, the rest from Q (about 235 total verses).

The Two-Source theory also argues that Matthew and Luke wrote independently of each other. Often associated with the Two-Source theory is M and L material; that is, both Matthew and Luke have in addition to Mark and Q their own special material (about 30 percent of Luke is L material and about 20 percent of Matthew is M material). M material (for example, Matt 2:1–12, the visit of the magi) and L material (for example, Luke 24:13–35, the road to Emmaus) are thought to be a combination of written and oral sources, as well as material from the evangelists' own hands. The inclusion of the M and L material supplements the model of the Two-Source theory as follows:

Two-Source Theory with M and L

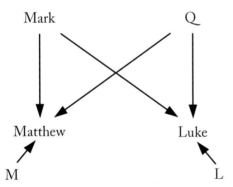

The Two-Source theory is not without its critics. Two major competing theories regarding the literary relationship among Matthew, Mark, and Luke are the Farrer theory and the Griesbach theory.

The Farrer theory maintains the Markan priority of the Two-Source theory; however, because the Farrer theory argues that Luke knows both Mark and Matthew, the need for a Q-source is, in the words of Austin Farrer, "dispensed" with.[7]

Farrer Theory

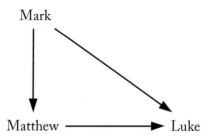

Scholars who object to the Farrer theory maintain that because Matthew and Luke use Mark so differently, it is quite difficult to see how Luke was influenced by Matthew's use of Mark. A third competing theory attempting to resolve the Synoptic Problem is the Griesbach theory, named after J. J. Griesbach in the early eighteenth century. Griesbach is credited with producing the first "synopsis," laying parallel Gospel accounts side by side for comparison. After his production of the Gospel synopsis, Griesbach offered a version of a fourth-century solution to the Synoptic Problem: namely, Matthew wrote first, then Luke edited Matthew, and finally Mark condensed both Matthew and Luke.

Greisbach Theory

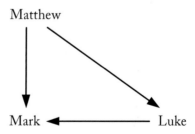

As the historical-critical methods of biblical interpretation grew throughout the nineteenth and twentieth centuries, and "Markan priority" gained solid ground, the Griesbach theory has for the most part lost support, despite William Farmer's attempts to revive it in the 1960s.[8]

Three Competing Theories on the Synoptic Gospels

One theory on the literary relationship among Matthew, Mark, and Luke is the Griesbach theory. Originated in the early eighteenth century by J. J. Griesbach (1745–1812), and revived by William Farmer in the 1960s, this theory holds that Matthew wrote first and that Mark is a conflation (blending) of Matthew and Luke. This view of "Matthean priority" dates back to the North African Church Father Augustine in the late fourth century CE.

The most widely accepted theory on the literary relationship among the Synoptic Gospels is the Two-Source theory. Originating in the early nineteenth century, this theory argues that Mark wrote first ("Markan priority") and that Matthew and Luke used Mark along with another unknown source, Q. The Two-Source theory was expanded by B. H. Streeter (1874–1937) to include M and L (material found only in the Gospels of Matthew and Luke) as additional sources for Matthew and Luke.

Recent debate about the hypothetical Q source has led to the Farrer theory. Originated by Austin Farrer (1904–1968) in an article published in 1951, "On Dispensing with Q," Farrer maintained the Markan priority, but argued that Luke knew and used the Gospel of Matthew as a source for his Gospel, thus, in effect, "dispensing" with much of what was thought to be Q. The Farrer theory has gained some scholarly support in recent years.

The majority of scholars today embrace the Two-Source theory as the most satisfactory solution to the Synoptic Problem. Furthermore, nearly all scholars support the Markan priority; that is, Mark was the first of the three written Gospels in the New Testament.

Modern Methods for Interpreting the Gospels

Modern methods for interpreting the New Testament Gospels are rooted in the nineteenth and twentieth centuries. In the wake of the eighteenth-century Age of Enlightenment and Age of Reason in Europe and America, Western culture began thinking differently about many things, including the nature of history and faith itself. The period of the Enlightenment and Reason had a profound impact on Western perceptions of reality, including of the Bible itself. It is in this context that the contemporary methodological approaches to the Gospels were first developed.

Today there exist many different methods for interpreting the Gospels. Most of these approaches tend to fall into one of three categories: *historical-critical, literary*, or *ideological.*

Historical Approaches

Methods for interpreting the Gospels that attempt to better understand the Gospels' historical development and sources are referred to as historical-critical methods. Chief among these are *source criticism, form criticism*, and *redaction criticism.*

Source critics ask the questions: what were the written and oral sources available to the Gospel writers, and in what ways did these writers use the sources for the composition of their Gospels? The three major theories attempting to solve the Synoptic Problem (what is the literary relationship among Matthew, Mark, and Luke) are examples of source criticism in action.

Whereas source critics are interested in stage three of the development of the Gospels (that is, the written traditions about Jesus), form critics focus on the oral traditions about Jesus. Form critics are less interested in the Gospels as a whole and more interested in the individual units (pericopes) and distinct literary forms that make up the Gospel narratives. The Gospels contain many different literary forms (for example, miracle stories, parables, and genealogies). Form critics seek to trace how and where these forms developed and circulated within the oral traditions that existed before the written Gospel, or among the written sources incorporated into the Gospels. One presupposition of form criticism is that early traditions about Jesus were preserved because they served a particular purpose in the *Sitz im Leben* (German for "setting in life") of the community and experiences of the early Christians. Accordingly, form critics ask the questions: what specific literary form (genre) is a given unit and in what *Sitz im Leben* was the pericope used by the original Christians (for example, in liturgical worship, baptismal preparation, preaching, and so on)?

Redaction criticism works with the written Gospels in the form we have them today. In several European languages, including German, redaction means "editing" and seeks to understand better the editorial process by which the written Gospels came together in their final form. Redaction critics build upon the theories of the source and form critics and are dependent upon their work. Redaction critics explain why a

Gospel writer uses and edits the available sources (written and oral) in the composition of his Gospel. In doing so, redaction critics can better understand the theology and worldview of the Gospel author. Whereas source and form criticism tend to regard the evangelists as passive compilers of traditional materials, redaction criticism recognizes the authors' active roles in shaping their presentations of Jesus in consideration of particular theological and pastoral concerns. A further implication of this advance in scholarship—recognizing the evangelists as authors—may be seen in literary approaches to the Gospels.

Literary Approaches

The popularity and success of redaction criticism in the twentieth century have led to continued efforts by biblical scholars to work with the Gospel narratives in the final forms we have today. Literary approaches to the Gospel are less interested in the historical-critical issues associated with the formation and oral transmission of the Gospels and instead focus exclusively on the Gospels as narratives.

Two current literary approaches to understanding the Gospels are *narrative criticism* and *reader-response criticism*. These methods have been developed in recent decades and bring a whole new set of questions to the Gospels. Narrative critics look at various features of the Gospels such as character, plot, and setting, as well as bring attention to rhetorical dimensions such as irony and symbolism. Narrative critics ask such questions as what is the role and function of the narrator of the Gospel story, and how are characters developed in the unfolding plot of the Gospel? Reader-response critics are interested in examining how readers interact with the Gospel narratives. Reader-response critics ask questions such as how is the reader being manipulated by the text, and is there a "correct" way of reading and interpreting the plot?

Ideological Approaches

Two of the major ideological approaches to the Gospels, *feminist* and *cross-cultural analyses*, examine the ideological biases and presuppositions that underlie contemporary interpretation. Unlike the historical-critical and literary approaches to the Gospels, which employ a clearly defined methodology, ideological approaches ask a different set of questions. Feminist criticism examines the Gospels in ways that seek to uncover the patriarchal bias embedded within the Gospel narratives. Cross-cultural criticism examines how people from different cultures today read and interpret the Gospels, depending on their social, political, and religious context. Cross-cultural critics ask such questions as how do African Americans tend to read the Gospel of Mark, and in what ways do Western cultures read the Gospels differently than Middle Eastern cultures?

The second part of this chapter has examined a variety of assumptions that biblical scholars employ as they examine the New Testament Gospels, as well as many of the modern methods for interpreting the Gospels. As we now move into an analysis of each of the New Testament Gospels, these scholarly assumptions and methodological approaches will help us to interpret the Gospels within their proper historical, theological, and literary contexts.

Summary of Interpreting the Gospels

Core Concepts

- The three stages of development of the New Testament Gospels were overlapping and complex.
- The "Synoptic Problem" involves addressing the similarities and differences among Matthew, Mark, and Luke.
- Three possible solutions for solving the Synoptic Problem are the Two-Source theory, the Farrer theory, and the Griesbach theory. Most scholars favor the Two-Source theory.
- Modern methods for interpreting the Gospels include historical, literary, and ideological approaches.

Supplemental Information

- The Gospels were originally written in Koine Greek, the common language in eastern portions of the Roman Empire.
- Synoptic means "seen together with the same eye."
- Most scholars today believe that Mark was the first written New Testament Gospel.
- Modern methods for interpreting the Gospels emerged in the eighteenth and nineteenth centuries.

Questions for Review

1. What are *anachronism* and *ethnocentrism* and why are they to be avoided in reading the Gospels?
2. Why is the figure of King David (circa 1000 BCE) important for understanding Hebrew Scriptures and depictions of Jesus in the New Testament Gospels?
3. What dates and events defined the first one hundred years of the New Testament period?
4. What are some examples of the social distance needed to travel between the people of the ancient Mediterranean and us, if we are to better understand the Hebrew Scriptures and the New Testament Gospels?
5. What is *Hellenism* and how did it affect the Palestinian world of Jesus?
6. Name the major Palestinian Jewish groups in the first century CE.
7. Describe how Jerusalem and the Temple have been the center of Jewish identity?
8. Explain how the formation of the New Testament Gospels occurred in stages.
9. What is the Synoptic Problem and how does the Two-Source theory address this problem?
10. What are some of the modern approaches to interpreting the Gospels?

Questions for Reflection

1. What do you think will be some of your biggest challenges in avoiding an anachronistic and ethnocentric reading of the Gospels?
2. In what ways (social, political, or religious) do you see our modern world as different from that of the ancient Mediterranean?
3. What insights do the theories addressing the Synoptic Problem offer about the formation of the Gospels of Matthew, Mark, and Luke?
4. Of the modern approaches to interpreting the New Testament Gospels, which interests you the most and why?

Recommendations for Further Reading

Goodacre, Marc. *The Synoptic Problem: A Way through the Maze.* London and New York: T & T Clark, 2001.

Goodacre challenges some of the basic assumptions that underlie many of our theories on the literary relationship between Matthew, Mark, and Luke, often termed the "Synoptic Problem." Maintaining Markan priority and arguing against the existence and necessity of Q, Goodacre presents an intriguing and viable alternative to the standard Two-Source theory that many Gospel scholars take for granted. This book is written with the undergraduate in mind, providing summaries, charts, and tables that make the "maze" of the Synoptic Problem manageable for the beginning student.

Johnson, Sarah Iles, ed. *Religions of the Ancient World: A Guide.* Cambridge, Mass.: Harvard, 2004.

This book offers a wide range of topics and scholarly perspectives on religions in the ancient world. Presented in three major categories—encountering ancient religions, histories behind various ancient religions, and key topics—this book covers an enormous amount of ground and material. Under the category of encountering ancient religions, topics such as monotheism, polytheism, and magic are covered. Under the category of histories, ancient religions, including those found in Egypt, Iran, Greece, and early Christianity generally, are covered. Key topics include sacred time and space, rites of passage, and religion and politics.

Malina, Bruce J. *The New Testament World: Insights from Cultural Anthropology.* 3d ed. Louisville, Ky.: Westminster John Knox Press, 2001.

Malina provides students with a solid and readable introduction to the cultural context of the ancient Mediterranean in the New Testament period. Malina provides helpful categories for students (for example, honor and shame, kinship and marriage, clean and unclean) that can be used to gain insights into the cultures and peoples who occupied the world of the New Testament period. This is a widely read book by those taking a social-scientific approach to understanding the New Testament.

Roetzel, Calvin J. *The World That Shaped the New Testament.* Rev. ed. Louisville, Ky.: Westminster John Knox Press, 2002.

An engaging treatment of the political, social, institutional, economic, and religious issues of the Second Temple period (515 BCE–70 CE) that gave rise to the New Testament. This is an excellent resource for beginning students who wish to more fully understand the forces that shaped the writings of the New Testament.

Tuckett, Christopher. *Reading the New Testament: Methods of Interpretation.* Philadelphia: Fortress, 1987.

This is one of the best recent books introducing students to various historical-critical approaches to studying the New Testament. Using primarily examples from the Gospels, Tuckett presents many of the basic aims of these methods and introduces newer methods for interpreting the Gospels that emerged in the last decades of the twentieth century (for example, structuralism and canonical criticism).

Endnotes

1 Bruce J. Malina, *The New Testament World: Insights from Cultural Anthropology* (3d ed.; Louisville, Ky.: Westminster John Knox, 2001), 10: "(*Ethnocentrism*) entails imposing your own cultural interpretations of persons, things, and events on other people. When applied to history, such ethnocentrism is called *anachronism*—imposing the cultural artifacts, meanings, and behavior of your own period on the people of the past."

2 A recent series of social-science commentaries seek to minimize anachronistic and ethnocentric readings of New Testament texts. See Bruce J. Malina and Richard L. Rohrbaugh, *Social-Science Commentary on the Synoptic Gospels* (2d ed.; Minneapolis: Fortress, 2003). Also of value is Malina and Rohrbaugh's companion volume *Social-Science Commentary on the Gospel of John* (Minneapolis: Fortress, 1998).

3 "Overcoming the distance between us and them" is a concept adopted from the introduction of Malina and Rohrbaugh, *Social-Science Commentary on the Synoptic Gospels*: "We must also recognize, as indeed recent social-scientific studies of the New Testament have begun to do, that the distance between ourselves and the Bible is social as well as temporal and conceptual," 2.

4 Ibid., 10: "We will have to voluntarily enter the world that they presumed existed when they wrote. We will have to be willing to do what is necessary in order to bring to our reading a set of mental scenarios proper to their time, place, and culture instead of importing ones from modern America."

5 The categories of honor and shame, first-century personality, limited good, and purity laws are taken from some of the chapter headings in Malina, *The New Testament World*. See Wayne A. Meeks, *The First Urban Christians: The Social World of the Apostle Paul* (2d ed.; New Haven and London: Yale University Press, 2003) for one of the pioneering studies on the social world of the New Testament period.

6 See Alan Millard, *Reading and Writing in the Time of Jesus* (Sheffield: Sheffield Academic Press, 2000), for an excellent resource on the issue of literacy in antiquity.

7 See Austin Farrer, "On Dispensing with Q," in *Studies in the Gospels: Essays in Honor of R. H. Lightfoot* (ed. D.E. Nineham; Oxford: Basil Black, 1951), 55–88. Two of the more prominent Farrer theory advocates today are Michael D. Goulder and Mark Goodacre. See Goulder, *Luke: A New Paradigm* (JSNTS Sup 20; Sheffield: Sheffield Academic Press, 1989) and Goodacre, *The Case against Q: Studies in Markan Priority and the Synoptic Problem* (Harrisburg, Pa.: Trinity Press International, 2002). In a series of articles from the *Journal of Biblical Literature (JBL)*, Goulder has established himself as a credible voice of opposition to the Q hypothesis: see Michael D. Goulder, "Is Q a Juggernaut?" *JBL* 115 (1996): 667–81; "Self-Contradiction in the IQP," *JBL* 118 (3, 1999): 506–17; "The Derrenbacker-Kloppenborg Defense," *JBL* 121 (2002): 331–36. Goulder wrote this 2002 *JBL* article in reaction to Derrenbacker and Kloppenborg's 2001 article, "Self-Contradiction in the IQP? A Reply to Michael Goulder," *JBL* 120 (2001): 57–76.

8 See William R. Farmer, *The Synoptic Problem: A Critical Analysis* (2d ed.; Macon, Ga.: Mercer University Press, 1976). Further modern advocates of the Griesbach hypothesis include David Dungan, *A History of the Synoptic Problem: The Canon, the Text, the Composition, and the Interpretation of the Gospels* (New York: Doubleday, 1999) and *Beyond the Q Impasse: Luke's Use of Matthew* and Alan J. McNicol, David L. Dungan and David B. Peabody, eds., *Demonstration by the Research Team of the International Institute for Gospel Studies* (Valley Forge, Pa.: Trinity International Press, 1996).

The Gospel of Mark: Jesus as the Suffering Messiah

2

Introduction

In this chapter we examine the Gospel of Mark. Part 1 considers the historical setting of this Gospel, while part 2 highlights how Mark tells the story of Jesus and includes such features as the "messianic secret," the miracles of Jesus, and Mark's portrayal of the Twelve. This brief presentation cannot cover the entire content of Mark's Gospel; rather, it offers background information to facilitate a more insightful reading of Mark.

First Written Gospel on the Life of Jesus

Our journey through the four New Testament Gospels begins with the Gospel of Mark. Despite the canonical order of the Gospels as Matthew, Mark, Luke, and John, scholars almost unanimously agree that Mark was written first. As you read in chapter 1, the Two-Source and Farrer theories subscribe to "Markan priority" (that is, Mark wrote first, and Matthew and Luke used Mark as a source). Mark's genius was to take the various oral traditions and sparse written materials about Jesus and commit these testaments to writing. At the time

Mark wrote, Jesus' story was known primarily by word-of-mouth; it is important for us today to see Mark's narrative as being read aloud within this predominantly oral culture. Prior to the Gospel of Mark, no single unified written narrative on the life of Jesus existed.

Mark's Story about Jesus

Mark's story is action-packed, containing eighty-eight passages that emphasize Jesus' deeds over his words. Yet of the four New Testament Gospels, Mark is actually the shortest, with 678 verses as compared to Matthew's 1,071, Luke's 1,151, and John's 869.[1] As we will see in the next chapters, Matthew and Luke expand Mark's original story significantly.

The central event of Mark's Gospel is the "passion," or suffering and death, of Jesus. Early in this Gospel narrative, Mark informs his audience of Jesus' impending death: after Jesus healed a man's withered hand, "The Pharisees went out and immediately took counsel with the Herodians against him to put him to death" (3:6). This Markan feature led to the classic characterization of this Gospel as "a passion narrative with an extended introduction."[2]

As we will see when we consider historical setting, Mark likely used oral and written sources for the story he tells. But these sources do not determine its composition. Mark's creativity as an author is key to how he constructed his Gospel.

Part 1: Historical Setting of Mark's Gospel

With each of the four New Testament Gospels, we first address the following historical questions: Who wrote the Gospel? When was the Gospel written? What sources did the writer use to compose his Gospel? Who was the intended audience? Answering these questions for the Gospel of Mark is challenging and requires careful study, because none of this information is directly provided by the Gospel.

Authorship

The author of the Gospel of Mark never directly identifies himself in his work. The reasons for his anonymity are unclear; it could be as simple as he wants the "good news" of Jesus Christ to speak for itself,

Outline of Mark's Gospel

1:1–13	**The preaching and activities of John the Baptist in Judea** The Gospel of Mark begins with the preaching of John the Baptist in the southern region of Palestine, Judea. (See map of Palestine in chapter 1.) Included is Jesus' baptism and temptation in the wilderness. Together these few passages serve as the introduction to the Gospel of Mark.
1:14–8:21	**The preaching and activities of Jesus in Galilee** Mark presents Jesus' public ministry largely in the northern region of Palestine, Galilee. Jesus ventures back and forth across the sea of Galilee, alternating between Jewish and Gentile territories, preaching the kingdom of God, and healing those he encounters.
8:22–10:52	**Jesus' journey to Jerusalem and the passion predictions** The central section of Mark's Gospel includes Jesus' journey from Galilee to Jerusalem in Judea. Jesus predicts his upcoming suffering, death, and Resurrection to his disciples. Jesus attempts to instruct the disciples about what it means to follow him; the disciples fail to grasp Jesus as the *suffering* Messiah.
11:1–13:37	**The preaching and activities of Jesus in Jerusalem** Jesus' anticipated arrival in Jerusalem is met with support from the crowds but opposition from the religious leaders of Jerusalem and the Temple. Jesus is publicly questioned and challenged by the Jewish leaders. In his eschatological discourse, Jesus speaks of the "end-times," including the destruction of the Temple, future persecutions and tribulations, and the Son of Man who is to come at the imminent end of the world.
14:1–16:8	**The suffering, death, and Resurrection of Jesus in Jerusalem** The suffering, death, and Resurrection of Jesus take place just as Jesus had predicted. The religious leaders in Jerusalem hand Jesus over to be crucified by the Roman authority, Pontius Pilate. Jesus willingly goes the way of the cross, followed by reports of an empty tomb.

(cont'd.)

(outline of Mark cont'd.)

	Added Resurrection narrative
16:9–20	Added in the second century to the original ending of Mark's Gospel (the empty tomb, 16:1–8) are two Resurrection narratives written by someone other than the original author of Mark: the "longer ending" (vv. 9–20) and the "shorter ending." The "longer ending" reports Jesus' appearance to Mary Magdalene and the two disciples, his commissioning of the eleven disciples, and his Ascension into heaven. The "shorter ending" is quite different, stating: "[And they reported all the instructions briefly to Peter's companions. Afterwards Jesus himself, through them, sent forth from east to west the sacred and imperishable proclamation of eternal salvation. Amen.]"

or it could be that his intended audience knew him and therefore no direct identification of authorship was necessary.[3]

Historical Questions

In searching for answers to questions of authorship, date of composition, sources, and intended audience, scholars look for clues, or internal and external evidence. Internal evidence is what we can glean from the Gospel itself to help us answer these historical questions. Each Gospel writer leaves behind clues (often unintentionally) that help us answer these questions. External evidence is found in what the early Christians thought or said. Here we draw from the other New Testament books and from the Church fathers, largely from the second and third century CE.

The tradition of naming the first written Gospel as "according to Mark" is first reported by Papias of Hierapolis in Asia Minor, about 130–140 CE. Papias speaks of Mark as the "interpreter of Peter."[4] Later Church fathers, including Irenaeus of Lyon and Clement of Alexandria, would echo this association and identify Peter's supposed interpreter with one of the Marks named elsewhere in the New Testament (1 Pet 5:13; Phmn 24; Col 4:10; 2 Tim 4:11; Acts 12:12, 25; 13:13; 15:35–38). Such associations between "Mark" and the apostle Peter, however, are based on little evidence. The same Church fathers, Ireneaeus and Clement of

Alexandria, also claimed that "Mark" wrote in Rome before Peter's martyrdom there (Clement cited by Eusebius, *Church History*, 2.15.2) or after (Irenaeus, *Against Heresies*, 3.12).

Turning to the internal evidence, we may ask what the Gospel of Mark reveals about its anonymous author. He is convinced that Jesus is the Jewish Messiah and the Son of God. He has knowledge of Jewish culture and of the Jewish Scriptures, as well as knowledge of Greek and Roman culture. Given what Mark accomplished in successfully creating the first written Gospel from developing oral traditions and limited written materials, it is fair to characterize Mark as a gifted author and theologian.

Date of Composition

The most common time frame for the composition of Mark's Gospel is during the Jewish Revolt against Rome, 66–73 CE. The internal evidence for the dating of Mark to the Jewish Revolt comes primarily from Mark 13, Jesus' eschatological discourse concerning the destruction of Jerusalem and the imminent end of the world. This chapter refers to the destruction and desolation of the Temple in Jerusalem (13:2) and the fleeing of people to the mountains (13:14), events commonly associated with the Jewish Revolt in 70 CE.[5] Mark 13 also speaks directly of hardships that some followers of Jesus in Palestine faced in the midst of this revolt (13:9–13).

Sources

Scholars have traditionally characterized the author of Mark as a conservative editor of the oral and written sources that he incorporates into his Gospel.[6] Examples of the written sources available to Mark would include materials clustered around a similar theme or idea: the string of controversy stories in 2:1–3:6; the series of parables in 4:1–34; the collection of miracle stories associated with the Sea of Galilee in 3:7–12, 4:35–5:43, and 6:32–56; the eschatological discourse in chapter 13; and above all, the passion narrative. All of these may be evidence of a written source or sources that Mark is incorporating into his Gospel. Oral sources would include whatever word-of-mouth traditions developed in the four decades between Jesus' life and the writing of Mark's Gospel, as well as any remaining eyewitnesses to the ministry of Jesus.

Audience and Place of Composition

The original recipients of Mark's Gospel were likely a mix of Jews and Gentiles.[7] Mark's heavy reliance on the Hebrew Scriptures implies an audience knowledgeable about Jewish teachings and beliefs. Mark's need to explain specific Jewish Palestinian customs also implies that Mark is writing to Gentiles (and perhaps Diaspora Jews) unfamiliar with some of these Jewish customs and practices in Palestine (see Mark 7:3; 14:12; 15:42). Also Mark's writing in Greek—transliterating and translating Aramaic sayings of Jesus (see 3:17; 5:41; 7:11; 15:22, 34)—implies that Mark's audience is outside of Palestine, possibly in Rome, and is a mix of Diaspora Jews and Gentiles.

While many scholars identify Rome as Mark's place of composition, studies in recent decades have offered alternative possibilities: Galilee, southern Syria, or Palestine.[8] Furthermore, even more recent studies have proposed the possibility that Mark—from the very beginning—was written not so much for a specific audience (such as the Christian community in Rome) as it was for much wider audiences and communities throughout the Greco-Roman Empire.[9]

Summary of Historical Setting for Mark's Gospel

Author:	unknown; later Christian tradition names "John Mark," a coworker of Paul and the "interpreter of Peter"
Date of composition:	about 66–73 CE, during the Jewish Revolt against Rome
Sources:	primarily oral traditions; maybe some early written materials clustered around a theme or an idea
Audience:	mix of Jews and Gentiles living outside Palestine
Place of composition:	possibly Rome

Part 2: How Mark Told the Story

Prominent features such as the Markan "messianic secret," Mark's portrayal of the Twelve, the organizational structure and rhetorical devises used in Mark, and his theological emphases make this Gospel distinctive within the fourfold Gospel tradition. Critical to more fully understanding Mark is to appreciate his portrayal of Jesus as the "suffering Messiah."

Beginning and Ending of Mark

One of the more striking aspects of Mark's narrative is that he does not begin with any birth or infancy stories for Jesus. Rather, Mark begins his narrative with the preaching and activities of John the Baptist in Judea. Whether Mark does not know details of the birth and infancy of Jesus, or knows and chooses not to include these details, is uncertain. Mark begins his narrative of Jesus' life with Jesus as an adult, being baptized by John the Baptist, the latter's activities in the Judean wilderness linked to the Old Testament prophets Isaiah and Malachi.

No less unusual is the double ending we find in the Gospel of Mark, the first climactic ending being the empty tomb (16:1–8), the second containing Resurrection narratives between Jesus and his disciples (16:9–20).

The fact that Mark ends so suddenly in 16:8 — in Greek, apparently in the middle of a sentence — leads some scholars to wonder about the "original ending" of Mark's Gospel. In Mark 16:1–8, the women (Mary Magdalene; Mary, the mother of James; and Salome) first visit and then flee from the empty tomb, telling no one what they saw because they are afraid. Even though the words of the "young man" to the women at Jesus' tomb (vv. 6–7) fulfill what Jesus promised his disciples at the Last Supper (14:28), some scholars suspect that the original ending to Mark's Gospel may have been lost. Most scholars today, however, see 16:8 as the original ending.

> ### Brackets [ ]
>
> From time to time when you read the New Testament, you will come across words in square brackets. The opening verse of the Gospel of Mark contains these square brackets:
>
> > The beginning of the gospel of Jesus Christ [the Son of God] (1:1).
>
> Square brackets indicate that there are questions about a word or phrase. In the above example, the phrase is missing from many early manuscripts; the bracketed words are either attested to in later manuscripts or supplied by scholars when no text tradition is available.

A secondary ending (16:9–20) is found in nearly all of the earliest manuscripts. This ending contains elements found in the Resurrection narratives of Matthew (28), Luke (24), and John (20): the appearance to Mary Magdalene (only in John 20) and the two disciples, the commissioning of the remaining eleven apostles, and the Ascension of Jesus. But the distinctive vocabulary and style of 16:9–20 suggests that a later author added these verses.[10] This author apparently knew and made use of the Resurrection narratives of Matthew, Luke, and John and added these verses, perhaps as a reaction against Mark's abrupt ending with Jesus' empty tomb and as an explanation of how Jesus' Resurrection became known to others.[11] The inclusion also puts Mark more on a par with the other Gospels.

Clustered Materials

Mark's Gospel tends to cluster materials that have a similar theme or focus. One cluster involves a series of five stories about controversies between Jesus and the Pharisees in 2:1–3:6. The subject of the controversy varies (for example, the authority to forgive sins, dietary laws, sharing table fellowship with tax collectors, and so on), but the controversies consistently center on the religious authorities of Galilee (and, later, of Judea in chapters 11–12) challenging Jesus' words and deeds. Another example of clustered material in Mark occurs with Jesus' parables (4:1–34). Mark records several parables: the parable of the sower, the parable of the lamp, and the parable of the mustard seed. Except for the parables clustered together in Mark 4, the only other parable in this Gospel is the parable of the tenets (12:1–12). Another example of clustered material is Jesus' eschatological sayings in Mark 13. Some scholars have argued that this clustered material may be evidence of sources that Mark received and simply incorporated intact into his Gospel.

Summary Statements

Scattered throughout the first half of Mark's Gospel are summary statements. These statements largely concern Jesus' ministry in Galilee (1:14–8:21) and highlight his enormous popularity and power to heal. Some examples:

1:28 "His fame spread everywhere throughout the whole region of Galilee."

1:34 "He cured many who were sick with various diseases, and he drove out many demons, not permitting them to speak because they knew him."

1:39 "So he went into their synagogues, preaching and driving out demons throughout the whole of Galilee."

1:45b "He remained outside in deserted places, and people kept coming to him from everywhere."

6:56 "Whatever villages or towns or countryside he entered, they laid the sick in the marketplaces and begged him that they might touch only the tassel on his cloak; and as many as touched it were healed."

Rhetorical Devices: Intercalation, Metaphor, and Irony

The Gospel of Mark contains a variety of rhetorical devices. As with the Markan clustered materials, we do not know if these rhetorical devices are the work of our Markan author or if they were already present in the oral or written sources received by Mark.

One rhetorical device in Mark is *intercalation*; that is, inserting one story within another. Mark (or a received written source) sometimes begins telling a story about Jesus, only to interrupt that story by inserting another story before completing the first. For example, Mark 5:21–43 contains two separate healing stories. One story involves the healing of Jairus' twelve-year-old daughter by Jesus (vv. 21–24, 35–43). Inserted into this story is another, the story of Jesus healing a woman who has been hemorrhaging for twelve years (vv. 25–34). Similar elements are found in each of these two healing stories (for example, the number twelve, females being healed, neither person healed is named), which may account in part for the connecting of these two stories. However, even more significant is the role faith plays in each healing. It is the faith of Jairus and the faith of this woman that bring about the healing. Intercalating these two stories reinforces Mark's theology that Jesus' power to heal is directly connected to the faith of people (see 2:1–12, vv. 3–5; 10:46–52,

vv. 51–52). Other intercalations in Mark occur at 3:20–35 (division within Jesus' family and opposition from the scribes), 6:1–30 (the calling and mission of the Twelve, interrupted by the death of John the Baptist), and 11:12–25 (Jesus cursing the fig tree and the incident in the Temple).

Metaphors occur throughout the Gospel of Mark, often in parables, as Jesus attempts to bring listeners to the deeper meaning of his message. For example, in Mark 4:30–32, Jesus describes the kingdom of God to the Twelve by comparing its growth to that of a mustard seed. Like the mustard seed that starts out small only to blossom and spread, the kingdom of God starts small with Jesus and his disciples, and then spreads as Jesus and the disciples share the "good news" of the kingdom of God with others. In 9:33–37, Jesus again uses metaphor—this time the figure of a child to describe true discipleship.

Irony also figures prominently in Mark, as statements, expectations, and events are often other than and even opposite of what might be expected—yet these ironies always contain within them an underlying truth. Sometimes the irony is subtle, as when Jesus' own kin in Nazareth reject him (6:1–6). It is ironic that those who know Jesus best—his relatives—show no faith in him. In fact, Mark reports, "they (Jesus' family) took offense at him" (6:3). Other times the irony is dramatic, as when the chief priests and scribes mock Jesus as he is dying on the cross, saying, "He saved others; he cannot save himself. Let the Messiah, the King of Israel, come down from the cross that we may see and believe" (15:31b–32). In Mark, the Jewish religious leaders of Jerusalem fail to grasp that it is *because* of his suffering and death on the cross that Jesus is the Messiah, the King of Israel. Seeing and believing in the crucified Messiah is key to understanding Mark's theology.

Jesus as Suffering Messiah

In the Gospel of Mark, no other image better captures who Jesus is than the suffering Messiah. Throughout this Gospel, Mark draws attention to the fact that Jesus' destiny is to suffer and die. Sometimes Jesus' impending suffering and death is subtle (2:20). At other times his upcoming suffering and death is inferred by the actions of others

Jesus' Passion Predictions

8:31	9:31	10:33 – 34
He began to teach them that the Son of Man must suffer greatly and be rejected by the elders, the chief priests, and the scribes, and be killed, and rise after three days.	He was teaching his disciples and telling them, "The Son of Man is to be handed over to men and they will kill him, and three days after his death he will rise."	"Behold, we are going up to Jerusalem, and the Son of Man will be handed over to the chief priests and the scribes, and they will condemn him to death and hand him over to the Gentiles who will mock him, spit upon him, scourge him, and put him to death, but after three days he will rise."

(3:6; 14:1). Most importantly, Jesus speaks of his own inevitable suffering and death in the so-called passion predictions, 8:31–33, 9:30–32, and 10:32–34:

The suffering and death of Jesus did not fit easily into first-century Jewish images of the Messiah and the messianic age; it was a major stumbling block for many among the first generation of believers, sometimes referred to as "the scandal of the cross." Perhaps in opposition to the attempts of some would-be followers of Jesus to downplay the cross and focus instead on other aspects of Jesus' public ministry and message, Mark highlights the scandal of the cross. For Mark, being a true follower of Jesus carries two demands: acknowledging that Jesus is the Jewish Messiah because he suffered and died and being willing to suffer as Jesus did—by taking up one's cross (8:34).

The Kingdom of God

The "kingdom of God" and kingdom language is used throughout Mark's Gospel:

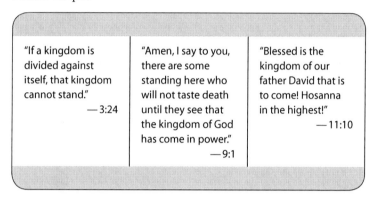

| "If a kingdom is divided against itself, that kingdom cannot stand."
—3:24 | "Amen, I say to you, there are some standing here who will not taste death until they see that the kingdom of God has come in power."
—9:1 | "Blessed is the kingdom of our father David that is to come! Hosanna in the highest!"
—11:10 |

The importance of the kingdom of God is accentuated with the first words spoken by Jesus in the Gospel of Mark: "This is the time of fulfillment. The kingdom of God is at hand. Repent, and believe in the gospel" (1:15).

The kingdom of God was often the focus of Jesus' ministry. Jesus' vision of the kingdom of God is frequently described metaphorically as, for example, a seed that is planted and sprouts from the ground (4:1–9, 26–29, 30–34), a lamp to be placed on a lamp stand for all to see (4:21–25), or an innocent child who simply trusts (10:13–16).

For the Markan Jesus, the kingdom of God has a present dimension in Jesus' ministry (see 10:14–15, 23–31) and a future dimension to be realized imminently (see 9:1; 13:24–27; 14:22–25). During his ministry, Jesus taught his disciples (4:10-20) as well as the crowds (8:34–9:1) about the kingdom of God. Moreover, Jesus taught that he, as Son of Man, would finish ushering in the kingdom of God at some undisclosed future time (9:1; 14:25, 62).

The term *kingdom* (in Greek, *basileia*) is more accurately rendered as "reign," "rule," or "kingship." Jesus' use of this language in his public ministry added a political dimension to his preaching that would have been perceived as a threat, especially to Roman authorities, because for Jesus, it was God who was to "rule" over all. In Mark's Gospel, Jesus comes to establish God's kingdom in the world. But Jesus' public ministry comes to an end with a political charge brought against him. He is executed on the order of Pontius Pilate with the charge that he is "The King of the Jews" (15:26).

Jesus as Eschatological Prophet

The Gospel of Mark also presents Jesus as an eschatological prophet, ushering in the kingdom of God throughout Galilee with a sense of urgency. We have seen how Jesus' first words emphasize the importance of time in the present: "This is the time of fulfillment" (1:15). But Jesus also emphasizes time in the future: "Amen, I say to you, there are some standing here who will not taste death until they see that the kingdom of God has come in power" (9:1). It is Jesus' sensitivity to time—present and future—that creates the image of Jesus as an eschatological prophet who has come to announce the kingdom of God.

> ### Eschatology
>
> The word *eschatology* refers to the "end-times" and is derived from the Greek adjective *eschatos*, meaning "last or final."

In Mark's Gospel, an urgency to Jesus' message about the kingdom of God adds to this sense of a "last" or "final" time. This urgency is seen in the narrative speed of Mark's Gospel, especially in the opening chapters. In the two chapters immediately following Jesus' baptism and temptation in the wilderness, Mark presents Jesus moving quickly throughout Galilee—preaching, healing, and creating controversy with his message and his actions.

After Mark 3:6, the narrative speed of Mark slows dramatically as the Gospel story unfolds and Jesus' Galilean ministry comes to an end in Mark 8. Mark 1–10 covers about one year of Jesus' public ministry in and around Galilee. Mark 11–16 covers the final week of Jesus' life in Jerusalem, with a much slower pace for the passion narrative and ultimate crucifixion.

The Twelve

The Gospel of Mark presents a rather unflattering portrayal of a select group of Jesus' followers, often referred to as "the Twelve." In chapters 3 and 6, Jesus sends out the Twelve, charging them to heal the sick, exorcise demons, and preach the kingdom of God.

A Feminist Interpretation of Mark: The Syrophoenician Woman (7:24–30)

Feminist interpretation emphasizes certain aspects of a biblical text, especially aspects that speak to the feminine. Such interpretations have usually been ignored or even silenced.

The incident between Jesus and the Syrophoenician woman provides a good example. Although a miracle story of Jesus exorcising a demon, this story also highlights the faith of this Gentile woman. Desperate for her daughter's healing, this woman steps outside accepted cultural and social norms by making a public request of Jesus, a man.

A feminist interpretation might also emphasize another feature of this story. Despite comparing this woman to a "dog," Jesus approves of her faith, her questioning, and her challenging traditionally male hierarchal religious structures.

The first disciples called by Jesus initially respond to him unconditionally (1:16–20). But it soon becomes apparent that these disciples have little understanding of who Jesus is (4:41; 6:52; 8:21), despite receiving authority and power from him to preach and to heal (3:13–15; 6:7–13, 30–33), having private conversations with him and receiving his instructions (4:10–20, 34; 8:27–30), and witnessing events that no one else sees (9:2–8). Furthermore, as the disciples begin to comprehend Jesus' true identity (8:29), they argue among themselves regarding who is the greatest (9:33–37), rebuke children for approaching Jesus (10:13–16), and seek their own future reward (10:35–45). Even worse, the Twelve abandon Jesus upon his arrest (14:50), thereby failing to live up to Jesus' expectations of true discipleship: "Whoever wishes to come after me must deny himself, take up his cross, and follow me" (8:34).

The negative portrayal of the Twelve is further reinforced by Mark's consistent presentation of others who follow Jesus and exemplify a strong faith in him, among them a leper (1:40–45), a hemorrhaging woman (5:25–34), the Syrophoenician woman (7:24–30), a blind man named Bartimaeus (10:46–52), and the woman who anoints Jesus' body for burial (14:3–9). In effect, these followers of Jesus—and not the Twelve—are the role models of discipleship in the Gospel of Mark.

The Miracles of Jesus

One of the hallmarks of Jesus' public ministry is his ability to perform "powerful deeds" (in Greek, *dunameis*). In fact, the extensive focus on Jesus' miracles, especially during Jesus' Galilean ministry (Mark 1–8), results in Mark emphasizing Jesus' deeds more than his words.

Several features about Jesus' miracles in the Gospel of Mark are noteworthy. Jesus' ability to work miracles shows that he has power and authority from God (3:23–30), which gives him the authority to preach about the kingdom of God as well as forgive sins (2:1–12, 18–22). His miracles are visible signs that the kingdom of God has arrived in and through Jesus' public ministry. Also, Jesus' power to perform miracles at times seems almost limitless (1:32–34; 1:41; 3:5; 5:1–20; 6:34–44, 53–56; 8:1–10). Often the faith of the person receiving the miracle is central to Jesus performing it (5:21–34; 10:46–52). In fact, in regard to Jesus' rejection at Nazareth (6:1–6), Mark tells us that Jesus "was *not able* to perform any mighty deed there" because of the Nazarenes' lack of faith (6:5, emphasis added).

One of Jesus' most-often performed miracles in the Gospel of Mark is exorcism. The first miracle Jesus performs is an exorcism (1:21–28). Mark presents Jesus in conversation with demons, controlling them and commanding them to follow his orders (1:34; 5:1–20; 6:7; 9:14–29). According to Mark, it is Jesus' ability to control the demons that helps him gain widespread fame throughout Galilee (1:28). One of the more

Jewish Belief in Supernatural Evil

The Jewish belief in evil as a supernatural force in opposition to God came late in Jewish biblical history. It was not until the influence of the Persian religion Zoroastrianism that Jewish theology began to speak of demons as a supernatural evil in opposition to God (Persian period, 539–330 BCE). Zoroastrianism taught dualism — the idea that the universe is divided between Good and Evil, light and darkness. These dual forces fought each other in the invisible order and were adversaries to humans in the seen order. Jewish biblical books emerging from this period (for example, Zech 3:1–10, Job 1–2) begin, for the first time in the Hebrew Scriptures, to speak of supernatural evil (Satan) in opposition to humans.

interesting features of Jesus' dialogues with the demons is that the demons know Jesus' true identity:

1:23   "What have you to do with us, Jesus of Nazareth? I know who you are—the Holy One of God!"

1:34   "[H]e (Jesus) drove out many demons, not permitting them to speak because they knew him."

3:11   (Summary statement of what demons would say to Jesus): "You are the Son of God."

5:7   (A "legion" of demons possessing a man): "What have you to do with me, Jesus, Son of the Most High God?"

Form Criticism and the Interpretation of Miracles[12]

You may recall from chapter 1 that form criticism, as applied to the New Testament Gospels, arose in the early twentieth century, building on the work of source critics. Source criticism examines the possible sources the Gospel writers used. Form criticism, on the other hand, is interested in the individual units (pericopes) and distinct literary forms that are combined to create the Gospels as a whole (for example, miracles stories, parables, and the passion narrative), as well as in the history of these forms in the life of early Christian communities prior to their becoming embedded within longer Gospel narratives.

Leading form critics such as Martin Dibelius (*From Tradition to Gospel*, 1919; English translation, 1935) and Rudolf Bultmann (*History of the Synoptic Tradition*, 1921; English translation, 1963) focus on the many literary forms in the Gospels. Dibelius and Bultmann seek to trace how and where these forms developed and circulated within the oral traditions that existed before the written Gospels. They presuppose that early oral traditions about Jesus were preserved because they served a particular purpose in the *Sitz im Leben* (German for "setting in life") of the community and experiences of the early Christians. For example, both Dibelius and Bultmann are convinced that before the written Gospels, teachers and storytellers were using the miracle form mainly for the purpose of teaching and telling stories about the life of Jesus.

Dibelius is interested in the narrative material of the Synoptic Gospels and asserts that after the passion narrative, which came first in the oral tradition, there followed paradigms (short stories of events in Jesus' life suitable for sermons), tales (miracles), legends, myths, and sayings of Jesus. Bultmann, on the other hand, divides the Synoptic Gospels into two categories: discourses of Jesus and narrative materials. Jesus' discourses were divided into apophthegms (short stories containing Jesus' words, similar to Dibelius' paradigms) and

(cont'd.)

(form criticism cont'd.)

dominical sayings (proverbial, prophetic, and apocalyptic sayings of Jesus, as well as parables). Narrative materials included two major groups: miracle stories and historical narratives and legends.

The work of form critics has helped us understand that the miracles of Jesus, which likely circulated in the oral tradition, fall into three main categories (or microgenres):

1. *Healings and exorcisms:* Jesus interacts with either demons (exorcisms), for example, Mark 1:21–28, or sick people (healings), Mark 1:29–31.
2. *Conflict narratives:* a healing or exorcism sets the stage for a confrontation between Jesus and certain Jewish leaders; for example, Mark 2:1–12, the healing of the paralytic and the controversy about healing on the Sabbath.
3. *Nature miracles:* nonhealing (and nondemonic) events occur that often reveal something about who Jesus is. Examples include the stilling of the storm (Mark 4:35–41), the feeding of the 5,000 (Mark 6:34–44), and walking on water (Mark 6:45–52).

Furthermore, form critics have shown us that the reports of Jesus' healings and exorcisms tend to contain the following elements:

- the introduction of a sick or afflicted person and a description of the malady or its effects on others (for example, family members);
- the words and/or actions of Jesus to remedy the disease, death, or demon possession; and
- confirmation that the healing or exorcism has (suddenly) taken place.

The consistent presence of these elements in Jesus' healings and exorcisms point to the stability with which these oral forms took shape in order to survive in the life of the early Church.

According to form critics, each of these categories of miracles had a corresponding purpose in the life of early Christians. Nature miracles were "epiphanies" that allowed the early Christians to teach others about who Jesus is. For example, nature miracles, such as Jesus' stilling of the storm, point to Jesus' divinity and encourage readers to reflect upon the dual nature of Jesus as human and divine. Conflict narratives taught the early Christians some principles by which one could defend the faith. Healings and exorcisms provided dramatic stories of Jesus' power, not unlike nature miracles in this respect. Dibelius did not believe that the miracle form served the early Church in sermons like paradigms; rather, the miracle form was created and survived in the oral tradition because of its spectacular quality.

(cont'd.)

(form criticism cont'd.)

In terms of Jesus' miracles, form criticism offers us important insights and interpretive strategies. Within the developing oral tradition, the early Church sometimes preserved (healings and exorcisms) and other times created (nature miracles) stories of Jesus' miracles as a means of teaching and evangelizing. Paying close attention to the form in which a miracle is preserved allows the reader to move beyond more literal questions of historical accuracy and into deeper issues of meaning. For example, the conflict narrative of Jesus healing the man with the withered hand (Mark 3:1–6) may have been preserved in the oral tradition to teach early Christians to view Sabbath law in a new light.

The "Messianic Secret"

One of the more enigmatic features of the Gospel of Mark, particularly in the first eight chapters, is the secrecy motif. According to Mark, Jesus spoke to the Twelve about "the mystery of the kingdom of God" (4:11), explaining to them in private about the meaning of his publicly spoken parables (4:34). Furthermore, Jesus commands many to silence about his activities and his identity: the disciples (5:43; 8:30; 9:9), the demons (1:34; 3:12), even those whom he heals (1:44; 7:36; 8:26). While the demons obey Jesus, many of those whom Jesus heals are unable or unwilling to remain silent, and subsequently tell others of their encounter with Jesus.

Dubbed the "messianic secret" in 1901 by William Wrede, the Markan secrecy motif has long interested scholars. Wrede's original hypothesis was that the historical Jesus never claimed to be the Jewish Messiah and therefore had no need to command silence on this matter. Instead, it was the early Christians who came to believe in Jesus as the Jewish Messiah after his death and invented the secrecy motif, placing in Jesus' mouth commands for silence as a way of affirming their post-Easter belief in Jesus. Not all scholars today accept Wrede's original "messianic secret" hypothesis; however, Wrede's study fundamentally changed how scholars appreciate Mark as a theologically crafted and apologetic work rather than as "real history."

Titles for Jesus

The opening line in the Gospel of Mark presents a title used in reference to Jesus, "Christ": "The beginning of the gospel of Jesus Christ [the Son of God]." (Although "Son of God" is a title that Mark will use for Jesus, recall that the square brackets indicate uncertainty as to whether Mark actually wrote "Son of God" for Jesus here.) Two other major titles used for Jesus are "teacher" and "Son of Man." For Mark, Jesus is simultaneously the Christ, the Son of God, the Son of Man, and teacher. Each of these titles indicates Mark's theological understanding of Jesus. Let's unpack what each title meant to Mark within first-century Judaism.

Today Christians use the terms *Jesus* and *Christ* so interchangeably that many are probably unaware that Christ is actually a *title* ascribed to Jesus. For Mark, who writes in Greek, Christ means "anointed." The Hebrew equivalent for the term *Christ* is "messiah." The terms *Christ* and *messiah* had various connotations for first-century Judaism. One idea of the Jewish messiah would have included a warrior king in the line of David, a messiah who would be "anointed" by God to restore Israel's "golden age," as in the days of King David. But Jewish messianic expectations were diverse, ranging from priest to prophet to teacher.[13] In Mark's Gospel, Jesus as messiah would have met some of these expectations.

It is easy, and even logical, to see why many would have referred to Jesus as the Christ, the anointed one, because Mark often refers to Jesus as "teacher" (4:38; 5:35; 9:17, 38; 10:17, 20, 35; 12:14, 19, 32; 13:1; 14:14), with Jesus' public ministry and message centered on establishing "the kingdom (reign) of God." Political and perhaps even military connotations could have been associated with such a phrase as "the kingdom of God." When Jesus asks his disciples,

Collective Identity

Mark 8:27

"Who do people say that I am?"

Jewish people of the ancient Near East had a strong sense of collective identity as compared with today's Western individualism. People came to know who they were through what *others* said of them. This is why Jesus poses the question to his disciples, "Who do people say that I am?" The question makes perfect sense in a culture where one comes to know oneself by the consensus of the group's perception.

"[W]ho do you say that I am?" Peter responds, "You are the Messiah" (8:29). It may be that Peter had in mind the political and military implications of this title. It seems almost certain that Peter did not envision Jesus as a suffering Messiah (8:31–33). According to Mark, it is also this confusion over the nature of Jesus' messiahship that ultimately leads to Jesus' execution under Pontius Pilate, who was the representative of the Roman political and military presence in Judea. Pilate crucifies Jesus with the official "charge" that Jesus is "The King of the Jews" (15:26). Thus, the Roman justification for executing Jesus was the charge that he claimed to be a "king" (the same Greek word, *basileus*, was used for the Roman emperor, or Caesar), who somehow threatened Rome's dominion.

An equally important title for Jesus in Mark's Gospel is "Son of God." Twice Mark records the "voice" (God himself) referring to Jesus as "my Son, the beloved," at Jesus' baptism and at Jesus' transfiguration (1:11; 9:7). Both scenes can be read as God's "anointing" of Jesus as his Son. Thus, two of Mark's titles converge: Jesus as Christ and Jesus as Son of God. Ironically, although even the demons know Jesus as God's Son (1:24; 5:7), neither Jesus' own disciples nor any other people in the Gospel of Mark know Jesus as God's Son. Nor does Jesus use this title in reference to himself in Mark, although in 14:61–62, asked by the Sanhedrin whether he is "the Messiah, the son of the Blessed One," Jesus answers, "I am." After Jesus has died on the cross, a Roman centurion says, "Truly this man was the Son of God!" (15:39), although whether this is a confession of faith or more mockery, we cannot know.

The identification of Jesus' suffering death as Son of God is closely connected to another title for Jesus used in the Gospel of Mark: "Son of Man." This title holds a place of distinction: it is the only title that Jesus uses for himself. In Mark's Gospel, Jesus never refers to himself directly as the Christ or as the Son of God. Son of Man is used in three different ways in the Gospel of Mark. First, Jesus uses this title in reference to his ministry (for example, "But that you may know that the Son of Man has the authority to forgive sins on earth" 2:10). Second, the title is used in reference to his impending suffering (for example, "The Son of Man is to be handed over to men and they will kill him, and three days after his death he will rise" 9:31). Third, the title is used in reference to the cosmic figure coming in the future to usher in God's judgment (for example, "Whoever is ashamed of me and of my words in this faithless and sinful generation, the Son of Man will be ashamed of when he comes in his Father's glory with the holy angels" 8:38).

It is this third use of the term, Jesus as the Son of Man as cosmic judge, which is of particular importance in Mark's Gospel. In his appearance before the Jewish council (14:53–65), Jesus speaks of himself as the Son of Man in the sense of future cosmic judge (14:62). The high priest declares this "blasphemy" and the council "all condemned him as deserving to die" (14:64). In the first half of the Gospel, Jesus has concealed his true identity; here he reveals it, a climactic moment that seals his fate even as it reveals his identity as the Son of Man, cosmic judge.

> ## Additional Titles for Jesus
>
> Besides the four major titles for Jesus in the Gospel of Mark—Christ, Son of God, Son of Man, and teacher—the following titles are also used for Jesus:
>
> *Rabbi/Master:* 9:5; 10:51; 11:21; 14:45
>
> *Lord:* 2:28; 5:19; 7:28
>
> *Son of David:* 10:47; 12:35

Finally, as already noted, the title "teacher" is often used in reference to Jesus, and it may have been understood as part of the Jewish expectations of the messiah. Yet aside from the frequent use of this title, Mark does surprisingly little with the content of Jesus' teachings. Nonetheless, the title "teacher" may reflect the most historically grounded reference to Jesus because teaching, especially about the kingdom of God, was a major activity in the public ministry of the historical Jesus.

Summary of Themes, Events, and Passages in Mark's Gospel

Core Concepts

- Jesus as the suffering Messiah is the dominant image of Jesus in the Gospel of Mark.
- The kingdom of God is the centerpiece of Jesus' public ministry.
- Jesus is portrayed as an eschatological prophet, conscious of the "end-time."
- "Christ," "Son of God," "Son of Man," and "teacher" are major titles assigned Jesus in Mark's Gospel.

(cont'd.)

(summary of Mark's Gospel cont'd.)

Supplemental Information

- The Gospel of Mark has no infancy narrative, and two different endings were added in the second century to round off its abrupt conclusion at 16:8.
- Mark employs a variety of literary devices including intercalation, metaphor, and irony.
- Faith in Jesus is essential for true discipleship in Mark's Gospel.
- Mark presents a negative portrait of the Twelve.
- Jesus' miracles point to his authority and power as Christ, Son of God, and Son of Man.

Questions for Review

1. What do we know about the author(s) of the Gospel of Mark?
2. When was Mark likely composed, and how does this affect our reading of this Gospel?
3. What was the likely makeup of Mark's audience, and how do we know this?
4. What is noteworthy about the beginning and the ending(s) of Mark?
5. What use does Mark make of literary devices?
6. What does it mean to say Jesus is portrayed as an eschatological prophet?
7. How are the Twelve portrayed in the Gospel of Mark?
8. What is the problem of the "messianic secret" in Mark's Gospel?
9. Explain the significance of the titles Mark uses for Jesus.
10. How does Mark highlight Jesus as the suffering Messiah?

Questions for Reflection

1. What is your reaction to Mark's abrupt ending at 16:8? Do you prefer the addition of the longer ending, 16:9–20?
2. Which prominent themes and passages do you find most engaging in the Gospel of Mark?

3. What is your reaction to the portrayal of Jesus as the *suffering* Messiah?

4. What is your reaction to the negative portrayal of the Twelve?

Recommendations for Further Reading

Harrington, Daniel J., S.J. *What Are They Saying about Mark?* New York: Paulist, 2004.

Harrington surveys some of the best research and scholarship on the Gospel of Mark from 1985 to the present. For the research and scholarship on the Gospel of Mark from 1960 to 1985, see Frank J. Matera's *What Are They Saying about Mark?* (Mahwah, N.J./New York: Paulist Press, 1987). Harrington divides the last twenty years of Markan work into three categories: literary studies, theological studies, and historical studies. He concludes with recommended readings on Mark that include feminist and political readings as well as readings for spirituality and preaching. This is an excellent starting point for the study of Mark's Gospel.

Horsley, Richard A. *Hearing the Whole Story: The Politics of Plot in Mark's Gospel.* Louisville, Ky.: Westminster John Knox Press, 2001.

Horsley is widely acknowledged as one of the leading voices in researching the sociopolitical environment of first-century Galilee. In this engaging interpretation of Mark, Horsley interprets the first Gospel in terms of the political conflict between the peasants of Galilee and the religious leaders of Jerusalem. *Hearing the Whole Story* offers a new perspective on reading Mark.

Rhoads, David, Joanna Dewey, and Donald Michie. *Mark as Story: An Introduction to the Narrative of a Gospel.* 2d ed. Minneapolis: Fortress, 1999.

Rhoads, Dewey, and Michie have collaborated in revising the original *Mark as Story* by Rhoads and Michie from 1982. Using the latest developments in narrative criticism and examining the narrator, settings, plot, and characters of Mark's Gospel, this book is an excellent introduction to reading this Gospel as a *story.* The authors begin their narrative analysis of Mark by providing their own translation without chapter and verse subtitles. This makes for a fresh approach to a storyline that has become all too familiar for many.

Tolbert, Mary Ann. *Sowing the Gospel: Mark's World in Literary-Historical Perspective.* Minneapolis: Fortress, 1989.

Tolbert offers one of the early, influential interpretations of the Gospel of Mark with an analysis of the literary unity of Mark in its original historical (social) setting. Tolbert argues that Mark's Gospel belongs to the genre of the ancient novel. As such, the Gospel of Mark is not so much a biography of Jesus as an attempt by Mark to persuade his audience to sow the gospel of the kingdom of God that Jesus proclaimed in his public ministry.

Tuckett, Christopher, ed. *The Messianic Secret*. Philadelphia: Fortress, 1983.

Tuckett offers a variety of scholars' positions on William Wrede's original proposal of the messianic secret in Mark's Gospel. This is an excellent resource for assessing how twentieth-century scholarship has responded to Wrede and the general idea of Mark as a theologian.

Endnotes

1 K. Aland and B. Aland, *The Text of the New Testament: An Introduction to the Critical Editions and to the Theory and Practice of Modern Textual Criticism* (trans. E.F. Rhodes; Grand Rapids, Mich.: Eerdmans/Leiden: Brill, 1987), 29.

2 See Martin Kähler, *The So-Called Historical Jesus and the Historic Biblical Christ* (trans. Carl E. Braaten; Philadelphia: Fortress, 1964), 80. Kähler wrote in German and originally published his book in 1892.

3 Robert A. Guelich, *Mark 1:1–8:26* (WBC 34A; Dallas, Tex.: Word Books, 1989), xxvi, following Hengel, argues that the ascribed title of the Gospel, "The Gospel according to Mark," indicates the early Church saw "the 'gospel' as an entity in itself not derived from any one author," communicating the idea that the Gospels were the "gospel *of* God."

4 Papias, as quoted by the fourth-century Church historian Eusebius. For commentators' survey of the internal and external evidence for authorship, see Guelich, xv–xxix; William L. Lane, *The Gospel According to Mark* (Grand Rapids, Mich.: Eerdmans, 1974), 21–24; Ben Witherington, *The Gospel of Mark: A Socio-Rhetorical Commentary* (Grand Rapids, Mich.: Eerdmans, 2001), 20–31; John R. Donahue and Daniel J. Harrington, *The Gospel of Mark* (SP 2; Collegeville, Minn.: Liturgical, 2002), 8–12.

5 Contrast Lane, 17–21, who sees the date of Mark's composition during the early stages of the war (65–68 CE), with Witherington, 31, who posits the latter stages of the war, 70 CE, during the fall of Jerusalem.

6 Guelich, xxxii–xxxv; Witherington, 16–18. For an extended discussion on this view of Mark as a conservative editor, see Ernst Best, "Mark's Preservation of the Tradition," in *The Interpretation of Mark* (ed. W.R. Telford; Edinburgh: T & T Clark, 1995), 153–68.

7 Lane, 17, 24–25; Guelich, xxix–xxxii; Donahue and Harrington, 41–46.

8 While Donahue and Harrington favor Rome as the place of composition, they also provide a brief summary of the alternative locations, concluding: "We acknowledge during the late 1950s that there have been tendencies to move the composition of Mark's Gospel toward the East and to give attention to events in Palestine during the First Jewish Revolt (66–73 CE)," 44.

9 See Richard Bauckham, *The Gospel for All Christians: Rethinking the Gospel's Origins* (ed. Richard Bauckham; Grand Rapids, Mich.: Eerdmans, 1998). Some of the leading scholars in Gospel studies today have contributed to this book (Bauckham, Michael Thompson, Loveday Alexander, Richard Burridge, Steven Barton, and Francis Watson). See especially Bauckham's opening essay, "For Whom Were the Gospels Written?" 9–48. See Witherington, 29–31, who speaks of this "new thesis" about the wider targeted audiences of the New Testament Gospels.

10 On the non-Markan authorship of Mark 16:9–20, see James A. Kelhoffer, *Miracle and Mission: The Authentication of Missionaries and Their Message in the Longer Ending of Mark* (WUNT 2.112; Tübingen: Mohr Siebeck, 2000), 48–122.

11 See further, Kelhoffer, *Miracle and Mission*, 123–56.

12 Although dated, one of the best introductions to form criticism remains Edgar V. McKnight, *What Is Form Criticism?* (Philadelphia: Fortress, 1969). For a good resource on miracles, see Wendy Cotter, *Miracles in Greco-Roman Antiquity: A Sourcebook* (London/New York: Routledge, 1999). Cotter provides a collection of Jewish, Greco-Roman, and Christian primary sources on miracles.

13 See John J. Collins, *Scepter and the Star: The Messiahs of the Dead Sea Scrolls and Other Ancient Literature* (New York: Doubleday, 1995). Collins explores the various images and ideas of the Messiah in first-century Judaism, concluding that Jews had a diversity of messianic expectations.

The Gospel
of Matthew:
Jesus as
the New Moses

3

Introduction

In the last chapter we examined the Gospel of Mark, focusing on Mark's historical setting and how the story of Jesus is told in this first written Gospel. In this chapter we will do the same with the Gospel of Matthew. Given that most scholars believe the author of Matthew used Mark as a major source for his Gospel, we will apply the method of redaction criticism, discussed in chapter 1, to see how Matthew revises and updates the story of Jesus found in Mark's Gospel.

Why Begin with Matthew?

Students sometimes ask why the New Testament begins with Matthew, if Mark was written first. The order of the New and Old Testament writings simply corresponds to an early Greek manuscript, *Codex Vaticanus*. Other manuscripts from the early Church preserve some or all of the New Testament writings in a variety of sequences. As the early centuries of Christianity unfolded, Matthew eventually emerged as the most popular of the four New Testament Gospels.

Why Matthew Wrote His Gospel

If our reconstruction of the chronological sequence of the written Gospels is correct, Mark wrote the first Gospel around 70 CE, followed by Matthew. As discussed in chapter 1, both the Two-Source and Farrer theories argue for Markan priority and believe that Matthew used Mark as one of his major sources. Matthew not only relied heavily on materials from Mark but also expanded considerably the length of Mark's Gospel, from 678 verses to 1,071 verses, supplying infancy and Resurrection narratives along with additions to the sayings of Jesus. Whatever were Matthew's motives in writing his Gospel, it stands somehow *in response* to Mark and to Matthew's own circumstances. Matthew had to balance the needs of his particular audience, the changing and evolving world of the first century, and, most importantly, his own theological vision of Jesus, which he may have felt Mark insufficiently represented.

Although Mark became a template of the written Gospel for Matthew as well as Luke, Matthew was a gifted author in his own right. Matthew took Mark's story and edited and expanded it, adapting it to the complex world in which he lived. The opening decades of Christianity unfolded in dramatically changing circumstances. Mark and Matthew took the same subject matter—and many of the same characters—and tell dramatically different stories.

An Outline of Matthew
The following sketch highlights Matthew's storyline.

1:1 – 2:23	**The birth of Jesus** The Gospel of Matthew begins with a genealogy of Jesus and stories associated with Jesus' birth. Told from Joseph's point of view, the opening passages assert that Jesus' coming is the fulfillment of Old Testament prophecy.
3:1 – 7:29	**Jesus begins proclaiming God's kingdom** Matthew associates the preaching and activities of John the Baptist with the start of Jesus' public ministry. After reporting

(cont'd.)

(outline of Matthew cont'd.)

3:1 – 7:29	the baptism and temptation of Jesus, Matthew includes some early activities of Jesus, including his lengthy Sermon on the Mount, Jesus' first major discourse. Matthew begins to portray the disciples as "men of little faith."

The preaching and activities of Jesus in Galilee

8:1 – 11:1	After the Sermon on the Mount, Matthew resumes reporting the ministry and message of Jesus in Galilee, highlighting Jesus' powerful deeds. Jesus then delivers his second major discourse, commissioning and instructing the Twelve, and warns the disciples of coming persecutions.

Opposition to Jesus' message and ministry

11:2 – 13:53	Matthew continues reporting the public ministry and message of Jesus, emphasizing the growing opposition to Jesus from Jewish leaders. Many of Jesus' parables are included in this section as his third major discourse.

Jesus' teaching on the kingdom of heaven and the Church

13:54 – 18:35	Jesus' words and powerful deeds frame this section, with much focus on the kingdom of heaven and Jesus' words concerning Peter and the "church," Jesus' fourth major discourse. Jesus also delivers two of his three passion predictions.

Jesus' public ministry in Judea and Jerusalem

19:1 – 25:46	After Jesus arrives in Judea and the city of Jerusalem, opposition to him and his message continues. Jesus continues to speak in parables as the religious leaders of Jerusalem challenge his authority. In his fifth and final discourse, Jesus strongly denounces the Jewish ruling elites of Jerusalem.

The suffering, death, and Resurrection of Jesus in Jerusalem

26:1 – 28:20	The suffering, death, and Resurrection of Jesus proceeds just as Jesus foreshadowed to his disciples. Matthew includes a Resurrection narrative in Galilee and concludes with Jesus' "great commission" to his disciples.

Part 1: Historical Setting of Matthew's Gospel

To address questions of authorship, date of composition, sources, and intended audience, we will look at the *internal evidence* from the Gospel of Matthew and the *external evidence* from other New Testament writers and early Church witnesses. As discussed in the previous chapter on Mark, internal evidence is what we can glean from the Gospel itself: each Gospel writer leaves behind clues (often unintentionally) that help us answer these questions. External evidence is what the early Christians thought about these modern questions, as evidenced by the other New Testament books and the Church fathers, the latter largely from the second and third century CE.[1]

Authorship

Like the author to the Gospel of Mark, the author of Matthew does not reveal his identity directly in his Gospel. Concerning the purported identity of Matthew, Eusebius, a Church historian from the fourth century, cites the second-century author Papias of Hierapolis as follows: "Matthew put together the oracles [of the Lord] in the Hebrew (or Aramaic) language, and each one interpreted them as best he could" (Eusebius, *Church History* 3.39.15). If nothing else, this testimony reveals that already in the early second century, a writing about Jesus was attributed to someone named Matthew. You will note, however, that Papias refers to a writing composed in Hebrew, the main language of the Jewish Scriptures, or Aramaic, the mother tongue of Jesus. This cannot, however, refer to our canonical Matthew, which was composed in Greek and whose Greek style does not at all suggest that this Gospel is a translation of an earlier Hebrew or Aramaic writing.

The internal and external evidence concerning the authorship of this Gospel is limited. Unlike Mark, where there are numerous references to a "Mark" (or "John Mark") throughout other New Testament writings (1 Peter, three Pauline letters, and Acts of the Apostles), references to Matthew in the New Testament are restricted to the Synoptic Gospels. First, we have the call of Matthew (or Levi), the tax collector (see Mark 2:13–17; Matt 9:9–13; Luke 5:27–32) and, second, we have Matthew (subsequently) listed as one of the twelve Apostles (see Mark 3:13–19; Matt 10:1–4; Luke 6:12–16).

Most likely, second-century Christianity surmised that the apostle Matthew wrote this Gospel out of a concern to establish an apostolic authority for the Gospel. But as with the Gospel of Mark, attributing this Gospel to the apostle Matthew does not work. If we are correct in dating the Gospel of Matthew a decade or more after the Gospel of Mark, it is hard to imagine that the apostle Matthew could have been active enough to write a Gospel so late in his life (if he were even alive). Thus, it follows that both the name "Matthew" and this author's alleged apostolic identity are unsubstantiated by the surviving evidence.

The internal evidence reveals a bit more about this author, even if we do not know his name. Our author was almost certainly a Jew; that is, he believed in the tenets of the Jewish faith as known in the first century CE. And because he believed in Jesus as the Jewish Messiah, we refer to him as Judaic Christian. Although, as a conscientious Jew, he was not afraid to highlight his criticism of the Jewish authorities (see Matthew 23), this did not in any way detract from his support for the Jewish Law, or Torah (Matt 5:17–19; 17:12). Furthermore, the author of Matthew emphasizes Jesus' mission to "the lost sheep of the house of Israel" (Matt 10:6; 15:24). And our author's knowledge, use, and integration of the Jewish Scriptures throughout his Gospel—especially his fondness for prophetic quotations—shows him to have been thoroughly conversant with those Scriptures. This evangelist shows himself to have been an accomplished author and theologian, who edited the Gospel of Mark and expanded it with additional resources to create a replacement for Mark's Gospel.

Date of Composition

The Gospel of Mark was written about 70 CE. So if Matthew used Mark as a primary source, then Matthew's Gospel was written sometime after 70 CE.[2] A few internal factors also point to a post-70 CE date for the writing of this Gospel. The author seems to have been aware of the destruction of Jerusalem and its Temple (see, for example, 24:2; see also the parable of the great supper, 22:1–10, esp. v. 7). External evidence shows that Matthew was circulating in the early second century, because numerous second-century Church fathers knew and used Matthew (see, for example, the *Epistle of Barnabas* 4:14 and Polycarp).

This internal and external evidence places the writing of Matthew at 70–100 CE. Because this Gospel is in part a *response* to Mark, we should account for the time it would have taken for the Gospel of Mark to circulate and become known by the Judaic Christians who comprised Matthew's intended audience. Thus, scholars of the authorship of Matthew's Gospel commonly hold a date of 80–85 CE.

Sources

The dominant view today is that Matthew relied largely on three sources to write his Gospel: (1) Mark, (2) Q (a hypothesized source to account for written material shared by Matthew and Luke—about 230 verses—that is not derived from Mark), and (3) M (additional oral and written sources peculiar to Matthew). In other words, as we noted with Mark in the last chapter, Matthew used both written and oral sources to compose his Gospel.[3] This source theory accounts for the vast majority of material found in the Gospel of Matthew.[4]

When we lay the Gospels of Mark and Matthew side by side, and presume that Matthew knew and used Mark, we can see that Matthew absorbs almost all of Mark (90 percent) into his Gospel. Matthew relies heavily on Mark's sequence of events in the ministry of Jesus, preserving many of Jesus' words and deeds as recorded in Mark, much of it verbatim.

Examples of Matthew's Use of Mark: Sequence of Events and Words and Deeds of Jesus

Sequence of events

MARK		MATTHEW	
1:2–8	Preaching of John the Baptist	3:1–12	Preaching of John the Baptist
1:9–11	Baptism of Jesus	3:13–17	Baptism of Jesus
1:12–13	Temptation of Jesus	4:1–11	Temptation of Jesus
1:14–15	Beginning of the Galilean ministry	4:12–17	Beginning of the Galilean ministry
1:16–20	Call of the first disciples	4:18–22	Call of the first disciples

(cont'd.)

(examples of Matthew's use of Mark cont'd.)

Words and deeds of Jesus

MARK 2:21–22
No one sews a piece of unshrunken cloth on an old cloak. If he does, its fullness pulls away, the new from the old, and the tear gets worse. Likewise, no one pours new wine into old wineskins. Otherwise, the wine will burst the skins, and both the wine and the skins are ruined. Rather, new wine is poured into fresh wineskins.

MATTHEW 9:16–17
No one patches an old cloak with a piece of unshrunken cloth, for its fullness pulls away from the cloak and the tear gets worse. People do not put new wine into old wineskins. Otherwise the skins burst, the wine spills out, and the skins are ruined. Rather, they pour new wine into fresh wineskins, and both are preserved.

Redaction criticism looks for changes that Matthew made to Mark that can reveal something of Matthew's theology. Notice how Matthew adds the words, "and both are preserved," to the ending of Jesus' saying on wine and wineskins. The metaphor of wine and wineskins can be heard as a reference to Jesus' message (wine) and those who are listening (old and new wineskins, that is, Jews and Gentiles). Matthew's additional words at the end of this saying point to Matthew's emphasis on Jesus' saving words for both Jews and Gentiles.

In addition to including such Markan materials, Matthew expands Mark by adding an infancy narrative (1:1–2:23), a Resurrection narrative (28:1–20), and five major blocks of discourse material (chapters 5–7, 10, 13, 18, 24–25). Much of this added material comes from the Q- and M-sources. Matthew's combining written Jesus materials (Mark, Q, and M), as well as his editorial expansion of these materials, evidences the growth and development of these traditions as the first century unfolds.

Audience and Place of Composition

Attempts to establish Matthew's intended audience are closely tied to theories of the place of composition for the Gospel of Matthew. Numerous features in this Gospel indicate a Judaic-Christian audience (that is, Jews who came to believe that Jesus was the Jewish

Messiah). Here are three such features: the author presents the primary missionary field for the earthly Jesus and his disciples as the nation of Israel (10:5–6; 15:24), the author assumes an understanding of Jewish customs and practices (15:2; 23:5), and the Gospel is highly critical of the Pharisees (for example, 23:1–36) and uses the language of "their synagogues" (4:23; 9:35; 10:17; 12:9; 13:54) and "our church" (16:18; 18:17). Such evidence suggests an audience of Judaic Christians as distinguished from Jews who did not believe that Jesus was the Jewish Messiah.

The conclusion that Matthew has targeted a Judaic-Christian audience and the fact that Matthew writes in Greek have led scholars to identify potential places of composition for the Gospel that had heavily Jewish, Greek-speaking populations. Syria and Palestine are often identified, with Antioch of Syria most often mentioned.[5] Other sites that fit this audience profile and deserve consideration include Galilee and Damascus. Finally, we cannot rule out the possibility that Matthew envisioned a much broader audience, one throughout the Roman Empire, which had a large population of Greek-speaking Jews.

Summary of Historical Setting for Matthew's Gospel

Author:	unknown; later Christian tradition would name "Matthew" (Levi) the tax collector and apostle of Jesus
Date of composition:	approximately 80–85 CE, after the Gospel of Mark
Sources:	primarily Mark, Q, and M (with M being sources available only to Matthew)
Audience and place of composition:	predominantly Judaic Christians; place of composition perhaps Antioch in Syria

Part 2: How Matthew Told the Story

Matthew's particular arrangement and use of many materials from Mark, Q, and M result in his telling the story of Jesus differently than Mark. Attending to such features as Jesus' Sermon on the Mount, the portrayal of Peter's role, the Gospel's groundbreaking concept of "Church," and its partial rehabilitation of the disciples will help us to appreciate Matthew's distinctive message.

The First Verses of Matthew and Mark

A comparison between the opening verses in Matthew and Mark shows that both connect their narratives to Old Testament Scriptures, albeit in different ways:

MARK 1:1–4	MATTHEW 1:1
The beginning of the gospel of Jesus Christ the Son of God. As it is written in Isaiah the the prophet . . . John [the] Baptist appeared in the desert proclaiming a baptism of repentance for the forgiveness of sins.	The book of the genealogy of Jesus Christ, the son of David, the son of Abraham.

Whereas Mark begins by connecting John the Baptist to the Hebrew prophets, Matthew begins by linking Jesus' identity with two of Israel's most significant figures, David and Abraham. For Matthew, Jesus fulfills the covenant that God made with Abraham (Gen 12:2, "I will make of you a great nation, and I will bless you; I will make your name great, so that you will be a blessing") and with David (2 Sam 7:12, "I will raise up your heir after you, sprung from your loins, and I will make his kingdom firm"). From the opening verse, Matthew places an emphasis on Jesus' Jewish ancestry.

The Infancy and Resurrection Narratives

Matthew begins and ends his Gospel differently than Mark. Matthew begins with a genealogy and a series of stories surrounding the birth and early years of Jesus, the so-called infancy narrative (Matt 1:1–2:23), and ends with a Resurrection narrative (Matt 28:11–20). None of the material in the infancy and extended Resurrection narratives comes from Matthew's primary source, the Gospel of Mark. Scholars assign the material present in Matthew, but not in the Gospels of Mark or Luke, to Matthew's M-source.

Following Matthew's opening verse is his genealogy of Jesus (1:2–17). Matthew traces Jesus' roots to venerated Jewish ancestors and to key moments in Israel's salvation history from Abraham to David (about 2000–1000 BCE), from David to the Babylonian exile (about 1000–587 BCE), and from the Babylonian exile to the Messiah (about 587–4 BCE). Genealogies were an important indice of identity in the ancient Mediterranean. The Jewish Scriptures contained numerous genealogies. Matthew's inclusion of Jesus' genealogy established his identity as the Jewish Messiah who has descended from the royal bloodline of David.

One interesting feature in Matthew's genealogy is its inclusion of five women: Tamar (1:3); Rahab and Ruth (1:5); Bathsheba ("wife of Uriah," 1:6); and Mary, the mother of Jesus (1:16). What links these five women from Israel's history is that each bore sons in unusual circumstances. For example, Tamar, having been unjustly treated by her father-in-law, Judah, had to trick Judah into bearing twin sons (see Gen 38). Matthew's audience would have been familiar with the stories associated with each of these mothers and their sons. This would have helped Matthew's community better understand the most unusual circumstance of the birth of Mary's son. For Matthew, the strange and unprecedented

Miraculous Births in Antiquity

Matthew's narration of the union between the human (Mary) and the divine (Holy Spirit) that results in the birth of Jesus (1:18–25) was unprecedented in Jewish Scriptures. But such unions and conceptions were not unheard of in Greek literature. Those familiar with Greek literature would not have seen Matthew's narration of the birth of Jesus as strange or unprecedented.

birth of Jesus is actually part of God's historical pattern of working salvation through irregular unions.

Following the genealogy are the stories of Jesus' birth, the visit of the magi, the flight to Egypt, the slaughtering of the infants, and the return from Egypt (1:18–2:23). These events recall the birth of Moses and the experience of the Exodus, which are central to the story of the Torah. Further, each narrative event is punctuated with prophecies from the Hebrew Scriptures (1:22–23; 2:5–6, 15, 17–18, 23), demonstrating that Jesus' birth fulfills Israelite prophecy.[6] For example, Matthew reports that Herod ordered the massacre of all

Matthew's Fulfillment Prophecies

Scattered throughout Matthew's Gospel are twelve "fulfillment prophecies." Matthew often inserts predictions from the Old Testament prophets into his narrative to serve as "fulfillment prophecies," because the events reported by Matthew are shown to "fulfill" what was predicted by the prophets of the Hebrew Scriptures:

Matthean text	Prophet and text
1. 1:22–23	Isaiah 7:14
2. 2:5–6	Micah 5:1
3. 2:15	Hosea 11:1
4. 2:17–18	Jeremiah 31:15
5. 2:23	Unknown text, possibly connected to a portion of the Old Testament in a manuscript or Jewish writing that has not survived.
6. 4:14–16	Isaiah 8:23
7. 8:17	Isaiah 53:4
8. 12:17–21	Isaiah 42:1–4
9. 13:14–15	Isaiah 6:9–10
10. 13:35	Psalm 78:2
11. 21:4–5	Isaiah 62:11; Zechariah 9:9
12. 27:9–10	Zechariah 11:12–13

The heaviest concentration of the prophetic fulfillment citations (five of the twelve) occurs in the infancy narrative toward the beginning of this Gospel. Generally speaking, the number twelve could function as an allusion to the twelve tribes of ancient Israel, now exemplified by the twelve Apostles and perhaps as well by the aforementioned twelve citations of the Old Testament in Matthew.

boys in Bethlehem two years old and younger (2:16–18), and then inserts this prophetic text:

> Then was fulfilled what had been said through Jeremiah the prophet:
>
> > "A voice was heard in Ramah,
> > sobbing and loud lamentation;
> > Rachel weeping for her children,
> > and she would not be consoled,
> > since they were no more."
> > —Matthew 2:17

Matthew not only begins his Gospel differently than Mark but he also ends it differently. Matthew inserts a Resurrection narrative that includes the report of the empty tomb as found in Mark's Resurrection narrative (compare Mark 16:1–8 with Matt 28:1–10). Matthew then supplements the Markan Resurrection narrative with the report of the Roman soldiers guarding the tomb where Jesus was buried (vv. 11–15) and the resurrected Christ's commission to the disciples (vv. 16–20). Unlike Mark, therefore, Matthew does not end his Gospel at the empty tomb. Among other things, Matthew's extended Resurrection would serve to defuse rumors that Jesus' disciples "invented" the Resurrection of Jesus, because Matthew presents the crucified Jesus alive again, in dialogue with his disciples as the resurrected Christ.

M-Source and Q-Source Materials in Matthew

In addition to revising the Gospel of Mark, Matthew added a substantial amount of new material, creating a Gospel nearly twice the length of Mark's. Scholars commonly identify the non-Markan materials that occur only in the Gospel of Matthew as belonging to Matthew's M-source. Here are some examples of M-source materials:

Opening:

1:1–2:23   The entire infancy narrative, including the genealogy

Parables:

13:24–30   Parable of the weeds among the wheat
13:44–45   Parable of the treasure
13:46   Parable of the pearl

13:47–48   Parable of the net

18:23–35   Parable of the unforgiving servant

20:1–1   Parable of the laborers in the vineyard

21:28–32   Parable of the two sons

25:1–13   Parable of the ten virgins

Sayings:

7:6   Pearls before swine

10:21–23   Coming persecutions

16:17–19   Blessing of Peter

18:15–20   Brother who sins

23:15–22   Denunciation of the Pharisees

27:52–53   Resurrection of the saints

Miracles:

9:32–34   Demon-possessed man who could not speak

17:24–27   Coin in the fish's mouth

Events:

14:28–31   Peter tries to walk on water

27:19   Dream of Pilate's wife

28:11–20   Extended Resurrection narrative

In addition to material from Mark and M, Matthew used a large amount of Q-source material (that is, material not found in Mark but occurring in both Matthew and Luke) to write his Gospel. Because these materials are so exhaustive (more than two hundred verses), many scholars posit that Matthew and Luke made use of one or more sources in addition to Mark. You read about this in chapter 1, in the section on the Two-Source theory. Recall that the Two-Source theory contends Mark was the first written Gospel ("Markan priority") and that Matthew and Luke used Mark as one of their written sources, as well as Q. Examples of Q material in Matthew include:

Parables:

13:31–33   Parable of the mustard seed and leaven (cf. Luke 13:18–21)

18:12–14   Parable of the lost sheep (cf. Luke 15:1–7)

22:1–14   Parable of the wedding feast (cf. Luke 14:15–24)

25:14–30   Parable of the Talents (cf. Luke 19:11–27)

Sayings:

     5:3–12   Beatitudes (cf. Luke 6:20–23)

     7:7–11   Asking and receiving (cf. Luke 11:9–13)

     8:19–22   Would-be disciples (cf. Luke 9:57–60)

     9:6–13   Lord's Prayer (cf. Luke 11:2–4)

     10:34–36   Divisions in the family (cf. Luke 12:51–53)

     12:43–45   Return of an unclean spirit (cf. Luke 11:24–26)

     23:37–39   Lament over Jerusalem (cf. Luke 13:34–35)

Miracles:

     8:5–10, 13   Healing of the centurion's servant (cf. Luke 7:1–10)

Other examples:

     3:7–10   Preaching of John the Baptist (cf. Luke 3:9)

     4:1–11   Temptation of Jesus (cf. Luke 4:1–13)

     11:1–19   John the Baptist questions Jesus (cf. Luke 7:18–35)

The Lord's Prayer

Only the Gospel of Matthew (6:9–13) and the Gospel of Luke (11:2–4) contain what we call the Lord's Prayer. This is referred to as "double-tradition material" and is therefore Q-source, according to the Two-Source theory. Much attention is paid to the differences between these two versions of the Lord's Prayer. If both Matthew and Luke derive this prayer from Q, it is difficult to determine which is closest to the "original" Q version. For example, did Matthew expand Q or did Luke abridge Q?

Such source-critical questions are particularly difficult, because Q materials do not survive independently of these two Gospels. It is possible that Matthew and Luke received versions of Q (that is Q^{Matt} and Q^{Luke}) that had already been edited in different ways. This explanation could account for at least some of the different depictions of Q material in the Lord's Prayer and elsewhere.

Jesus as the New Moses

Matthew's stories of the birth and infancy of Jesus parallel those of two major figures in the Hebrew Scriptures: Moses and Joseph. Matthew's audience would have noticed that some of the stories Matthew includes about Jesus' birth and infancy (the flight to Egypt, the massacre of the infants, and the return to Egypt, 2:13–23) parallel those of the birth of Moses found in Exodus 1:8–2:25. Like Moses, Jesus has his life threatened as an infant, only to be saved by his parents, fleeing to Egypt. The presentation of Jesus as the New Moses continues elsewhere in Matthew, for example, in the Sermon on the Mount (Matt 5–7), with Jesus interpreting the Mosaic Law, and in Jesus' sayings concerning the twelve Apostles as the future judges of the twelve tribes of Israel (Matt 19:27–29) and his blood as the "blood of the covenant" (Matt 26:28).

Matthew presents the story of Jesus' birth and ministry to evoke this image of the Exodus and Moses. By doing so, Matthew associates the birth and ministry of Jesus with some of Israel's most significant events: the Exodus and the giving of the Torah. These events were foundational to Jewish identity and their history as a people.

In addition to associating Jesus with Moses, Matthew's audience may also have connected the dreams that inform and direct Joseph (1:20; 2:13, 19, 22) with those of another Joseph famous for dreams in the Hebrew Scriptures: Joseph, the son of Jacob (Gen 37–50). The latter Joseph became known in Israel's history as a great interpreter of dreams (see, for example, Gen 40–41, where Joseph correctly interprets the Pharaoh's dream and saves Egypt during a famine). Both of these dreamer Josephs proved salvific for the people of Israel.

God's Abiding Presence

A distinctive theme in the Gospel of Matthew is that of God's ongoing presence, which is experienced either directly or through Jesus. At the beginning of the Gospel, at the birth of Jesus, the words of the prophet are recalled and applied to Jesus: "'and they shall name him Emmanuel,' which means, 'God is with us'" (1:23). In the middle of the Gospel, Jesus tells his disciples, "For where two or three are gathered together in my name, there am I in the midst of them" (18:20). And the last words of the resurrected Christ at the end of the Gospel convey this ongoing presence, "And behold, I am with you always, until the end of the age" (28:20b). It was important for Matthew to assure his Judaic-Christian community of God's continuing presence with them. Note also that Jesus' final words indicate his departure, yet Matthew does not narrate the assumption of Jesus, unlike Luke and John.

The Sermon on the Mount and Jewish Law

Matthew 5–7 is commonly referred to as Jesus' famous Sermon on the Mount because Jesus delivers it on a mountain (5:1). The setting of Jesus' sermon merits comparison with the setting of Moses delivering the Law to the people of Israel at the base of Mount Sinai.

Narrative and Discourse Material

The Gospel of Matthew alternates between narrative and discourse material. Matthew inserts five large blocks of discourse material in his narrative, as follows:

The Infancy Narrative: 1:1 – 2:23

Proclamation of the Kingdom: 3:1 – 7:29
        — Jesus' Sermon on the Mount (*discourse 1*): [5:1 – 7:29]

Ministry and Mission in Galilee: 8:1 – 11:1
        — Jesus' missionary discourse (*discourse 2*): [10:1 – 42]

Opposition from Israel: 11:2 – 13:53
        — Jesus' parables (*discourse 3*): [13:1 – 52]

Jesus, the Kingdom, and the Church: 13:54 – 18:35
        — Jesus' community (*discourse 4*): [18:1 – 35]

Ministry in Judea and Jerusalem: 19:1 – 25:46
        — Jesus' eschatological discourse (*discourse 5*): [24:1 – 25:46]

The Passion and Resurrection Narratives: 26:1 – 28:20

In Matthew, narrative material characterized by action propels the plot whereas the discourses are speeches that Jesus delivers at various points. Often, a narrative and the discourse within it share a similar theme.

For Matthew, Jesus' Sermon on the Mount is the new interpretation of the Mosaic Law that all Judaic Christians must now follow. Jesus covers a remarkable range of subjects in this sermon (for example, anger and retaliation, adultery and divorce, almsgiving and prayer). He also develops numerous metaphors for discipleship (for example, salt and light) and lays out the demands for discipleship (love of enemies, proper prayer, and dependence on God).

Two sayings in Jesus' Sermon on the Mount best summarize the main point of this extended discourse: "Do not think that I have come to abolish the law or the prophets. I have not come to abolish but to fulfill" (5:17), and "Do to others whatever you would have them do to you. This is the law and the prophets" (7:12). For Matthew's Judaic-Christian community, the Mosaic Law remains a requirement that is to be informed and supplemented by the golden rule of benevolence toward others.

With the Sermon on the Mount, Matthew presents Jesus as fulfilling the Law, not replacing it. The Matthean Jesus, and Matthew's community, still followed the fundamental tenets of the Law and the prophets.

Parables of Jesus

You may recall that the Gospel of Mark contained only a few parables of Jesus, which were clustered together in Mark 4. The Gospel of Matthew contains many more of Jesus' parables, including several that are unique to Matthew:

13:24–30	Parable of the weeds among the wheat
13:44	Parable of the treasure
13:45–46	Parable of the pearl
13:47–48	Parable of the net
18:23–35	Parable of the unforgiving servant
20:1–16	Parable of the laborers in the vineyard
21:28–32	Parable of the two sons
25:1–13	Parable of the ten virgins

Some of these parables are elaborate stories, whereas others are little more than one-liners. Matthew includes these parables because they describe "the kingdom of heaven," the centerpiece of Jesus' message, as in Matthew 13:44: "The kingdom of heaven is like a treasure buried in a field, which a person finds and hides again, and out of joy goes and sells all that he has and buys that field."

The additional parables in Matthew's Gospel may be simply vehicles for Matthew to communicate his messages, which include God's abiding presence in the community and the need for openness to Gentile inclusion.

Form Criticism and the Interpretation of Parables[7]

As we noted in chapters 1 and 2, in the early twentieth century New Testament scholars began investigating the smaller literary microforms that were incorporated into the Gospels. Form critics focused largely on the Synoptic Gospels.

Scholars such as C. H. Dodd (*The Parables of the Kingdom*, 1935) and Joachim Jeremias (*The Parables of Jesus*, 1947; translated into English in 1954) produced groundbreaking form-critical work on the parables of Jesus.

Challenging the then-prevalent assumption that Jesus' parables were allegories, Dodd applied form-critical principles (matching oral forms to a "setting in life" for Jesus and the early Church) to the parables. In contrast to Rudolf Bultmann, another leading form critic, Dodd concluded that the parables are best understood as rooted in the historical Jesus and his life setting. Jesus' parables centered on the kingdom of God as present in the here and now. Dodd was convinced that the parables must be interpreted in the context of the eschatological (end-time) preaching of Jesus. Dodd referred to this as "realized eschatology." Jeremias carried on the work of Dodd, arguing that the parables go back to Jesus' original "life setting." But Jeremias disagreed with Dodd's one-sided concept of the kingdom of God as a *present* reality (realized eschatology). Jeremias spoke of Jesus' parables as both rooted in the historical Jesus and, as Bultmann had argued, influenced by the early Church. For Jeremias, "principles of transformation" (how the early Church may have "transformed" an original parable by Jesus to better meet their needs of teaching and evangelizing) must be applied to the parables in order to recognize the effect of the early Church on their transmission.

Form critics have helped us recognize that Jesus' parables are short stories or similes that can have many meanings. Jesus' parables include the following:

- Metaphorical aphorisms, or one-liners, such as Matthew 13:44: "The kingdom of heaven is like a treasure buried in a field, which a person finds and hides again, and out of joy goes and sells all that he has and buys that field."

(cont'd.)

(form criticism cont'd.)

- Metaphorical narratives, or extended short stories, such as Matthew 20:1 – 16 wherein Jesus talks with the laborers in the vineyard.

Form critics rightly stress the importance of not reducing the parables to mere fables or allegories that offer only moral instruction. Rather, they argue, the life settings of Jesus and the early Church must also be considered and the theological implications of the parables, recognized. For example, the parable of the laborers in the vineyard (Matt 20:1 – 16) may have circulated in the early Church to encourage Judaic Christians to be more open to Gentile inclusion. The pithy parable of the buried treasure (Matt 13:44, quoted above) is plausibly rooted in the historical Jesus, who hoped to capture the imagination of his followers regarding the remarkable value of the kingdom of heaven.

The Kingdom of Heaven

As Matthew narrates the beginning of Jesus' Galilean ministry, he summarizes Jesus' basic message: "Repent, for the kingdom of heaven is at hand" (Matt 4:17b). You may recall how Jesus' first words are presented in Mark: "This is the time of fulfillment. The kingdom of God is at hand. Repent, and believe in the gospel" (1:15). Here and elsewhere, Matthew consistently changes Mark's "kingdom of God" to "kingdom of heaven." This reflects Matthew's Jewish religious piety, which involved avoiding saying God's name directly. For Jews, God is the Holy Other; saying God's name directly would be a sign of disrespect.

Separating Sheep from Goats (25:31 – 46)

In the ancient Mediterranean, sheep and goats were traditionally considered more than domesticated animals: they symbolized the social values of honor and shame. Sheep symbolized honor, and goats symbolized shame.

In his eschatological discourse (Matt 24 – 25), Jesus' discussion of the end-times — the *eschaton* — is informed by this tradition, as sheep are seated at the right hand of the Son of Man (a place of honor), and goats are seated at his left hand (a place of shame and judgment).

Matthew and Mark on Jesus' Rejection at Nazareth

In the ancient Mediterranean, where collective identity was more highly valued than individual identity, the rejection by one's own kinship group would have been a devastating experience. One's kinship group strongly shaped and defined one's identity. The Synoptic Gospels record the story of Jesus' rejection at Nazareth (Mark 6:1–6; Matt 13:54–58; Luke 4:16–30). We can only imagine how difficult this rejection may have been for Jesus personally.

In his account of Jesus' rejection at Nazareth (13:53–58), Matthew follows Mark's account (6:1–6) closely. When you lay these episodes side by side, you can see that Matthew often follows Mark word-for-word, making only minor changes (for example, compare "the synagogue" [Mark 6:2] to "their synagogue" [Matt 13:54]). But one seemingly minor change that Matthew makes to Mark has profound theological implications:

MARK 6:5	MATTHEW 13:58
So he was not able to perform any mighty deed there, apart from curing a few sick people by laying his hands on them.	And he did not work many mighty deeds there because of their lack of faith.

Whereas Mark limits Jesus' ability to do "mighty deed[s]" (miracles) in Nazareth, Matthew emends this idea of limited power, suggesting instead that Jesus chose not to do "mighty deeds" (miracles) in Nazareth.

Peter and the Church

Matthew is the only Gospel writer to use the term *church*. Matthew uses the term three times in two different passages:

"And so I say to you, you are Peter, and upon this rock I will build my church, and the gates of the netherworld shall not prevail against it." —16:18	"If he refuses to listen to them, tell the church. If he refuses to listen even to the church, then treat him as you would a Gentile or a tax collector." —18:17

Matthew introduces the "church" as a structure that Jesus begins to build in his ministry. Matthew's use of *church* has led scholars to imagine Matthew's community as "the church across the road from the synagogue." Apparently Matthew's Church community had a recognized leadership (18:15–20) and high expectations for its members, including continued adherence to the Mosaic Law (5:17), humility (18:1–5), unconditional forgiveness of each other (18:21–35), and a willingness to sacrifice everything for the kingdom of God (16:24–28; 18:6–9).

Peter figures prominently in Matthew's Gospel (see 14:28–33; 15:15–20; 16:16–20; 16:22–23; 17:1-8; 17:24–27; 18:21–35) and is even portrayed as the spokesman for the other disciples and one whose opinion Jesus solicits and respects (16:17–19; 17:24–27). Jesus, in fact, hands Peter the "keys to the kingdom of heaven" (16:19), informing him, "You are Peter, and upon this rock I will build my church" (16:18). Yet Matthew also portrays Peter as one who lacks sufficient faith, sinking in the water out of fear and requesting Jesus' help (14:28–30). This characterization of Peter teaches the Matthean community about the relationship among Peter, Jesus, and the Church: Peter may be the rock of the Church, but Jesus is the object of its faith.

Rehabilitating the Disciples (Partially)

A subtle but significant change that Matthew makes to Mark is his characterization of the disciples as "men of little faith" (see Matt 6:30; 8:26; 14:31; 16:8; 28:17). Whereas Mark portrays the disciples as largely ignorant of Jesus' identity, Matthew consistently portrays the disciples in a slightly more positive way as "men of little faith." We see this portrayal in passages from the beginning of Jesus' public ministry to his glorious Resurrection. It begins with the episode of Jesus stilling the storm (compare Mark 4:35–41 with Matt 8:23–27), when Jesus questions Peter after Peter fails to walk toward him on water: "Why are you terrified, O you of little faith?" (Matt 8:26). Even in the final episode of Matthew's Gospel, we are told: "When they (the disciples) saw him (the resurrected Christ), they worshiped, but they doubted" (Matt 28:17).

This portrait of the disciples as "men of little faith" recurs throughout Matthew's Gospel. It may be that this characterization mirrors Matthew's own community, just as Mark's portrayal of the disciples as lacking an understanding of Jesus' identity may have mirrored that evangelist's community.

The Problem of Gentile Inclusion

An intriguing aspect of the Gospel of Matthew is its inconsistency regarding the issue of Gentile inclusion. Matthew offers positive and negative portrayals of Gentiles. For example, in the story of the healing of the Canaanite (or Gentile) woman's demon-possessed daughter (Matt 15:21–28), Jesus initially refuses to exorcize the girl, saying, "I was sent only to the lost sheep of the house of Israel" (v. 24). Matthew has added this line to his Markan source for this story (compare Mark 7:24–30). But in the Resurrection narrative, the departing words of the resurrected Christ to his disciples are, "Go, therefore, and make disciples of all nations" (Matt 28:19), thus supporting the idea of Gentile inclusion.

These varying portraits of Gentiles and of the Gentile mission may reflect issues within Matthew's community regarding Gentiles. Although Matthew's community may have been largely Jewish in membership, it is likely that the growth of early Christianity, with its marked influx of Gentiles, was a reality that this Judaic-Christian community had to face, however reluctantly.

The Great Commission

In the final episode of Matthew's extended Resurrection narrative (Matt 28:16–20), Jesus commissions his disciples to evangelize, commanding them to go and baptize "all nations . . . in the name of the Father, and of the Son, and of the holy Spirit" (28:19). Matthew encourages his intended audience of primarily Judaic Christians to be open to Gentile inclusion while maintaining their Jewish loyalty to the unchanging requirements of Mosaic Law (see Matt 5–7).

With this great commission, Matthew is able to bring his Gospel full circle, ending with what scholars refer to as an *inclusio* (Matt 10:5–6), where the mission, once limited to Israel, is directed to all nations.

Summary of How Matthew Told the Story

Core Concepts

- The Gospel of Matthew presents Jesus as the New Moses who fulfills God's historic promises made to Israel through the prophets.
- Matthew wrote his Gospel to update and correct Mark's Gospel and to supplement Mark with numerous materials from M and Q.
- For Matthew, Mark's account was insufficient for the needs of his Judaic-Christian audience.
- The opening verse of Matthew (1:1) emphasizes Jesus' identity as a descendent of Abraham and David.

Supplemental Information

- Both Matthew and Mark begin their Gospels with references to the Old Testament.
- Matthew adds infancy and Resurrection narratives to Mark's account. Whereas Mark focuses on the prophets, Matthew focuses on Abraham and David.
- Matthew's Gospel emphasizes God's abiding presence with the community and the issue of Gentile inclusion.
- Matthew's infancy and Resurrection narratives are comprised of M materials, and his five blocks of discourses integrate numerous materials from Mark, M, and Q.
- Matthew portrays the disciples as "men of little faith," a slight improvement over their depiction as men of little understanding in Mark.
- The Gospel of Matthew is the only Gospel that uses the term *church* to describe the community of believers in Jesus.
- Modern methods for interpreting the Gospels emerged in the eighteenth and nineteenth centuries.

Questions for Review

1. What sources does Matthew use to write his Gospel?
2. List five examples of material that Matthew adds to the Gospel of Mark. What effect do you think these additions have on his overall narrative?

3. Who is Matthew's intended audience?

4. How does Matthew's opening verse connect his narrative with the Jewish Scriptures? Compare this with Mark's opening verses.

5. How does Matthew communicate the theme of God's abiding presence?

6. How do the birth stories of Jesus in Matthew resemble the birth stories of Moses in the Hebrew Scriptures?

7. Why might Matthew prefer the phrase "the kingdom of heaven"?

8. How is Peter's role enhanced in the Gospel of Matthew?

9. Compare the depictions of the disciples in Matthew and Mark. Cite passages to support your comparisons.

10. Discuss passages that demonstrate Matthew's theme of Gentile inclusion.

Questions for Reflection

1. How does Matthew's portrayal of Jesus as the New Moses revise Mark's portrayal of Jesus?

2. Is Matthew's Gospel targeted to Judaic Christians? Defend your response. Explain how this question of audience affects your reading of Matthew.

3. What might have motivated Matthew to slightly rehabilitate the portrayal of the disciples as found in the Gospel of Mark?

4. The Catholic Church would ultimately embrace both Matthew and Mark as Scripture. How do you think the author of Matthew would have viewed Mark's Gospel?

Recommendations for Further Reading

Kingsbury, Jack Dean. *Matthew as Story*. Rev. and enl. ed. Philadelphia: Fortress, 1988.

Kingsbury is one of the leading voices on the literary analysis of the Gospel of Matthew. He explains his literary method for examining Matthew and then applies it to the story of Jesus, the religious leaders, and the disciples. Kingsbury takes up special topics such as the title "Son of Man" and the speeches of Jesus. This easy-to-read book helped define the method of narrative criticism for Gospel studies.

Neyrey, Jerome H. *Honor and Shame in the Gospel of Matthew*. Louisville, Ky.: Westminster John Knox Press, 1998.

Neyrey offers a fresh approach to reading the Gospel of Matthew within its first-century context. Neyrey provides an extended discussion of honor and shame — the fundamental cultural values of the ancient Mediterranean — in Matthew's Gospel, highlighting the rhetoric of praise for Jesus that is evidenced throughout, from Jesus' birth and ministry to his death. An analysis of honor and shame in Matthew's Sermon on the Mount concludes this volume.

Overman, J. Andrew. *Matthew's Gospel and Formative Christianity: The Social World of the Matthean Community*. Minneapolis, Minn.: Fortress, 1991.

Among the best introductions to the Gospel of Matthew, Overman examines this Gospel from the social and historical perspective of the ancient Near East. Overman analyzes Matthew's community from within the first-century social and religious environment from which this Gospel emerged.

Senior, Donald. *What Are They Saying about Matthew?* Rev. and enl. ed. New York: Paulist, 1996.

Revising his original work, *What Are They Saying about Matthew?*, Senior surveys recent research on the Gospel of Matthew, incorporating more than ninety newly published books and articles on Matthew. Senior brings readers up-to-date on some of the best Matthean scholarship from 1985 to 1995, emphasizing what scholars are saying about the setting, sources, and structure of this Gospel, as well as the Matthean view of salvation history, use of the Old Testament, attitude toward the Law and Christology, and view of discipleship and Church. An excellent starting point for the academic study of Matthew.

Wainwright, Elaine M. *Shall We Look for Another? A Feminist Rereading of the Matthean Jesus*. Maryknoll, N.Y.: Orbis Books, 1998.

Wainwright presents a convincing case that one's gender makes a difference in how one reads and interprets the Bible. Focusing on key texts in the Gospel of Matthew, for example, 1:1–2:23 (the genealogy and birth narratives), 15:21–28 (the Canaanite woman), and 16:13–20 (Peter's confession), Wainwright offers a credible method for reading these texts that brings fresh insights into the Gospel of Matthew. This book is an excellent example of feminist interpretation.

Endnotes

1 The internal and external sources for the identity of Matthew are limited. See W.F. Albright and C.S. Mann, *Matthew* (AB; New York: Doubleday, 1971), clx–cxc; Daniel J. Harrington, *The Gospel of Matthew* (SP 1; Collegeville, Minn.: Liturgical, 1991), 8–10; Ulrich Luz, *Matthew 1–7: A Continental Commentary* (Minneapolis: Fortress, 1992), 93–5; Donald A. Hagner, *Matthew 1–13* (WBC 33A; Dallas, Tex.: Word Books, 1993), lxxv–lxxvii; Donald Senior, *Matthew* (Nashville: Abingdon Press, 1998), 21–4; W.D. Davies and Dale C. Allison, *Matthew: A Shorter Commentary* (New York and London: T & T Clark International, 2004), xi–xii.

2 Weighing all the internal and external factors for dating the Gospel of Matthew, most scholars settle on the date *after* Mark (70 CE): Davies and Allison, "most likely between 80 and 95," xii; Harrington, "around A.D. 85," 8; Luz, "one should not put the date for the Gospel of Matthew long after 80," 93.

3 While most commentators mention other source theories (especially the Griesbach theory that Matthew wrote first), in the end most side with the Two-Source theory. See Davies and Allison, xiii–xxii; Senior, 25–26; Harrington, 4–7; Luz, 74–76; and Hagner, xlvi–l.

4 The minority of scholars who support the idea of Matthean priority (i.e., Matthew is the first evangelist to write and Mark uses Matthew) have not convinced most Gospel scholars. See, for example, William R. Farmer, *The Synoptic Problem: A Critical Analysis* (2d ed.; Macon, Ga.: Mercer University Press, 1976); David Dungan, *A History of the Synoptic Problem: The Canon, the Text, the Composition, and the Interpretation of the Gospels* (New York: Doubleday, 1999); E.P. Sanders and M. Davies, *Studying the Synoptic Gospels* (London: SCM Press; Valley Forge, Pa.: Trinity Press International, 1989).

5 Davies and Allison, xiii; Hagner, lxxv; Luz, 90–2; Harrington, 9–10. The external evidence reinforces the location of Antioch. The Jewish historian Josephus speaks of the large Jewish population in Antioch (Josephus, *Jewish Wars* 7:43), and Ignatius, the bishop of Antioch, seems to know the Gospel of Matthew as is indicated by one of his letters: Phil 5.1–2, 8.2.

6 The question of the historicity of events associated with the birth of Jesus (e.g., the visit of the magi, the slaughtering of the infants) comes into particular focus when one compares Matthew's infancy narrative with that of Luke. Though both narratives are self-contained stories that foreshadow the theology of each author's larger Gospel narrative,

Luke and Matthew offer numerous differing details surrounding the birth of Jesus.

7 Much scholarly work continues on the interpretation of the parables of Jesus. An excellent work is John Dominic Crossan, *In Parables: The Challenge of the Historical Jesus* (New York: Harper and Row, 1973). Crossan offers thirteen ways of looking at Jesus' parables. For a more recent work on parables, see Luise Schottroff, *The Parables of Jesus* (trans. Linda M. Maloney; Minneapolis: Fortress, 2006). Schottroff divides his book into three parts: "Learning to See," "In Search of a Non-Dualistic Parable Theory," and "Jesus the Parable-Teller: The Parables in the Literary Context of the Gospels."

The Gospel of Luke: Jesus as the Universal Savior

Introduction

As with the chapters on the Gospels of Mark and Matthew, this chapter examines Luke's historical setting, as well as some of its unique features, such as its focus on women and emphasis on the innocence of Jesus. The author of Luke's Gospel, like that of Matthew's, probably used Mark as one of his major sources. And like Matthew, Luke revises and updates the story of Jesus as found in the Gospel of Mark. But as we will see, Luke brings to the story of Jesus a new and different perspective from those of Mark and Matthew.

Luke-Acts: One Author, Two Volumes

Just as Matthew was writing partly in response to Mark, so too Luke was writing in response to a developing oral and written Gospel tradition. Most scholars today agree that one author wrote both the Gospel of Luke and the Acts of the Apostles. In other words, Luke's "good news" is embodied in two volumes, Luke *and* Acts, or "Luke-Acts."[1] So it is not only the story of Jesus that interests Luke, as is the case with Matthew, Mark, and John, but also the story of the early Church. Luke is writing the story of Jesus *and* the origins of the early Christian movement. This sets him apart from the other evangelists.

Together, Luke's Gospel and Acts comprise the story of how Christianity, rooted in the Jewish Messiah, came to be embraced and eventually dominated by the Gentiles. These two writings narrate what Luke sees as Christianity's core message: the God of Israel provides universal salvation for all people throughout the world.[2]

Emphasis on Historical Context

With this significantly different aim, Luke expands and revises Mark, providing a historical context for the story of Jesus and the early Church. Luke is careful, for example, to place the activities of John the Baptist and Jesus within their historical and chronological context (see Luke 1:5; 2:1–2; 3:1–2). Luke again applies this historical sensitivity in Acts by frequently tracking the activities of Peter, Stephen, Philip, Paul, and others within their historical, social, and geographic contexts (see Acts 4:5–6; 6:8–10; 8:26–27; 12:1–3; 13:1, 13–14). Luke's interest in presenting the story of Jesus and the early Church in its historical context lies, at least in part, in his wish to defend and explain the inclusion of Gentiles into Christianity.[3]

Luke traces this new development in the salvation history of Israel within its specific historical context. His two-volume work encompasses the first sixty years of Church history and comprises about one-fourth of the New Testament.[4]

Time Line for Luke-Acts

We are fortunate that Luke has provided historical figures (for example, the Roman ruler, Tiberius Caesar) with which to date the early events in Church history. Note that Luke and his contemporaries do not mark time the way we do in the modern period.

4 BCE Births of Jesus and John	The births occur in the days of Herod, King of Judea (Luke 1:5). See also Matt 2:19.
28–30 CE Public ministries of John and Jesus	Luke situates these ministries in the fifteenth year of the reign of Tiberius Caesar (28 CE), when Pontius

(cont'd.)

(time line for Luke-Acts cont'd.)

28–30 CE Public ministries of John and Jesus	Pilate is governor of Judea and Herod is Tetrarch of Galilee, during the high priesthood of Annas and Caiaphas (Luke 3:1–2).
30 CE Birth of the Church in Jerusalem	Main historical marker offered by Luke in Acts for the birth of the Church is the period of forty days between the Resurrection and the Ascension (Acts 1) followed by Pentecost (Acts 2).
48 CE Conference of Jerusalem: the Gentile inclusion	Prior to the death of James in 44 CE (Acts 12:2), no historical marker is offered by Luke in Acts for the conference of Jerusalem (Acts 15).
64 CE Paul's house arrest in Rome	Having entered Rome, Paul is placed under house arrest and is guarded by a soldier (Acts 28:16).

A Synoptic Outline

We refer to the Gospels of Matthew, Mark, and Luke as the Synoptic Gospels (*syn-optic* means "seen together"). A comparative sketch of each Gospel illustrates how their presentations overlap.

MATTHEW	MARK	LUKE
1:1–2:23 Birth of Jesus		1:1–2:52 Prologue and birth of John and Jesus
3:1–7:29 Jesus begins proclaiming God's kingdom	1:1–13 Preaching and activities of John the Baptist in Judea	3:1–4:13 Preaching of John and beginning of Jesus' ministry
8:1–11:1 Preaching and activities of Jesus in Galilee	1:14–8:21 Preaching and activities of Jesus in Galilee	4:14–9:50 Preaching and activities of Jesus in Galilee
		(cont'd.)

(Matthew cont'd)	(Mark cont'd)	(Luke cont'd)
11:2–13:53 Opposition to Jesus' message and ministry	8:22–10:52 Jesus' journey to Jerusalem and the passion predictions	9:51–19:44 Travel narrative to Jerusalem
13:54–18:35 Jesus' teaching on the kingdom of heaven and the Church	11:1–13:37 Preaching and activities of Jesus in Jerusalem	19:45–21:38 Preaching and activities of Jesus in Jerusalem
19:1–25:46 Jesus' public ministry in Judea and Jerusalem	14:1–16:8 Suffering, death, and Resurrection of Jesus in Jerusalem	22:1–23:56 Passion narrative in Jerusalem
26:1–28:20 Suffering, death, and Resurrection of Jesus in Jerusalem	16:9–20 Added Resurrection narrative	24:1–53 Resurrection and Ascension narrative

Mark created the paradigm for the written Gospel. The most noticeable changes made by Matthew and Luke are to the beginning and ending of Mark, where they added birth and Resurrection narratives. Furthermore, whereas Matthew and Luke highlight Jesus' preaching and healing in Transjordan (a north-south strip of land east of the Jordan Valley), Mark omits a Transjordan section.

Outline of Luke's Gospel
Following are highlights in the storyline of the Gospel of Luke.

	Prologue
1:1–4	Luke opens his Gospel with a four-verse prologue that provides his reader, Theophilus, with background information about his research and writing strategy.

(cont'd.)

(outline of Luke's Gospel cont'd.)

1:5 – 2:52	**Infancy narrative of Jesus and John the Baptist** Luke presents the announcements and births of John the Baptist and Jesus. Told largely from Mary's point of view, Luke's infancy narrative is adorned with songs from Zechariah, Mary, the angels, and Simeon. Luke includes a story of Jesus as a boy at age twelve.
3:1 – 4:13	**Preaching of John and beginning ministry of Jesus** Like Matthew, Luke connects the preaching of John the Baptist with the start of Jesus' public ministry. Luke also includes a genealogy of Jesus (different from Matthew's) and Jesus' baptism and temptation as the events that initiate Jesus' ministry.
4:14 – 9:50	**Preaching and activities of Jesus in Galilee** Luke presents Jesus' ministry throughout Galilee. Like Matthew and Mark, Luke highlights Jesus' powerful deeds and his message of the kingdom of God. Jesus delivers two of his three passion predictions during his Galilean ministry.
9:51 – 19:44	**Travel narrative to Jerusalem** Luke provides a lengthy description of Jesus' departure from Galilee and his journey to his destiny in Jerusalem, a destiny that will include the Last Supper, Gethsemane, arrest, trials, suffering, death, Resurrection, Ascension, and Pentecost. The implications for what it means to follow Jesus are daunting. Along the journey, Jesus performs mighty deeds and preaches to the crowds, his disciples, and his opponents.
19:45 – 21:38	**Preaching and activities of Jesus in Jerusalem** Luke narrates how, upon Jesus' arrival in Jerusalem, Jesus directly challenges the religious leadership of the city and the Temple. Jesus forewarns his disciples of coming persecutions, the destruction of the Temple, and the coming of the Son of Man.
22:1 – 23:56	**Passion narrative in Jerusalem** Luke tells how, consistent with Jesus' passion predictions, Jesus is handed over to the religious leaders of Jerusalem, who in turn deliver him to be tried by Pontius Pilate. Jesus suffers and dies, but not before both Pontius Pilate and Herod Antipas find him innocent of the charges brought against him.

(cont'd.)

(outline of Luke's Gospel cont'd.)

24:1 – 53	**Resurrection and Ascension narrative** Luke offers an extended Resurrection narrative set in Judea (not Galilee, as Mark anticipates and Matthew narrates) that includes Jesus' Ascension into heaven, setting the stage for the second half of his narrative, the Acts of the Apostles.

Part 1: Historical Setting of Luke's Gospel

As with the chapters on the Gospels of Mark and Matthew, here we will look for internal evidence from the Gospel of Luke and external evidence from early Church witnesses and other New Testament texts to address questions of authorship, date of composition, sources, and intended audience. Unlike Matthew and Mark, the Gospel of Luke (1:1–4) supplies a prologue that offers us some historical footing. Indeed, Luke tells us about his sources, intended audience, and compositional strategy.

Authorship

Like the other writers of the Synoptic Gospels, Luke never directly identifies himself in his work. However, we do have some internal evidence that tells us about the author of Luke-Acts. Two major clues are found in the prologue (1:1–4). First, the evangelist identifies himself as a Christian of the later first century who was not himself witness to the events he narrates. Second, Luke writes that he has sought out "eyewitnesses and ministers of the word" for the "events that have been fulfilled among us" and adds that he "investigated everything accurately anew . . . [in order] to write" an "orderly sequence . . . so that you may realize the certainty of the teachings you have received." These are carefully communicated details about the strategy and thinking that our author employed in writing Luke-Acts.

The author also seems to want to bolster his credibility by writing himself into the narrative in the so-called we-passages of Acts (see Acts 16:10; 20:6; 21:8; 27:1; 28:14b); however, most scholars today dismiss the historicity of his claims. The insertion of the we-passages in the second half of Acts, which focuses on Paul, leaves the impression that the author was traveling with Paul on at least some of Paul's extensive journeys. The we-passages also indicate that the author or his source has considerable knowledge of the geography of the Roman Empire. From the opening of the Gospel in Jerusalem to the closing of Acts in Rome, Luke covers the geographic region from "Jerusalem . . . to ends of the earth" (Acts 1:8).

The obstacle in identifying the authors of the New Testament Gospels is that all were written anonymously. As with "Mark" and "Matthew," the name "Luke" was attached to this writing in the second century CE. We do know that the Pauline letters refer to someone named Luke, about whom we know very little except that a Luke is named as a coworker by both Paul (Philemon 23–24) and two different Deutero-Pauline authors (Col 4:14 and 2 Tim 4:9–11). Some of the early Church fathers

> ## Literary Relationships in Greco-Roman Literature
>
> Patron-client relationships in antiquity were common and involved two parties of unequal social rank. Patrons were socially high-ranking people who had the means to grant "favors" to less socially privileged people. It was not uncommon for authors to dedicate literary works to the patrons who sponsored them. This may be the case with Luke-Acts, with Theophilus being the patron and Luke, his client. In both Luke (1:4) and Acts (1:1), Luke refers to Theophilus in the prologue as "most excellent Theophilus."
>
> We see a similar patron-client relationship between Josephus (a contemporary Jewish historian to Luke) and his patron, Epaphroditus, in Josephus' *Against Apion*:
>
> "In the history of Antiquities, most excellent Epaphroditus, I believe that I made sufficiently clear . . ."
> —*Against Apion* 1.1–3
>
> "In the first book of this work, most esteemed Epaphroditus, I proved the antiquity of our race . . ."
> —*Against Apion* 2.1

attempted to associate the Luke mentioned in the Pauline letters with the author of the Gospel of Luke (for example, second-century Justin Martyr and Irenaeus, as well as third-century Tertullian), but these surviving sources are too late and not sufficiently credible to establish this point of authorship. Furthermore, Luke was a common name in the Roman Empire at the time the Gospels were written.

Date of Composition

In the first words of his prologue, Luke distances himself from the events he narrates. He tells of a process of creating a narrative tradition that is well under way, informing us that "many" have been compiling narratives (v. 1) and that there "were eyewitnesses from the beginning and ministers of the word" prior to him and from whom he has been investigating the events anew, in a more orderly and accurate sequence (vv. 2–3). Luke's choice of words suggest that he is writing his Gospel and Acts sometime in the second half of the first century CE, although there is no evidence to exclude an early second-century date. Luke is writing after Paul's arrival in Rome (the final events narrated in Acts 27–28), which happened probably in the early 60s CE.

As with Matthew and Mark, Luke's Gospel contains an eschatological (end-time) discourse between Jesus and his disciples (see Luke 19:41–44; 21:20–24). This indicates an awareness of events that transpired post-70 CE, after the destruction of Jerusalem and the Temple by the Romans. Because most scholars believe Luke used the Gospel of Mark (composed about 70 CE) as one of his main sources, the most commonly cited date for the writing of Luke-Acts is sometime from 80 to 85 CE.

Sources

Luke's prologue tells us that "many" have undertaken the task of compiling narratives about Jesus. Scholars have concluded that among the many narratives Luke could access in writing his Gospel were Mark's Gospel and Q (the Two-Source theory). The extensive material found only in the Gospel of Luke (nearly 30 percent of the Gospel) is referred to as L-source material. This material was likely derived both from written materials that did not survive independently of their use in Acts and from material that Luke himself composed, perhaps out of oral traditions.[5]

Whereas Luke's L-source material is scattered throughout his Gospel, the Mark and Q-source material is distributed in an alternating pattern in specific sections of Luke's Gospel:

Luke 3:1–6:1	mostly Markan material
Luke 6:20–8:3	mostly Q-source material

Luke 8:4–9:50   mostly Markan material

Luke 9:51–18:14   mostly Q-source material

Luke 18:15–24:11   mostly Markan material

The insertions of Q-source material into the main Markan narrative, which Luke adopted, are commonly referred to as "the little interpolation" (6:20–8:3) and "the big interpolation" (9:51–18:14). Whereas Matthew chopped up his source material and rearranged it in five large blocks, Luke kept large chunks of material from his sources intact and tended to follow Mark's order. For this reason, scholars who accept the Q-hypothesis infer that Luke is a more reliable source for the original order of Q materials. Also unlike Matthew, who uses 90 percent of the Gospel of Mark, Luke uses only one-third of Mark's Gospel, completely omitting two sections: Mark 6:45–8:26 and Mark 9:41–10:12. The exclusions of these two sections by Luke are referred to as "the big omission" (6:45–8:26) and "the little omission" (9:41–10:12).

The author of Luke-Acts most likely had few sources available to him in the writing of Acts, certainly no written sources that we know of. But some scholars believe the we-passages in Acts may have come from Luke's (or someone else's) travel journal. Other scholars suggest that perhaps Luke had a "Jerusalem" source and an "Antioch" source for the opening chapters of Acts.[6] The sources for Acts will be discussed in more detail in chapter 5, "The Acts of the Apostles."

Audience and Place of Composition

We look last at the question of intended audience. Luke-Acts offers plenty of internal evidence indicating that his intended audience was largely Gentile Christian. It seems highly unlikely that Luke had only one reader (Theophilus) in mind. Indeed, his overarching focus on the Gentile mission, and the inclusion of Gentiles without requiring circumcision for male converts, strongly suggests Luke's intended audience included Gentiles. This by no means excludes the probability that Judaic Christians who embraced the validity of such a Gentile mission were also a part of Luke's intended audience. Indeed, Luke is writing to explain and perhaps defend the Gentile mission as a legitimate and divine initiative.

The content of Luke-Acts provides ample evidence for Luke's overarching concern for the Gentiles. Even if we limit our search to the three main figures in Luke-Acts (Jesus, Peter, and Paul), we see an emphasis on Gentile Christians. At Jesus' first speech in his rejection at Nazareth (Luke 4:16–30), Jesus tells his fellow Nazarene villagers that, just like the prophets Elijah and Elisha, his "good news" will be taken to the Gentiles, to non-Israelites (Luke 4:24–27). Peter's vision (Acts 10:9–16) leads to his insight, "In truth, I see that God shows no partiality" (Acts 10:34). This facilitates the full inclusion of the Gentiles into the Christian movement, a controversial issue that was settled at the conference of Jerusalem, according to Acts 15. With Paul's stop in the Antioch synagogue (Acts 13:13–52) on his first missionary journey, a pattern is set that repeats itself throughout the remainder of Acts: Paul brings the good news of Jesus to the Jews in their synagogues and then, after being rejected, tells the Jews, "It was necessary that the word of God be spoken to you first, but since you reject it and condemn yourselves as unworthy of eternal life, we now turn to the Gentiles" (v. 46).

A more vexing question concerns *where* Luke-Acts may have been written. On this, there is virtually no internal evidence and only scant external evidence. Indeed, the location of the writing of Luke-Acts remains uncertain.

Summary of Historical Setting for Luke-Acts

Author:	unknown; later Church tradition names "Luke," the traveling companion and coworker of Paul
Date of composition:	about 80–85 CE, after the Gospel of Mark
Sources:	according to the Two-Source theory, Mark, Q, and L (with L being a combination of oral and written sources available only to Luke)
Audience and place of composition:	Theophilus and predominantly Gentile Christians; unknown place of composition

Part 2: How Luke Told the Story

With his prologue and infancy narrative, his telling of Jesus' table fellowship, and his emphasis on the importance of Jerusalem and the Temple, Luke has a unique way of telling the story of Jesus. These aspects distinguish Luke from the other Synoptic Gospel writers, Matthew and Mark.

Luke's Infancy Narrative

Mark begins his story of Jesus with the appearance of John the Baptist, which is linked to a citation of the Old Testament prophets Isaiah and Malachi. But Luke, like Matthew, begins his narrative with the birth of Jesus. The infancy narratives of Matthew and Luke are self-contained stories that frame and foreshadow their upcoming narratives. Unlike Matthew, who narrates only the birth of Jesus (Matt 1:1–2:23), Luke sees the birth of John the Baptist as inseparable from the birth of Jesus. Both births must be told to demonstrate fully what the God of Israel was initiating in these two sons, not just for Israel but for all people, Jew and Gentile. The parallel structure within Luke's infancy narrative underlines this point:

JOHN'S BIRTH	JESUS' BIRTH
1:5 Historical setting identified for announcement of John's birth	2:1–2 Historical setting identified for announcement of Jesus' birth
1:5–25 Announcement of John's birth	1:26–38 Announcement of Jesus' birth
1:67–79 Canticle of John's father, Zechariah	1:46–55 Canticle of Jesus' mother, Mary
1:57–66 Birth of John	2:1–20 Birth of Jesus
1:80 Summary statement on John	2:40, 52 Summary statement on Jesus

A comparison between the infancy narratives of Luke and Matthew reveals numerous similarities and differences. Following is a partial list of these, with editorial rationale:

- Both infancy narratives rely heavily on the Hebrew Scriptures, indicating that Matthew and Luke viewed the birth of Jesus (and John, in Luke's case) as part of Israel's story of salvation.
- Both infancy narratives present the God of Israel as controlling the events leading to the birth of the Messiah.
- Matthew tells the infancy narrative from Joseph's point of view; Luke tells the infancy narrative from Mary's point of view. The authors' respective choices might exemplify and be understood as the attempt of the early Christian tradition to balance the perspectives of Mary and Joseph.
- Matthew tells the birth story of Jesus; Luke tells the birth stories of both John and Jesus.
- Matthew presents the magi as witnesses to the birth of Jesus; Luke presents the shepherds as witnesses.
- Whereas Matthew presents Jesus' infancy and youth as beginning in Bethlehem, moving to Egypt, and then settling in Nazareth, Luke presents them as beginning in Nazareth, moving to Bethlehem, and then returning to Nazareth.

These infancy narratives cannot be harmonized into a single, coherent narrative nor traced to the same Q-source. Therefore, scholars classify the infancy narratives of Matthew and Luke as M- and L-source material, respectively. Because the infancy narratives of Matthew and Luke function largely to foreshadow their particular stories of Jesus, we find, not surprisingly, two different presentations of Jesus' birth.

The core of Luke's infancy narrative is unique to Luke (L-source) and probably stems from the author "investigat[ing] everything . . . anew." The great canticles (songs) of Mary (Luke 1:46–55) and Zechariah (Luke 1:68–79) articulate not only how God's past promises to Israel are realized beginning with the births of John and Jesus but also how God's fulfilled promises bring about a great reversal of fortune for the strong and the weak, the privileged and the marginalized. The angelic visitations to Zechariah and Mary

(1:5–20; 1:26–38) and to the shepherds in the fields (2:8–14) reveal the true identity of John as prophet and forerunner of Jesus, Son of the Most High, the Lord and Messiah. The words of the prophets Simeon and Anna in Jerusalem's Temple (2:22–38) speak of God's salvation offered to both Jews and Gentiles and point to the "contradiction" (controversy) that will mark their ministries. The divine guidance that characterizes the ministry of Jesus and the early Church is suggested by Luke's description of the Holy Spirit "filling" John; John's parents, Elizabeth and Zechariah; and Simeon (1:15, 42, 67; 2:25, 27); and "overshadowing" Mary (1:35). The geographic references to Jerusalem, Nazareth, and Bethlehem (1:9, 26; 2:4, 22, 25, 38–39, 51) highlight the importance of these three places in the early Church: Bethlehem being the prophesied birthplace of the Messiah; Nazareth, the home of Jesus the Messiah; and Jerusalem, the capital city of the Promised Land and home of the Temple, the symbol of Israel's cultic and national identity.

The Boy Jesus, Luke 2:41–51

Luke's infancy narrative ends with a story of Jesus at age 12. In this episode, Luke foreshadows the entire storyline of the Gospel. All of the elements of Jesus' adult ministry are present:

- Jerusalem and the Temple are the main setting.
- Jesus' singular focus is on the affairs of his "Father's house."
- Observers of Jesus are "astounded" at him, as they will be later at his teachings (see, for example, 4:22; 5:26).
- Jesus' actions stir controversy (Mary and Joseph experience "great anxiety").
- "Three days" is a key time frame.

This is the only passage in the New Testament Gospels that mentions anything about Jesus' life between his birth and the beginning of his public ministry. As we shall see in chapter 8, some second-century extracanonical gospels reflect a greater interest in Jesus as a youngster.

Special Lukan Material

With 1,151 verses, the Gospel of Luke is the longest of the four New Testament Gospels. Nearly one-third of its contents occurs only in Luke. The following material, unique to Luke, is either taken from Luke's L-source(s) or composed by Luke himself:

Opening:

 1:1–2:52 Prologue and infancy narrative

Parables:

 10:29–37 Parable of the good Samaritan

 12:16–21 Parable of the rich fool

 13:6–9 Parable of the barren fig tree

 15:8–10 Parable of the lost coin

 15:11–32 Parable of the lost son

 16:1–8 Parable of the dishonest steward

 16:19–31 Parable of the rich man and Lazarus

 18:1–8 Parable of the persistent widow

 18:9–14 Parable of the Pharisee and the tax collector

Sayings:

 3:10–14 John the Baptist's reply to questions from the crowds

 14:7–14 Jesus' lesson to the Pharisees on conduct at table fellowship

 14:28–33 Counting the costs of discipleship

Miracles:

 5:1–11 Peter's catch of fish

 7:11–17 Raising of the widow's son

 13:10–17 Healing the crippled woman on the Sabbath

 14:1–6 Healing the man with dropsy on the Sabbath

Events:

 7:36–50 Pardon of the sinful woman

 8:1–3 Galilean women as followers and providers

 9:51–56 Rejection by Samaritan village

 10:38–42 Martha and Mary

 19:1–10 Zacchaeus the tax collector

 19:41–44 Jesus weeps over Jerusalem

 23:6–12 Jesus before Herod Antipas

 24:1–53 The extended Resurrection and Ascension narrative

The Genealogy of Jesus in Luke

Both Matthew 1:1−17 and Luke 3:23−38 provide genealogies for Jesus. In the first-century Mediterranean world, people were identified by their "three Gs": gender, geography, and genealogy. That Jesus is male (gender), born in Bethlehem, and raised in Nazareth (geography) is well attested in the Gospel tradition. Regarding Jesus' genealogy, however, Matthew and Luke stake out different theological positions. For Matthew, Jesus' genealogy moves forward in time, indicating that Jesus is the Jewish Messiah, son of Abraham and David, long awaited and orchestrated by the God of Israel. For Luke, the genealogy of Jesus moves backward in time, including and transcending his Jewish roots, to Adam, the first human father of all people, and to God, the heavenly Father of all, Jew and Gentile alike. Jesus is Lord, Messiah, and Son of God for all people.

Matthew and Luke also differ in their placement of the genealogies in their infancy narratives. Matthew begins his Gospel with a genealogy of Jesus, while Luke inserts his genealogy further into the narrative, between the baptism and the temptation of Jesus. Also, by tracing Jesus' genealogy back to Adam, the father of *all humanity*, Luke assures his audience that Gentiles too belong to Jesus' ancestry.

Luke 4:16 – 30: The "Gospel" within the Gospel

Luke begins the section on the preaching and activities of Jesus in Galilee with the rejection of Jesus at Nazareth, 4:16−30. The significance of this episode is hard to overstate, as Luke captures the entire plot of his Gospel within it; it is, literally, the "gospel" within the Gospel. Luke significantly expands and rewrites the rejection of Jesus at Nazareth as presented in Mark (6:1−6) and Matthew (13:54−58). Like the songs of Mary and Zechariah in Luke's infancy narrative, Jesus' speech in his Nazarene synagogue on the Sabbath offers a glimpse of God's salvific (that is, saving) work in the world. This shows well how Luke takes a historical event (Jesus' rejection at Nazareth) and presents it in light of a theological truth (universal salvation).

Jesus' first speech, which was delivered in Nazareth, describes the framework for his mission and ministry:

"The Spirit of the Lord is upon me, because he has anointed me to bring glad tidings to the poor. He has sent me to proclaim liberty to captives and recovery of sight to the blind, to let the oppressed go free, and to proclaim a year acceptable to the Lord."

—Luke 4:18–19

Old Testament prophecy, Jesus proclaims, is being fulfilled: "Today this scripture passage is fulfilled in your hearing" (4:21). Not only are God's past promises being fulfilled in Jesus' Spirit-driven ministry but also a great reversal is taking place wherein the socially marginalized and the Gentiles are now recipients of the "good news." What follows—the violent reaction of Jesus' own kin in Nazareth, who drive him from town and threaten to kill him, and Jesus' near miraculous escape (v. 30)—foreshadows Jesus' upcoming crucifixion, Resurrection, and Ascension.

Luke presents Jesus' ministry throughout Galilee as fulfilling some of the prophecies of the Hebrew Scriptures (Isaiah 60:1–2 in Luke 4:18–19). Salvation is offered to all, Jew and Gentile, rich and poor, powerful and marginalized. As Jesus travels throughout Galilee and the surrounding northern regions of Israel's Promised Land, the demon-possessed are freed (4:31–37; 8:26–39; 9:37–43), the sick and unclean are healed (5:12–16; 7:1–10; 8:43–48), the dead are raised to life (7:11–17; 8:40–42, 49–56), and even sins are forgiven (5:17–26). Jesus' Galilean ministry produces both astonishment (5:26; 7:16–17; 8:25, 56) and controversy (5:30–32; 6:1–11; 7:39). We hear how Jesus views John the Baptist (the greatest prophet of all, 7:26–28), and more significantly, how

Luke's "Orderly Sequence"

"I too have decided, after investigating everything accurately anew, to write it down in an orderly sequence . . ."
—Luke 1:3

The details and placement of Luke 4:16–30 provide a prime example of Luke reworking prior narratives anew.

Whereas Mark (and Matthew) place Jesus' rejection at Nazareth *after* his call of the disciples, Luke's investigation reveals that Jesus was rejected at Nazareth *before* his call of the disciples. Perhaps this revised "orderly sequence" stems from Luke's "eyewitnesses" and "ministers of the word" (1:2).

Jesus views himself—metaphorically, as physician and bride-groom (5:31, 34), and as prophet (4:24) and Son of Man (5:24; 7:34; 9:22, 26, 44).

Luke's Concern for Women

Women figure prominently in Luke's Gospel. He is often careful to balance men and women in his Gospel: for example, in the infancy narrative we have Zechariah and Mary, Simeon and Anna; and in Jesus' public ministry we have the healing of a woman on the Sabbath (13:10–17) and the healing of a man on the Sabbath (14:1–6). Luke also consistently presents Jesus' concern for widows: Jesus raises the widow's son from the dead (7:11–17), tells a parable about a persis-tent widow (18:1–8), decries scribes who take advantage of widows (20:45–47), and holds up widows as models of faith because they generously give to others in need (21:1–4).

Luke also mentions a select group of women who accompanied Jesus and the Twelve as they visited the towns and villages of Galilee:

> Accompanying him were the Twelve and some women who had been cured of evil spirits and infirmities, Mary, called Magdalene, from whom seven demons had gone out, Joanna, the wife of Herod's steward Chuza, Susanna, and many others who provided for them out of their resources.
>
> —Luke 8:2–3

These women (Mary Magdalene, Joanna, Susanna, and "many oth-ers") "provided" for Jesus and the Twelve "out of their resources." It was not uncommon for Pharisees to have financial support from women for their interests and activities. The women remain with Jesus through his public ministry, all the way to the Resurrection (24:1–12, esp. v. 10). Luke emphasizes the role of women in the life of Jesus in order to affirm the theological truth of God's invitation to universal salvation.

None of the evangelists records Jesus calling women to discipleship as he calls men. Yet, Luke (alone) shows Jesus praising Mary, the sister of Martha, for her decision to sit "beside the Lord at his feet listen-ing to him speak" (10:39). In the culture of Jesus' day, only men sat at their master's feet, assuming the position of disciple. Given the social (patriarchal) reality of Luke's day, this may have been the closest the author could come to telling his readers that Jesus had women disciples.

Jesus' Table Fellowship

One of the hallmarks of Jesus' public ministry was table fellowship. Although each Gospel presents Jesus in table fellowship with others, none presents Jesus eating and drinking as often as Luke. Nineteen times Luke shows Jesus eating meals with people ranging from sinners and outcasts to the religious elite (the Pharisees). Thirteen of these episodes are peculiar to Luke (that is, come from Luke's L-source). Furthermore, in the Gospel of Luke, Jesus often speaks about food and eating in parables (for example, 7:36–50; 14:7–14, 15–24; 16:19–30). Jesus' opponents see his practice of table fellowship as cause for criticism:

> For John the Baptist came neither eating food nor drinking wine, and you said, "He is possessed by a demon." The Son of Man came eating and drinking and you said, "Look, he is a glutton and a drunkard, a friend of tax collectors and sinners."
>
> —Luke 7:33–34

In Luke's Gospel, the clean and the unclean, the Jew and the Gentile, the sinner and the law-abiding are all welcome to share table fellowship with Jesus. Jesus' table fellowship highlights Luke's emphasis on Jesus as the universal savior. For Luke, Jesus' reclining at table was a public and visible sign—a clear message that all people are welcome in the kingdom of God.

Jesus' Travel Narrative in Luke

Luke 9:51–19:44 is commonly referred to as Luke's travel narrative. These ten chapters narrate Jesus' journey from Galilee to the city of Jerusalem in Judea and are an expansion of Mark 8:21–10:52. On the journey, Jesus teaches his disciples what true discipleship entails, confronts his opponents (mostly the Pharisees) for abusing their power and privilege, and challenges the crowds to accept his invitation to follow him. The following chart highlights these themes of teaching, confronting, and challenging found throughout the Lukan travel narrative.

Jesus teaching his disciples on the journey	Jesus confronting his opponents on the journey	Jesus challenging the crowds on the journey
9:51–56	10:13–16	9:57–62
10:1–12	11:37–54	10:25–37
10:17–20	13:10–17	11:14–23
10:21–24	13:18–19	11:24–26
10:38–42	13:20–21	11:29–32
11:1–4	13:31–33	11:33–35
11:5–8	14:1–6	12:13–21
11:9–13	14:7–14	12:54–56
12:1–9	14:15–24	12:57–59
12:10–12	15:1–7	13:1–5
12:25–38	15:8–10	13:6–9
13:22–34	15:11–32	13:22–30
13:35–48	16:8	14:25–35
13:49–53	16:14–15	17:11–19
16:1–12	16:16–17	18:15–17
17:1–4	16:19–31	18:35–43
17:5–6	17:20–21	19:1–10
17:7–10	18:9–14	19:11–27
17:22–37	18:18–30	18:31–34
18:1–8	18:28–30	

You will note from the preceding chart that Jesus speaks with rather equal frequency to his disciples, his opponents, and the crowds while traveling to Jerusalem. Whereas almost every episode within the travel narrative involves one of these three groups, the two exceptions are 13:34–35 and 19:41–44. In the first of these passages, Jesus laments Jerusalem's past and present and warns of future judgment; in the second, Jesus laments Jerusalem's historic rejection of prophets sent to Isreal by God and warns of the impending destruction of Jerusalem and the Temple. The centrality of Jesus' extended journey to Jerusalem in Luke reinforces both the geographic focal point of Jerusalem in Luke-Acts and the tragic consequences of Jerusalem's blindness to God's salvation, which is offered in the prophetic ministry of Jesus.

Jesus and Ezekiel

Luke 9:51–19:44 narrates Jesus' journey to Jerusalem. As Jesus commences this journey, Luke tells us, "he set his face to go to Jerusalem" (9:51b). Some translate this passage as "he resolutely determined to journey to Jerusalem," but that translation misses Luke's point, captured in the phrase "set his face." For Luke to say Jesus "set his face" calls to mind Ezekiel 21:7–8, where the Lord tells Ezekiel, "Son of Man, set your face against Jerusalem . . . prophesy against the land of Israel." For Luke, Jesus' message and ministry in Jerusalem were very much within and connected to the prophetic tradition of Israel.

As Jesus teaches his disciples and challenges the crowds on his journey, we learn much about Luke's definition of discipleship. For Luke, disciples are privileged witnesses (10:21–24, 38–42), people of prayer guided by the Holy Spirit (11:1–13; 12:10–12). They are "sent out" to preach the good news of the kingdom of God (10:1–12). But the cost of discipleship is high. A disciple of Jesus must keep a proper attitude toward possessions and wealth; this is a prominent Lukan theme—more prominent than in the other New Testament Gospels (see 12:13–21, 22–34; 14:25–38; 16:19–31; 18:18–23, 24–30; 19:1–10). The parable of the rich man and Lazarus (Luke 16:19–31) provides a good example of how Luke reinforces this theme of poverty and riches. A disciple must also serve others (see 10:29–37; 12:35–48; 17:7–10; 19:11–27), be humble (see 14:7–14; 18:9–14), and be willing to follow unconditionally (9:57–62) and "carry his own cross and come after" Jesus (14:25–38).

Other Lukan themes, such as the importance of mercy, repentance, and forgiveness, are highlighted in Luke 15 and the parables of the lost sheep, the lost coin, and the prodigal son. Note that two of these three parables are unique to Luke, highlighting the likelihood that he chose them because they reinforce themes important to his Gospel.

As Jesus speaks to his opponents in the travel narrative, we learn that a great reversal is taking place as the past promises that God made to Israel are being fulfilled in Jesus' mission and ministry. The hypocrisy of the Pharisees and scribes is exposed (see 11:37–54; 12:1; 13:10–17; 16:14–15; 18:9–14), and their privileged positions are being taken away (see 13:22–30; 14:15–24). God's invitation to salvation is no longer limited to Israel but is offered to all, Jew and Gentile alike, and especially to the marginalized and lost (see 14:1–6; 15:1–7; 15:8–10; 15:11–32; 18:35–43; 19:1–10).

Parables of Jesus in Luke's Travel Narrative

In Luke, Jesus tells the following 12 parables as he travels to Jerusalem. Of these, 9 are found only in Luke and are noted with an asterisk (*).

10:29–37*	The good Samaritan
12:13–21*	The rich fool
13:6–9 *	The barren fig tree
14:15–24	The great feast
15:1–7	The lost sheep
15:8–10*	The lost coin
15:11–32*	The prodigal son
16:1–8*	The dishonest steward
16:19–31*	The rich man and Lazarus
18:1–8*	The persistent widow
18:9–14*	The Pharisee and the tax collector
19:11–27	The ten gold coins

As you read these parables, consider whom Jesus is addressing (his disciples, his opponents, or the crowds). Knowing Jesus' audience often helps to understand the meaning of the parable and the theology of Luke.

The Importance of Jerusalem

Jerusalem is the geographic focal point for Luke as he narrates God's saving work for the world. The Gospel begins and ends in the Temple of Jerusalem (1:5–25 and 24:51–53). The entire middle section of the Gospel (9:51–19:44) depicts Jesus' journey to Jerusalem, with frequent reminders that Jerusalem is Jesus' destiny (9:51; 13:22; 17:11; 18:31; 19:11). Twice on his journey, Jesus weeps over Jerusalem, once as he approaches the city (13:34–35), and once as he arrives there (19:41–44). Jesus' death and Resurrection occur in Jerusalem (22–24). The birth of the Church (the opening episodes of Acts 1–7) begins in Jerusalem. And Peter and Paul consistently return to Jerusalem in the midst of their missionary work throughout Acts. Recall from chapter 1 how important Jerusalem and the Temple were to the national and cultic identity of first-century Jews.

Form Criticism and Interpreting the Passion Narrative

Each of the New Testament Gospels contains a "passion narrative" (a recounting of the suffering and death of Jesus): Matt 26–27, Mark 14–15, Luke 22–23, and John 18–19. The leading form critics of the twentieth century, such as Rudolf Bultmann and Martin Dibelius, argue that the passion narrative held a distinct place within the oral tradition of the early Church.[7]

You will recall from the discussions of form criticism in chapters 2 and 3 that form critics contend that many miracles and parables circulated independently in written form as distinct, individual units prior to their incorporation into longer Gospel narratives. The survival of these individual units was assured because they proved to be useful in the "life setting" (or daily life) of early Christian communities.

Form critics maintain that much of the material that was eventually incorporated into the Synoptic Gospels at first circulated independently, without a single, connected narrative of the life of Jesus like that in the Gospel of Mark. There was one exception to this general rule, however: the passion narrative.

Bultmann and Dibelius argue that a pre-Markan passion story of Jesus, connecting the events from the Last Supper to the death on the cross, circulated in written form at a very early point in the formation of the gospel tradition. This connected narrative of the passion of Jesus would be, then, the earliest written attempt to put the events of Jesus' life and death within a larger context.

A likely reason for this exceptional development would be the need of Jesus' followers to explain how Jesus could be betrayed by a trusted disciple (Judas) and executed as a disgraced criminal. The passion narrative gave context and conveyed meaning in a way that these incidents reported in isolation could not.

The Innocence of Jesus

More than any other evangelist, Luke presses the issue of Jesus' innocence of the capital crime for which he stands accused. Three times Pilate speaks of Jesus' innocence:

23:4 "I find this man not guilty."

23:15 "So no capitol crime has been committed by him."

23:22 "What evil has this man done? I found him guilty of no capitol crime."

Luke is also the only evangelist to report Jesus' standing accused before Herod Antipas:

23:14–15 "I (Pilate) have conducted my investigation in your presence and have not found this man guilty of the charges you have brought against him, nor did Herod, for he sent him back to us."

In Luke the centurion at the foot of Jesus' cross states:

23:47 "This man was innocent beyond doubt."

Luke is arguing for the legitimate status of the early Church. If Jesus deserved capital punishment, then the early Church would be an illegal organization. But both the political authorities (Pilate and the centurion) and the religious authorities (Herod Antipas) of Jesus' day found him innocent. By Luke exonerating Jesus and the religious authorities, the blame shifts to the Jews, which is a prominent theme in Acts. The innocence of Peter and Paul is also emphasized in Acts as they too stand accused of crimes.

Herein lies a good example of how one of Luke's theological themes (the innocence of Jesus and placing blame on the Jews) overrides the historical complexity of determining who was responsible for the death of Jesus. Missing this complexity and not appreciating the cultural conditions at the time the evangelists wrote have led to the sort of anti-Semitism decried by the Church today. This will be discussed in more detail in chapter 7, "The Historical Jesus."

The Ascension of Jesus

With the exception of Mark 16:19 (a second-century addition to Mark's Gospel), no other New Testament writer attests to the Ascension of Jesus. Luke, on the other hand, narrates Jesus' Ascension twice: once in the final episode in the Gospel of Luke (24:50–53) and again in the opening episode of Acts of the Apostles (1:6–11). Luke presents the Ascension of Jesus as the key event linking the ministry of Jesus to the birth of the early Church.

In Luke's Gospel the final words of Jesus before his Ascension offer a summary that integrates the Gospel's theological truths into a single statement for Theophilus and Luke's intended audience: "Thus is it written that the Messiah would suffer and rise from the dead on the third day and that repentance, for the forgiveness of sins, would be preached in his name to all nations, beginning from Jerusalem" (24:46–47).

Summary of How Luke Told the Story

Core Concepts

- The Gospel of Luke presents Jesus as the universal savior to all people, Jews and Gentiles, men and women, clean and unclean.
- Luke writes his Gospel subsequent to the appearance of, and as a correction to, "many narratives" so that Theophilus may know the "certainty" of his instruction.
- Jerusalem, and especially the Temple, is the geographic focal point of the Gospel of Luke.
- Luke 4:16–30 foreshadows and summarizes the story in Luke's Gospel.

Supplemental Information

- Luke's infancy narrative presents a parallel structure highlighting both Jesus and John the Baptist.
- Luke's genealogy (3:23–38) points to his interest in the Gentile mission by culminating in Jesus as "son of Adam, son of God," in whom all people are descendents.
- Most of Luke's parables are unique to this Gospel and tell us much about this author's theology.
- Women are prominent in Luke's Gospel.
- Luke's "travel narrative" of Jesus from Galilee to Jerusalem (9:51–19:44) is a unique literary feature within the Gospel tradition.
- Jesus spends much time in table fellowship in the Gospel of Luke.
- Luke emphasizes the innocence of Jesus.
- Luke is the only evangelist to narrate the Resurrection *and* Ascension of Jesus.

Questions for Review

1. What does the prologue to Luke's Gospel (1:1–4) tell us about this author?
2. What sources did Luke use in writing his Gospel?
3. Why is Luke seen as writing primarily for a Gentile audience?
4. Explain how Luke 4:16–30 (the story of Jesus' rejection at Nazareth) is "the gospel" within the Gospel.
5. How does Luke's genealogy differ from Matthew's?
6. What three groups does Luke organize his source material around for Jesus' journey to Jerusalem (Luke 9:51–19:44)?
7. How does Luke focus on women, the poor, and the marginalized?
8. How did Jesus use table fellowship in his public ministry?
9. Explain the importance of Jerusalem in Luke's Gospel.
10. How does Luke stress the innocence of Jesus? Whom does Luke blame for Jesus' execution?

Questions for Reflection

1. How does the prologue (1:1–4) aid in understanding the Gospel of Luke?
2. In Luke-Acts, how does Luke defend his belief that the Gentiles are to be included in Christianity?
3. Luke presents Jesus' radically inclusive vision of the Gentiles, the poor, and the unclean in the kingdom of God. Are there modern implications for such a vision? Explain.
4. How does Luke present Jesus as the savior to all people?

Recommendations for Further Reading

Johnson, Luke Timothy. *The Gospel of Luke*. Sacra Pagina 3. Collegeville, Minn.: The Liturgical Press, 1991; *The Acts of the Apostles*. Sacra Pagina 5; Collegeville, Minn.: The Liturgical Press, 1992.

A prolific scholar, Johnson specializes in Luke-Acts. These Sacra Pagina volumes on Luke and Acts offer up-to-date introductions, critical notes, interpretations, and comments for each individual episode (pericope).

Powell, Mark Allan. *What Are They Saying about Luke?* Mahwah, N.J.: Paulist, 1989.

As with each volume in the "What Are They Saying about . . ." (WATSA) series, this is an excellent starting point for the academic study of Luke. Powell presents current thinking about the author of Luke, the Gospel itself, and the community that Luke addresses. He starts with a look at how this evangelist has come to be viewed as a historian, theologian, and author and then details theories about the composition of Luke's Gospel, the concerns of Luke's community, and the theology that drives Luke (Christ and salvation). Powell concludes with a discussion of the political, social, and pastoral issues associated with the Gospel of Luke.

Reid, Barbara E. *Choosing the Better Part? Women in the Gospel of Luke.* Collegeville, Minn.: The Liturgical Press, 1996.

An established biblical scholar, Reid examines biblical texts from a feminist perspective. Here she uses feminist methodology and the standard historical-critical approach (author, audience, and purpose) to consider the women in the Gospel of Luke. She then focuses on women's participation in discipleship and mission in Luke and Acts. An analysis of specific women in Luke's Gospel, such as Elizabeth and Mary, Anna, Simon's mother-in-law, and the widow of Nain concludes the volume.

Talbert, Charles H. *Literary Patterns, Theological Themes, and the Genre of Luke-Acts.* Missoula: Scholars Press, 1974.

Another book for students interested in better understanding the literary dialogue among Lukan scholars as they research and write on Luke-Acts. Talbert's work is a standard in understanding the historical, theological, and literary dynamics of Luke-Acts.

Tannehill, Robert C. *The Narrative Unity of Luke-Acts: A Literary Interpretation.* Vol. 1, *The Gospel According to Luke.* Philadelphia: Fortress, 1986. Vol. 2, *The Acts of the Apostles.* Minneapolis: Fortress, 1990.

This two-volume work is a helpful introduction to the Gospel of Luke and the Acts of the Apostles. Tannehill organizes each volume differently (the Gospel, more thematically, the Acts, sequentially). Both provide plenty of insights into the literary composition of Luke-Acts.

Endnotes

1 Henry J. Cadbury articulated Luke's wider aim when he first coined the term "Luke-Acts" in his publication, *The Making of Luke-Acts* (New York: Macmillan, 1927). Subsequent decades of research and publication throughout the twentieth century solidified the treatment of the

Gospel and Acts as a single literary work with a unifying theological vision. Studies such as Charles H. Talbert's *Literary Patterns, Theological Themes, and the Genre of Luke-Acts* (SBLMS 20; Missoula, Mont.: Scholars Press, 1974) and Robert C. Tannehill, *The Narrative Unity of Luke-Acts*, 2 vols. (Philadelphia/Minneapolis: Fortress, 1986, 1990) have contributed to today's dominant perception of the Gospel of Luke and Acts of the Apostles as "Luke-Acts."

2 An often-quoted contemporary study on the relationship between these two biblical books is Mikeal C. Parsons and Richard I. Pervo, *Rethinking the Unity of Luke and Acts* (Minneapolis: Fortress, 1993). Parsons and Pervo do not challenge the idea of a shared authorship between Luke and Acts. Their challenge on the unity of Luke and Acts centers on issues of canonical ordering, genre affiliation, narrative features, and theological orientation. See the discussion by Steve Walton, "Acts: Many Questions, Many Answers," in *The Face of New Testament Studies: A Survey of Recent Research* (eds., Scot McKnight and Grant R. Osborne; Grand Rapids, Mich.: Baker Academics, 2004): 229–50, esp. 236. See for example Mark Allan Powell, *Fortress Introduction to the Gospels* (Minneapolis: Fortress, 1998), where Powell acknowledges that Luke wrote Acts as a sequel to his Gospel (87), but he does not group Luke with Acts as Luke-Acts in his introductory discussion of the Gospel of Luke. This approach to introductory matters on Luke-Acts is seen in Powell's earlier works, which focus on surveying the scholarly research, *What Are They Saying about Luke?* (Mahwah, N.J.: Paulist, 1989) and *What Are They Saying about Acts?* (Mahwah, N.J.: Paulist, 1991). See also, for example, scholarly commentaries treating Luke and Acts separately such as the Sacra Pagina Commentary series, Luke Timothy Johnson, *The Gospel of Luke* (SP 3; Collegeville, Minn.: Liturgical, 1991) and *The Acts of the Apostles* (SP 5; Collegeville, Minn.: Liturgical, 1992). Besides the work of noted scholars Cadbury, Talbert, and Tannehill, other influential studies that treat Luke and Acts together, see William S. Kurz, *Reading Luke-Acts: Dynamics of Biblical Narrative* (Louisville, Ky.: Westminster John Knox Press, 1993); Craig Evans and James A. Sanders, *Luke and Scripture: The Function of Sacred Tradition in Luke-Acts* (Minneapolis: Fortress, 1993). The extensive productivity of Lukan scholar L. T. Johnson is instructive here. In the Sacra Pagina Commentary series, Johnson treats Luke and Acts in separate volumes. But in his book, *The Writings of the New Testament: An Interpretation* (rev. ed.; Minneapolis: Augsburg, 1999), Johnson treats Luke and Acts together in his part-three discussion on the Synoptic tradition, 155–257, esp. 213–57.

3 Because of this Lukan concern, some scholars have even identified Luke-Acts as "apologetic history." Three leading proponents of Luke-Acts being apologetic history are Philip Esler, *Community and Gospel in Luke-Acts: The Social and Political Motivations of Lucan Theology* (SNTSMS 57; Cambridge: Cambridge University Press, 1987), see esp. 210–19; George Sterling, *Historiography and Self-Definition: Josephus, Luke-Acts, and Apologetic Historiography* (NTS 64; Leiden: Brill, 1992); Johnson, Luke, 8–10.

4 According to K. Aland and B. Aland, *The Text of the New Testament: An Introduction to the Critical Editions and to the Theory and Practice of Modern Textual Criticism* (trans. E.F. Rhodes; Grand Rapids, Mich.: Eerdmans/Leiden: Brill, 1987), 29, Luke's Gospel is the longest of the NT Gospels with 1,151 verses compared with Matthew's 1,071, John's 869, and Mark's 678.

5 The Farrer theory, discussed in chapter 1 as an alternative to the Two-Source theory, argues that the Gospel of Matthew may have been one of Luke's written sources.

6 See Raymond E. Brown, *An Introduction to the New Testament* (New York and London: Doubleday, 1997), 316–18.

7 Leading form critics of the twentieth century offer extended discussions of the passion narrative within the early oral tradition. See Martin Dibelius, *From Tradition to Gospel* (trans. B.L. Woolf; New York: Charles Scribner's Sons, 1935), 178–217; Rudolf Bultmann, *History of the Synoptic Tradition* (trans. John Marsh; New York: Harper and Row, 1963), 262–84.

5

The Acts of the Apostles: The Spirit-Driven Church

Introduction

When the Acts of the Apostles is read with the Gospel of Luke as a single narrative with a unifying theological vision, it becomes clear that Luke is telling his readers more than just the story of Jesus. The Gospels of Mark and Matthew provided that story. Luke is telling the story of the early Church as well. For Luke, explaining how so many Gentiles came to embrace Christianity, a religion rooted in God's historic and covenantal relationship with Israel, is central to the story of Jesus and the early Church. The Acts of the Apostles provides such an explanation.

The First Narrative "Church History"

In writing the Acts of the Apostles, Luke accomplished something neither Matthew nor Mark had: he produced the first narrative history of the early Church. This project, however, is not entirely unique within the New Testament. Paul, in his letter to the Galatians, also offers something of an account of Christian origins (see Gal 1–2). And John, in his Gospel, narrates Jesus' promise of the Paraclete (Holy Spirit) that will come to guide believers back to the earthly Jesus (see

John 14–16). Nonetheless, Luke's two-part narrative of Jesus and the early Church stands apart from the offerings of his predecessors.

Luke is not, however, a modern historian writing "objective" history for his readers. He is writing a continuation of the biblical history rooted in the Hebrew Scriptures and his focus is on the God of Israel and God's historic intervention in human history. The history of Jesus and the early Church is reported from the perspective of Luke's theological outlook, which posits that the mission and inclusion of Gentiles into Christianity are not historical accidents, but have been driven and directed by God.

Luke's style of writing is comparable to that of his contemporaries. Like other historians of his time, he uses prologues, summaries, speeches, and journeys to recall for his audience some of the key people and defining moments in the life of the early Church. But Luke is highly selective in what people and moments he highlights. Acts is "Church history" insofar as the Church is, from Luke's perspective, a continuation of the history between God and his people, Israel, who now include all the people of the world.

The Prologues to Luke and Acts

LUKE 1:1–4	ACTS 1:1–2
Since many have undertaken to compile a narrative of the events that have been fulfilled among us, just as those who were eyewitnesses from the beginning and ministers of the word have handed down to us, I too have decided, after investigating everything accurately anew, to write it down in an orderly sequence for you, most excellent Theophilus, so that you may realize the certainty of the teachings you have received.	In the first book, Theophilus, I dealt with all that Jesus did and taught, until the day he was taken up, after giving instruction through the holy Spirit to the apostles whom he had chosen.

Several important insights can be gained by laying these two prologues side by side. First, Luke establishes a literary continuity between the Gospel and Acts. Luke addresses Acts to the same reader to whom he addressed his Gospel: Theophilus (Luke's patron). And Luke's reference to his Gospel as "the first book" indicates that the Gospel and Acts were originally one continuous narrative separated into two rolls of papyrus.[1]

A second insight from seeing these prologues together is that Luke maintains a theological continuity between the Gospel and Acts. Luke is attentive to the Gentile phenomenon, from the Gospel's infancy and Resurrection narratives to the speeches in Acts. This inclusive attitude is apparent as Luke reports the following (emphasis added):

Simeon's prophecy to Mary and Joseph:	"for my eyes have seen your salvation, which you prepared in sight of *all the peoples*, a light for revelation to the *Gentiles*, and glory for your people *Israel*." —Luke 2:30–32
The final words of the resurrected Jesus to his disciples:	"Thus it is written that the Messiah would suffer and rise from the dead on the third day and that repentance, for the forgiveness of sins, would be preached in his name to *all nations*, beginning from Jerusalem." —Luke 24:46–47
Peter's speech in the home of Cornelius, the Gentile centurion:	"In truth, I see that God shows no partiality. Rather, in *every nation* whoever fears him and acts uprightly is acceptable to him." —Acts 10:34–35

Luke is also attentive to the role of the Holy Spirit, which for Luke guides the birth and ministry of Jesus in the Gospel, and the birth and mission of the Church and the apostles in Acts. It seems likely that Luke lived and wrote his Gospel in an already established

Was Theophilus a Real Person?

There is no external evidence of Theophilus' existence beyond the fact that his name was common among Jews and Gentiles. Some scholars have suggested that the name "Theophilus" itself gives us some insights into his identity. Because *Theo-phile* in Greek translates as "beloved of God," some believe that the name Theophilus is symbolic of all believing Christians who were open to catechesis.

Gentile Christian context and sought to trace his community's origins. A third insight can be inferred from these prologues. Because Luke does not state otherwise in the prologue to Acts, we can assume he is using the same principles for the composition of Acts that he used for the Gospel.[2] These principles are as follows: Luke (not an eyewitness himself) is relying on "eyewitnesses from the beginning and ministers of the word" (Luke 1:2) as sources for Acts; he is concerned for the proper "orderly sequence" when reporting the first three decades of the early Church; and he remains committed to assuring Theophilus of "the certainty of the teachings you have received" (Luke 1:4). Unlike the prologue to his Gospel where he tells us that "many have undertaken to compile a narrative" (1:1) of Jesus' life and works, in Acts Luke does not say if others have attempted to compile a narrative of the events of the early Church. Although Luke had sources for Acts, certainly oral and probably written ones, scholars agree that he was the first to write an extended narration of Church history. His history begins with the births of Jesus and John and concludes with Paul's preaching under house arrest in Rome, covering the years 4 BCE–64 CE.

Outline of the Acts of the Apostles

1:1–5	**Prologue and promise of the Holy Spirit** Luke opens Acts with a brief prologue and dedication to Theophilus. He refers to his Gospel and offers assurance of the arrival of the Holy Spirit.

(cont'd.)

(outline of the Acts of the Apostles cont'd.)

1:6 – 8:3	**Peter and the mission of the apostles in Jerusalem** The opening chapters of Acts center on activities occurring in Jerusalem, beginning with Jesus' Ascension and the descent of the Holy Spirit onto the disciples. Luke then reports on the preaching and activities of Peter and John in Jerusalem, culminating in the martyrdom of Stephen.
8:4 – 12:25	**Mission in Judea and Samaria** Persecution in Jerusalem forces the disciples' missionary work to move beyond Jerusalem and into the regions of Judea and Samaria. Luke next reports on the activities of Philip in Samaria, the call of Paul, the activities of Peter in Lydda and Joppa, the visions of Cornelius and Peter, and the persecutions of Herod Agrippa, who ruled in Judea, 41 – 44 CE.
13:1 – 14:28	**Paul's first missionary journey** Luke presents Paul's first missionary journey in Antioch, Cyprus, Antioch of Pisidia, Iconium, and Lystra. Paul preaches to both Jews and Gentiles with mixed results.
15:1 – 35	**Jerusalem council** The council at Jerusalem, the center of the story of Acts, takes up the question of the Gentiles. After much deliberation and a speech by Peter, the apostles decide to officially include Gentiles in the Christian movement, removing the requirement of circumcision. After this point, Peter and the other apostles completely disappear from Acts.
15:36 – 18:22	**Paul's second missionary journey** Beginning with Paul and Barnabas departing on separate missions, Luke reports on Paul's second missionary journey to Antioch, Asia Minor, and Greece. Timothy and Silas are now Paul's main coworkers.
18:23 – 21:14	**Paul's third missionary journey** Luke highlights the activities of Paul on his third (and in Acts, final) missionary journey, in which he revisits Greece and Asia Minor.

(cont'd.)

(outline of the Acts of the Apostles cont'd.)

21:15 – 28:31	**Paul's arrest in Jerusalem and journey to Rome** Luke details Paul's arrest in Jerusalem, followed by his imprisonments and defense speeches to various Jewish and Roman authorities. The last two chapters tell of Paul's journey to Rome, with Acts concluding as Paul preaches to Jews in Rome while under house arrest. Notably, the final fourth of Acts is devoted not to the expansion of the Christian movement but to Paul's journey to the empire's capital city and his largely unsuccessful attempt to preach to Jews there.

Part 1: Historical Setting of the Acts of the Apostles

In the previous chapter we addressed questions about the author, date, audience, and location of Luke-Acts. By way of review, these points are summarized again here.

Authorship

The author of Luke-Acts is unknown. Tradition rooted in the second-century CE, however, names the author as Luke, the traveling companion and coworker of Paul.

Date of Composition

How soon the author writes Acts after the Gospel of Luke is unknown. Most scholars think the composition of Acts occurred during roughly the same years as the Gospel, 80–85 CE.

Audience and Place of Composition

Given Luke-Acts' focus on the Gentile mission, it is likely that the author's intended audience was predominantly Gentile Christian. As with Luke's Gospel, the place of composition of Acts is unknown.

Sources

The question of sources, touched upon briefly in chapter 4, merits additional attention here. Unlike author, date, audience, and location, Acts is distinguished from the Gospel of Luke by its sources.

For his Gospel, Luke had access to oral sources ("eyewitnesses from the beginning and ministers of the word") and written sources (the Gospel of Mark, Q, L, and possibly the Gospel of Matthew). These written sources, especially the Gospel of Mark, gave Luke a model for telling the story of Jesus' life and work. But as far as we know, these Lukan sources were limited to the life of Jesus and did not address the opening decades of the early Church.

This is not to say that Luke had no sources for Acts. Although there is no general consensus, scholars tend to posit that Luke used oral and written sources for various parts of Acts. A three-source hypothesis is often suggested, encompassing some 75 percent of Acts:[3]

- Jerusalem source   Acts 1:6–2:40; 3:1–4:31; 4:36–5:11; 5:17–42; 8:5–40; 9:32; 11:18; 12:1–23
- Antioch in Syria source   Acts 6:1–6; 6:8–8:4; 11:19–30; 15:3–33
- Pauline source   Acts 9:1–30; 13:3–14:28; 15:35–28:31 (the we-passages and the speeches)

The Jerusalem- and Antioch-source theories derive from the fact that Acts can be divided into events associated with the city of Jerusalem (chapters 1–12) and events associated with the city of Antioch (chapters 6–8, 11, and 15). Luke may have tapped into oral or written sources that preserved events associated with these cities.

Did Luke know or use Paul's letters as a source for writing Acts?[4] If we are correct in dating Luke-Acts to 80–85 CE, then Paul's letters had been in circulation for nearly three decades at that time. (Paul wrote his letters in the 50s CE.) On the one hand, it is striking that Luke does not discuss Paul as a letter writer in Acts 9–28 where he focuses on Paul. Furthermore, central Pauline theological views developed in Paul's letters, such as those regarding faith and the Law and justification by grace, are not integrated into Acts. The numerous speeches by Paul in Acts would have been an ideal place for Luke to present Paul's theology. Instead, the author of Acts presents a Paul with a different theology in these speeches. On the other hand, some details in Acts find support from Paul's letters. For example, Paul does visit numerous cities identified in Acts. And Paul is clearly on a mission to the Gentiles that covers large geographic regions of the Roman Empire, as seen in Acts.

Given that Luke significantly edited his sources for his Gospel (Mark and Q), it is probable that he did the same with whatever sources and traditions he may have used to compose Acts.

Part 2: How Luke Told the Story of the Early Church

The prominent themes and passages in Acts strongly suggest the author had the Gospel of Luke in mind as he compiled his narrative of early Church history from Jesus' Ascension in Jerusalem to Paul's preaching in Rome.

The "Two Men" in Luke-Acts

At three key moments in Luke-Acts, "two men" suddenly appear:

- At the transfiguration of Jesus (Luke 9:30–31)

- At the Resurrection of Jesus (Luke 24:4)

- At the Ascension of Jesus (Acts 1:10)

Only at the transfiguration does Luke identify these "two men" as Moses and Elijah. Many scholars today agree that Moses symbolically represents the Law and Elijah symbolically represents the Prophets. For first-century Jews, the Hebrew Scriptures represented their Law and the Prophets.

For Luke, then, the Hebrew Scriptures bore witness to and affirmed for salvation history the key moments in Jesus' life, death, Resurrection, and Ascension.

The Beginning and Ending of Acts

The beginning of the Acts of the Apostles offers a smooth transition from the Gospel of Luke. The double narration of Jesus' Ascension (Luke 24:50–53; Acts 1:6–11) accentuates the importance of the Ascension for Luke. Given that no other New Testament author narrates Jesus' Ascension to heaven after the Resurrection,[5] this concept can be regarded as a distinctively Lukan innovation. In Acts, the Ascension of Jesus brings about the descent of the Holy Spirit. With the arrival of the Holy Spirit (2:1–4), the birth of the Church takes place.

Luke's closing Acts with Paul's preaching in Rome makes perfect sense. First, Jesus' final words from Acts 1:8 are now fulfilled: the "good news" of God's salvation offered to all has spread from Jerusalem, to Judea and Samaria, and has now reached Rome, the "ends of the earth." Second, Theophilus and the rest of Luke's intended audience now have a detailed explanation of how the early Church, originally a Judaic messianic movement, grew into a religion embraced by the Gentiles and began to spread throughout the Roman Empire.

For Luke, the Jesus movement takes the place of Judaism because the gospel has been preached to Jews in every key place, as exemplified by Rome. Now that the Jews have had their chance, the gospel can go to those Gentiles who will listen (see Acts 28:25–28). In fact, the ending of Acts reveals much about the purpose of Acts.

Parallel Structuring in Luke-Acts

As the following chart shows, the Gospel of Luke and Acts are notably parallel in structure:[6]

LUKE	ACTS
11:1–5 Prologue to Luke's patron, Theophilus	1:1–5 Prologue to Luke's patron, Theophilus
3:22 Holy Spirit descends upon Jesus	2:4 Holy Spirit descends upon the disciples
4:14–15 Jesus begins his mission in the power of the Holy Spirit	2:1–4 Peter/disciples begin mission filled with the Holy Spirit
4:16–30 Jesus announces prophecy is fulfilled	2:14–36 Peter announces prophecy is fulfilled
5:17–26 Jesus heals a crippled man, all are amazed	3:1–10 Peter heals a crippled man, all are amazed
7:1–10 Jesus comes by invitation to the home of a faith-filled Gentile (a Roman centurion)	10:1–23 Peter comes by invitation to the home of a faith-filled Gentile (a Roman centurion)
7:11–17 Jesus raises the widow's son from the dead	9:36–43 Peter raises widow from the dead
	(cont'd.)

(Luke cont'd.)	(Acts cont'd.)
10:1–12 Jesus sends disciples on mission to the Gentiles	13:1–19:20 Paul and Barnabas sent on mission to the Gentiles
9:51–19:44 Jesus travels to Jerusalem	19:21–21:17 Paul travels to Jerusalem
19:37–38 Jesus is welcomed in Jerusalem	21:17–19 Paul is welcomed in Jerusalem
20:27–39 Sadducees oppose Jesus but scribes support him	23:6–9 Sadducees oppose Paul but Pharisees support him
22:19 Jesus celebrates Eucharist: takes, blesses, breaks, and gives bread	27:35 Paul celebrates Eucharist: takes, blesses, breaks, and gives bread
22:54–23:47 Jesus is seized by angry mob, slapped, tried four times, found innocent three times, rejected by the Jews, accepted by the centurion	21:30–27:43 Paul is seized by angry mob, slapped, tried four times, found innocent three times, rejected by the Jews, accepted by the centurion
24:45–47 Gospel concludes with Jesus confirming that Scripture has been fulfilled; Gentile inclusion emphasized	28:23–28 Acts concludes with Paul confirming that Scripture has been fulfilled; Gentile inclusion emphasized

The effect of this extensive parallel structuring between the Gospel and Acts is that the ministry and mission of Peter and Paul neatly mirror the ministry and mission of Jesus. This connects the Gospel and Acts on literary, historical, and theological levels. It also reinforces Luke's assertion that together the story of Jesus and the history of the early Church provide a complete picture of the God of Israel's offer of salvation not just to Israel but to all people, Jew and Gentile alike.

Luke's parallel arrangement of events can also be seen *within* Acts with the presentations of Peter (chapters 1–12) and Paul (chapters 13–28).[7] In Acts this serves the purpose of presenting a unified picture of the Judean Church led by Peter and the Gentile Church led by Paul:

ACTS 1 – 12	ACTS 13 – 28
2:1–40 Holy Spirit descends and Peter delivers a speech	13:1–40 Holy Spirit descends and Paul delivers a speech
3:1–26 Peter heals a man crippled from birth and delivers a speech	14:8–17 Paul heals a man crippled from birth and delivers a speech
5:15 Peter performs extraordinary miracles of healing the sick and exorcising unclean spirits	19:12 Paul performs extraordinary miracles of healing the sick and exorcising unclean spirits
8:9–24 Peter confronts and curses Simon the magician	13:6–12 Paul confronts and curses Elymas the magician
9:36–43 Peter raises Tabitha from the dead	20:9–12 Paul raises Eutychus from the dead
7:1–10 Jesus comes by invitation to the home of a faith-filled Gentile (a Roman centurion)	10:1–23 Peter comes by invitation to the home of a faith-filled Gentile (a Roman centurion)
10–11 Divine guidance leads Peter on a mission to the Gentiles	13–21 Divine guidance leads Paul on a mission to the Gentiles
12:1–19 Peter is arrested, imprisoned, and miraculously escapes	16:16–40 Paul is arrested, imprisoned, and miraculously escapes

This parallel structuring is not just an aid for remembering and repeating the story of Luke-Acts, important as that would be for an oral culture. It is also a means for Luke to emphasize his assertions that the ministry of Jesus and the mission of the early Church fulfill the prophecy of the Hebrew Scriptures, are divinely guided, and are bringing about universal salvation.

By emphasizing such parallels between the apostle Peter and the figure of Paul, the author of Acts legitimizes Paul's authority as a leader of the mission to the Gentiles. Although Acts only rarely refers to Paul as an "apostle" (Acts 14:4, 6, 14, possibly from Luke's sources), Luke wishes to present Paul as an authoritative leader who enjoyed the same divine confirmation as the Twelve apostles.

Speeches in Acts

Speeches are one of the prominent literary features of Acts. Speeches alone make up nearly one-third of the storyline:

Peter:	2:14–36; 3:12–26; 4:8–12; 5:29–32; 10:34–43; 15:7–11
Stephen:	7:2–53
Paul:	13:16–41; 14:15–17; 17:22–31; 20:17–35; 22:1–21; 24:10–21; 26:2–23; 28:17–28

In the Gospel, Luke presents speeches by Mary (1:46–55), Zechariah (1:67–79), and Jesus (4:16–30; 6:20–49). In Acts, Luke presents many more speeches by Peter, Stephen, and Paul. In antiquity it was common for historians to have historical figures deliver speeches in their narratives. As with other ancient presentations of speeches, the speeches in Acts are not to be taken as exact transcripts of what Peter, Paul, and others said; rather, the speeches are colored by the historian's agenda, and in the case of Luke-Acts, Luke's theological and political agenda.[8]

Much like the speeches of Mary and Zechariah in Luke 1, which set the context for the Gospel, Peter's first speech to the Jews and Gentiles in the streets of Jerusalem (2:14–36) sets the context for Acts. Peter's speech confirms that through the life, death, Resurrection, and Ascension of Jesus, God has fulfilled past promises to Israel (see also Peter's speech at Solomon's Portico, 3:12–26). Peter's speech in the home of the Gentile centurion, Cornelius (10:34–43), affirms the Gentile inclusion into Christianity. And Peter's defense speeches before the Sanhedrin (4:8–12; 5:29–32) demonstrate that he is innocent of the charges that certain Jewish religious leaders have brought against him.

In Acts, Paul delivers three speeches on his missionary journeys: the first in a synagogue in Antioch Pisidia (13:16–41), the second at the Areopagus in Athens (17:22–31), and the third in Miletus before his final journey to Jerusalem (20:17–35). In each speech, Paul delivers his message that Jesus, the Jewish Messiah raised from the dead, brings salvation to all people. Acts also presents Paul giving three speeches before both the Jews and the Roman authorities: the first before the Jerusalem Jews (22:1–21), the second before Felix (24:10–21), and the third before King Agrippa (26:2–23). Paul not only defends Jesus as the resurrected Messiah, savior to all people, but he also defends his own call to apostleship to the Jews and the Gentiles by telling his life story and twice recounting his dramatic conversion from one who had formerly persecuted the early Church (22:3–16; 26:2–18). Once again, Paul is presented as innocent of the charges brought against him.

Summaries in Acts

With the summaries in Acts, Luke presents an idealized portrait of the early Church: a Church united under apostolic

Portraits of Paul before His Calling

What little Luke tells us about Paul before his call is disturbing. Three texts are key: Acts 7:58; 8:1–3; 9:1.

- 7:58: Luke introduces Paul by telling us that at the stoning of Stephen, the witnesses who were about to stone him "laid down their cloaks at the feet (*podas*) of . . . Saul." Laying their cloaks at Paul's feet is Luke's message that Paul was the acknowledged leader of the group. (See Acts 4:35 where the Christians would put their proceeds "at the feet (*podas*) of the apostles.")

- 8:1–3: Following Stephen's martyrdom, Luke tells us that a severe persecution of the Church began in Jerusalem. Paul began "to destroy the church," literally "dragging" men and women to prison (8:3).

- 9:1: Luke begins the story of Paul's call experience by telling us that Paul is "still breathing murderous threats against the disciples of the Lord." The adverb *eti* ("still") indicates that Paul persecuted followers of Jesus for some time before he met the resurrected Christ on the road to Damascus.

Portraying Paul as a man who "breathed murder" captures well the magnitude of Paul's internal conversion to his call.

leadership, guided by the Holy Spirit, growing and spreading through-out the Roman Empire. Consider the following quotes:

> They devoted themselves to the teaching of the apostles and to the communal life, to the breaking of the bread and to the prayers. Awe came upon everyone, and many wonders and signs were done through the apostles. All who believed were together and had all things in common; they would sell their property and possessions and divide them among all according to each one's needs. Every day they devoted themselves to meeting together in the temple area and to breaking bread in their homes. They ate their meals with exultation and sincerity of heart, praising God and enjoying favor with all the people. And every day the Lord added to their number those who were being saved.
>
> —Acts 2:42–47

> The community of believers was of one heart and mind, and no one claimed that any of his possessions was his own, but they had everything in common. With great power the apostles bore witness to the resurrection of the Lord Jesus, and great favor was accorded them all. There was no needy person among them, for those who owned property or houses would sell them, bring the proceeds of the sale, and put them at the feet of the apostles, and they were distributed to each according to need.
>
> —Acts 4:32–35

> Many signs and wonders were done among the people at the hands of the apostles. They were all together in Solomon's portico. None of the others dared to join them, but the people esteemed them. Yet more than ever, believers in the Lord, great numbers of men and women, were added to them. Thus they even carried the sick out into the streets and laid them on cots and mats so that when Peter came by, at least his shadow might fall on one or another of them. A large number of people from the towns in the vicinity of Jerusalem also gathered, bringing the sick and those disturbed by unclean spirits, and they were all cured.
>
> —Acts 5:12–16

The word of God continued to spread, and the number of the disciples in Jerusalem increased greatly; even a large group of priests were becoming obedient to the faith.

—Acts 6:7

The church throughout all Judea, Galilee, and Samaria was at peace. It was being built up and walked in fear of the Lord, and with the consolation of the holy Spirit it grew in numbers.

—Acts 9:31

Day after day the churches grew stronger in faith and increased in number.

—Acts 16:5

Thus did the word of the Lord continue to spread with influence and power.

—Acts 19:20

The Role of the Holy Spirit

In Luke-Acts the Holy Spirit plays a leading role in the events associated with the birth and ministry of Jesus and the birth and mission of the early Church. In the opening chapters of Luke's Gospel, the Holy Spirit: "filled" Zechariah, Elizabeth, and Simeon (Luke 1–2); "overshadowed" Mary, resulting in the conception of Jesus (Luke 1:35); led Jesus into the wild to be tempted by the devil (Luke 3:1); and remained present to Jesus in his ministry (Luke 4:18).

Likewise, in Acts the Holy Spirit facilitates the spread of the Jesus movement. Luke tells of the Holy Spirit acting not only on Jewish followers of Jesus (Acts 2:1–4) but also on Samaritans (8:14–17) and Gentile followers (10:44–48). The role of the Spirit remains integral throughout Acts, especially in Paul's mission to the Gentiles (see, for example, 16:6–10; 20:17–24; 21:7–14). For Luke, the descent and presence of the Holy Spirit to each of these different groups emphasizes the universal aspect of salvation that the God of Israel now offers to the world.

Discipleship and the Twelve in Acts

The reconstitution of the Twelve apostles was as important as the descent of the Holy Spirit to the formation of the Church. In fact, after the eleven apostles settled back into Jerusalem following their

---

The Listing of the Twelve Apostles in the Synoptic Gospels and Acts

MATTHEW 10:2–4

Simon called Peter, and his brother Andrew; James, the son of Zebedee, and his brother John; Philip and Bartholomew, Thomas and Matthew the tax collector; James, the son of Alphaeus, and Thaddeus; Simon the Cananean, and Judas Iscariot who betrayed him.

MARK 3:16–19

Simon, whom he named Peter; James, son of Zebedee, and John the brother of James, whom he named Boanerges, that is, sons of thunder; Andrew, Philip, Bartholomew, Matthew, Thomas, James the son of Alphaeus; Thaddeus, Simon the Cananean, and Judas Iscariot who betrayed him.

LUKE 6:14–16

Simon, whom he named Peter, and his brother Andrew, James, John, Philip, Bartholomew, Matthew, Thomas, James the son of Alphaeus, Simon who was called a Zealot, and Judas the son of James, and Judas Iscariot, who became a traitor.

ACTS 1:13

Peter and John and James and Andrew, Philip and Thomas, Bartholomew and Matthew, James the son of Alphaeus, Simon the Zealot, and Judas son of James.

The concept of the Twelve apostles was important even if the details (that is, their names) could vary. For example, Judas, son of James, is included in Luke and Acts but missing from Matthew and Mark, who include Thaddeus instead. Notice also that the Gospel of John does not include a list of the Twelve apostles.

Even though Paul refers to himself as an apostle (see Paul's greetings in his letters: Rom 1:1; 1 Cor 1:1; 2 Cor 1:1; Gal 1:1), Luke in Acts views Paul more as an authoritative Church leader than an apostle, albeit a divinely commissioned leader like the original Twelve.

witness of the Resurrection and Ascension of Jesus, the first order of business was to choose another apostle to replace Judas, who had committed suicide (Acts 1:18–19). For Luke, the public witness of the Twelve, so central to Jesus' ministry, was important for the continuity of the mission of Jesus and the early Church. In Acts, it is only after the Twelve are reconstituted that the Holy Spirit descends and the Church begins.

The Twelve quickly became an important part of an idealized portrait of the early Church. Of the Twelve apostles, Luke highlights Peter and John, and to a lesser extent, Philip. For Luke, the image of the Twelve had an important function in the narrative of Acts, especially in the first half of Acts.

The image of the apostles — and by extension all disciples (any follower of Jesus) — is thoroughly integrated into Acts. The presentation of the disciples also supports Luke's idealized portrait of the early Church. The apostles and the disciples are often shown at prayer (1:14; 2:42; 3:1; 4:24–30; 6:4) and being guided by the Holy Spirit (2:4; 4:8, 31; 7:55). The apostles, especially Peter and John, are "sent out" to preach the "good news" (1:14; 3:12; 4:7; 6:7; 8:1). The apostles and other disciples display a proper attitude toward wealth and possessions (2:44–45; 4:32–35, 36–37; 6:1–7). The Twelve also humbly serve others in their healing ministry (3:1–10; 4:29–30; 5:15–16) and distribution of wealth to the needy (2:45; 4:35). Finally, the apostles follow Jesus unconditionally (4:20; 5:42) and certainly carry

The Death of Judas

The Gospel tradition contains two different accounts of the death of Judas: Matthew 27:3–10 and Acts 1:18–19. In Matthew, Judas "deeply regretted" his betrayal of Jesus and commits suicide ("hanged himself"). In Acts, Luke tells us that Judas died by "falling headlong" whereupon "he burst open in the middle, and all his insides spilled out." This too appears to be a suicide, although of a different sort.

What Matthew and Acts have in common is the tradition that Judas died in a field called the "Field of Blood." Matthew tells us this was a potter's field (27:7). Because potters worked with clay, the name "Field of Blood" may have originated with the red clay of the field. But it is also possible that the name "Field of Blood" derives from Judas' own blood, which was spilled there, according to Luke's account. Tradition leaves the origins of the name "Field of Blood" unresolved.

their own crosses, with Peter and John being harassed and persecuted by the Sanhedrin (4:1–3, 21; 5:17–18, 40–41) and James paying the ultimate price of discipleship, which is death (12:2–3; see also the stoning of Stephen, 7:54–60).

Additionally, Luke's brief account of Philip's successful mission in Samaria and Judea, with the focus on Simon the magician (8:4–25) and the Ethiopian eunuch (8:26–40), provides a model of true discipleship. Philip gives witness to the Samaritans and Judeans (8:25, 40); Simon and the eunuch pray and are guided by the Holy Spirit (8:14–17, 22–24, 26, 29, 39), and both show the proper attitude toward wealth and possessions (8:18–24, 27).

Luke's Focus on Women in Acts

Women figure prominently in Luke's story of Jesus (see, for example, Luke 1–2; 8:1–3; 10:38–42). Likewise in Acts, women play a key role in the story of the early Church.

As in his Gospel (7:11–17; 18:1–8; 20:45–47; 21:1–4), Luke continues to show concern for widows in Acts 6:1–7, where the Twelve respond proactively to the needs of the Gentile widows. Peter even restores the widow Tabitha ("a disciple") to life (Acts 9:36–43). Luke also presents Paul in positive relationships with women; for example, after hearing Paul preach, Lydia, a wealthy woman, is baptized and offers her home to Paul during his travels (Acts 16:11–15). As in the Gospel, women in Acts are often portrayed as models of discipleship and leaders within the early Church (see Acts 18, where Priscilla and her husband, Aquilla, are presented as leaders of the Christian community in Corinth, in collaboration with Paul and his Gentile mission).

Peter: From Luke 5 to Acts 15

Peter makes a decisive entry and exit from Luke-Acts. From the moment Peter receives his call and commission from Jesus (Luke 5:1-11, "Do not be afraid; from now on you will be catching men," v. 10b), Luke-Acts builds up to the encounter between Peter, the leading Jew, and Cornelius, a god-fearing Gentile. Luke uses Peter in Luke-Acts to illustrate the tension and disconnect that defined the Jesus movement in its early years: a Jewish messianic movement with a large Gentile base.

In Acts 10:1–11:18, Luke presents Peter as coming to accept Gentile inclusion, albeit reluctantly. The visions of Peter and Cornelius (10:1–16) and the descent of the Holy Spirit onto Cornelius' home (10:44–49) assure the divine guidance and blessing at work in the Gentile mission of the early Church. The opening words of Peter's speech in Cornelius' home—"In truth, I see that God shows no partiality. Rather, in every nation whoever fears him and acts uprightly is acceptable to him" (10:34b–35)—illustrate Peter's support of Paul's mission to the Gentiles. Peter, the leading Jewish apostle of the Judaic messianic movement, comes to accept god-fearing Gentiles, as do the other apostles and brothers in Judea (11:1–18).

This characterization of Peter as initiating the Gentile mission further exemplifies the idealized portrait of the Church in Acts that we discussed earlier in this chapter. By contrast, in Galatians, Paul names Peter as "the apostle to the circumcision" (that is, to the Jewish followers of Jesus) and unfaithful to the cause of Paul's Gentile mission (see Gal 2:7–14). Yet in Acts, with the descent of the Holy Spirit onto the Gentiles, both the Jews (Acts 2:1–4) and now the Gentiles (Acts 10:44–49) have their own Pentecost experience. In Luke's chronology, all of this takes place before Paul becomes a follower of Jesus, and unlike Paul's portrayal of the situation in Galatians, in Luke-Acts we find no conflict between Peter and Paul.

The last we hear of Peter in Luke-Acts is the speech he delivers at the Jerusalem council, 15:1–35. The council is the attempt to resolve the growing tension between Judaic and Gentile Christians.

The Movement Known as "The Way"

Beginning with the story of Paul's call, Acts refers to the disciples of Jesus as belonging to "the Way" (see 9:2; 18:25, 26; 19:9, 23; 22:4; 24:14, 22). According to Acts, "the Way" was the name originally given to the early Jesus movement, which subsequently developed into what we recognize today as Christianity. In Acts this name probably highlights Jesus as "the Way" to salvation; we do not find "the Way" used elsewhere in the New Testament as a name for the spiritual path of those who follow Jesus.

Later in Acts, the term "Christians" is first applied to the community of Jews and Gentiles in Antioch in Syria who were united in their support for those suffering from famine in Judea (11:26).

The issues of faith and Law (circumcision of males) lie at the heart of this debate. Peter's final speech is instrumental in resolving the conflict:

> My brothers, you are well aware that from the early days God made his choice among you that through my mouth the Gentiles would hear the word of the gospel and believe. And God, who knows the heart, bore witness by granting them the holy Spirit just as he did us. He made no distinction between us and them, for by faith he purified their hearts. Why, then, are you now putting God to the test by placing on the shoulders of the disciples a yoke that neither our ancestors nor we have been able to bear? On the contrary, we believe that we are saved through the grace of the Lord Jesus, in the same way as they.
>
> —Acts 15:7–11

With this speech, Peter departs a hero in Luke-Acts, fulfilling his call and commission from Jesus (Luke 5:1–11). The apostles and presbyters in Jerusalem are convinced by Peter's speech and the testimony of Paul and Barnabas (Acts 15:12).

Persecution of the Christians

The Acts of the Apostles includes several instances of Jewish persecution of Jesus' followers. How Acts depicts this persecution offers a corollary to Luke's idealized portrait of the early Church as completely unified on the inside and facing opposition only from the outside by Jews. Historians are inclined to believe that the situations depicted in Acts were in truth far more complex: Church leaders would sometimes disagree (note the deeply irked apostle Paul in Gal 2:7–14), and many Jews did not fit into Acts' neat, dichotomous categories of either following Jesus or persecuting his followers.

Luke's depiction of persecutions also furthers his theological agenda. Shortly after Pentecost in Acts, Luke provides detailed accounts of the persecution of Peter and John by the Jewish leaders, including arrests and imprisonments, interrogations and warnings, even floggings (4:5–22; 5:17–42). Acts also offers an extended account of the stoning to death of Stephen (6:8–8:1) and tells of the first apostle, James, who was "killed by the sword" (12:2) during the reign of King Herod Agrippa.

Who Was the First Martyr?

Scholars have long debated who the first martyr, or protomartyr, was. The question is somewhat complicated, because in Greek the word *martys* usually designates a "witness" or one who gives "testimony" in a court of law. It was not until the late-second century *Martyrdom of Polycarp* that the Greek word *martys* was used in a novel way to designate a martyr, that is, a witness to Jesus who was killed because of his testimony. Scholars' proposals for the first martyr include the following:

1. Seven Palestinian Jewish brothers, who according to 2 Maccabees 7 were tortured and killed under the rule of the Greek king Antiochus IV Epiphanes (175 – 164 BCE) for refusing to eat swine's flesh, which the Old Testament forbids.

2. Jesus of Nazareth, whose death figures prominently in early Christian literature.

3. A deacon named Stephen, who, according to Acts 7, was killed by Jews outraged by his interpretation of the Jewish Scriptures and testimony about Jesus.

4. The apostles Peter and Paul, who, according to the late-second century writing *Acts of Peter*, were killed in Rome under the Emperor Nero in the early 60s CE. (See also Paul's letter to the Philippians 1:19 – 26, written while he was in a Roman prison and reflecting on the possibility of his death.)

5. Ignatius, bishop of Antioch in Syria (north of Palestine), who, after being arrested in Antioch, was brought to Rome and killed there around 110 CE. In his letters, Ignatius rejoices that he will soon die for Christ and even asks concerned Christians not to prevent this from happening.

6. Ignatius' disciple Polycarp, who was killed toward the middle of the second century for refusing to participate in a polytheistic sacrifice for the Roman emperor, whom many Romans honored as divine.

Each in their own way, the Jewish brothers, Jesus, Stephen, Peter, Paul, Ignatius, and Polycarp (among others), gave "witness" to their faith. The question we are left with is whether the novel use of the Greek word *martys* in the *Martyrdom of Polycarp* therefore makes Polycarp the first martyr. Alternately, could it make sense to apply the term *martyr* to one or more people who died for their faith prior to the late-second century? Moreover, for Christian writings the possible precedent of the seven Jewish brothers raises the question of whether early Christians borrowed an earlier concept of martyrdom from Judaism or even from Greco-Roman concepts of "noble death."

In addition to individual persecution, Acts speaks of a "severe persecution of the church in Jerusalem," led by Saul in the early 30s CE (8:1). This widespread persecution in Jerusalem scattered the Jesus movement "throughout the countryside of Judea and Samaria" (8:1). Luke devotes all of Acts 12 to narrating the persecutions of Christians by Herod Agrippa, including the gruesome details of Agrippa's demise (12:20–23). Luke consistently tells us that the persecutions did not crush the early Church, but quite to the contrary, "the word of God continued to spread and grow" (12:24).

Luke's portrayal of the persecution of Jesus' followers had another important function in Acts. Luke had to explain why the early Church and its communities were not more directly connected to the legalized and ancient religion of Judaism as well as justify its reaching out to Gentiles. The early Church would have needed this association and connection with Judaism to be viewed as legitimate (and legal) in the eyes of the Roman Empire. The speeches in Acts show how the Jesus movement was rooted in the ancient Hebrew Scriptures, and the pattern of rejection of Paul from the synagogues in Acts (discussed below) illustrates that the early Church desired a connection to the synagogue but was unjustly rejected and subsequently extended itself to the Gentile community.

The "Calling" or "Conversion" of Paul

Scholars debate whether Luke intended the encounter between Paul and the resurrected Christ to be understood as a call within Judaism or as a conversion from one religion to another, from Judaism to Christianity. Luke leaves this ambiguous. In this chapter, we have been using the term *call* to indicate that Paul was "called" by the resurrected Christ. Paul's response to this call resulted in his conversion from persecuting members of the Jesus movement to becoming a leader in supporting Gentile inclusion into the early Church.

We first hear about Saul (Paul) at 7:58 and 8:1–3 in the context of the stoning of Stephen. Saul is portrayed as not only supporting the stoning of Stephen but also as almost single-handedly "trying to destroy the church" (8:3). This sets the stage for the magnitude of his encounter with the resurrected Christ in 9:1–19. On three separate occasions, Luke narrates the call of Paul: on the road to Damascus to persecute Christians, Acts 9:1–19; as part of Paul's defense speech to the Jews in Jerusalem, Acts 22:3–16; and as part of Paul's defense speech to King Agrippa, Acts 26:2–18. The specific details of Paul's call story vary in each account, but one consistent feature is Jesus' words to him: "Saul, Saul, why are you persecuting me?" (9:4; compare 22:7; 26:14).

The words of the Lord to Ananias, the one tending to Paul's recovery after his encounter with Christ, are programmatic for Paul's mission in the rest of Acts: "Go, for this man is a chosen instrument of mine to carry my name before Gentiles, kings, and Israelites, and I will show him what he will have to suffer for my name" (9:15–16). This is in fact how the narrative of Acts ends (chapters 21–28), with Paul defending himself in front of "kings" (Governor Felix and King Agrippa), in Rome under house arrest, and debating and converting both Jews and Gentiles.

Just as Luke 4:16–30 provides an overview of Jesus' ministry in the remainder of the Gospel, Acts 9:19b–30 provides an overview of Paul's ministry

Two Names for Paul in Acts: Saul and Paul

In Paul's surviving letters, the apostle always refers to himself as Paul. In Acts, however, this person is first introduced with the Semitic name Saul, perhaps to emphasize his Jewish heritage. Acts refers to Paul as Saul before he becomes a follower of Jesus (Acts 7:58; 8:1–3; 9:1), and in one passage after (Acts 13:7, 9). Later in this narrative the name Paul (the Greek equivalent to Saul) reflects the Greco-Roman culture in which he was raised (according to Acts, the city of Tarsus outside the Promised Land of Israel, in the Diaspora). When the focus of Acts turns entirely to Paul (Acts 15–28), Luke consistently refers to him by that name. Many scholars doubt whether Luke's characterization of a previous name Saul is historical.

that is further detailed in Acts 13–28. The major elements of Paul's ministry are as follows: Paul was rooted in Jerusalem and on a mission with others, he boldly preached Jesus as Messiah, and he experienced persecution. As Luke summarizes in 9:31, the end of Paul's persecution brought "peace" to the growing Church throughout Judea, Galilee, and Samaria.

As we have seen already, discrepancies exist between Luke's presentation of Paul in Acts and Paul's self-description in his letter to the Galatians. In his ongoing effort to portray the early Church as a united movement, Luke presents Paul as immediately preaching about the risen Christ in Damascus and then traveling to Jerusalem and joining and supporting the apostles there. In Galatians, Paul writes that after his encounter with the resurrected Christ, "I did not immediately consult with flesh and blood, nor did I go up to Jerusalem to those who were apostles before me; rather, I went into Arabia and then returned to Damascus" (Gal 1:16b–17).

Paul's Three Missionary Journeys

According to Luke, Paul was the leading figure in spreading the Jesus movement to the cities of the Roman Empire, which he did on three missionary journeys: 13:4–14:27; 15:36–18:22; 18:2–21:16. Scholars estimate that Paul traveled nearly ten thousand miles for his missionary work, which lasted nearly thirty years, from about 34 to 64 CE.

Prior to depicting Paul in Acts, Luke uses a similar journey motif in his Gospel as he presents Jesus on his journey to Jerusalem, 9:51–19:44.

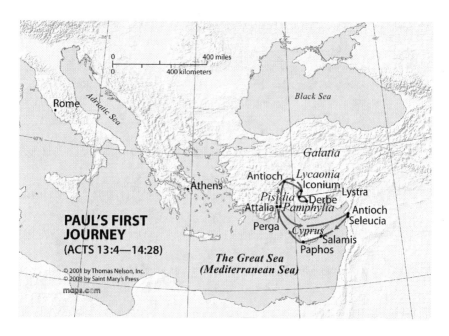

PAUL'S FIRST
JOURNEY
(ACTS 13:4—14:28)

© 2001 by Thomas Nelson, Inc.
© 2008 by Saint Mary's Press
maps.com

On Paul's first journey, a pattern of Jewish rejection and Gentile acceptance emerges. The first mission by Paul and Barnabas (Acts 13:4–14:28) involved journeying to the island of Cyprus (13:4–12) and the regions of Pamphylia, Pisidia, and Lycaonia, all in the province of Asia Minor. Paul and Barnabas established churches at Pisidian Antioch, Iconium, and Derbe (Acts 13:13–14:28). On this journey, Paul experiences a consistent pattern of rejection and even persecution by the Jews and acceptance by the Gentiles (Acts 13:44–52; 14:1–7, 8–20). In the midst of these experiences, Paul declares to his Jewish antagonists, "It was necessary that the word of God be spoken to you first, but since you reject it and condemn yourselves as unworthy of eternal life, we now turn to the Gentiles" (Acts 13:46). Paul's declaration here foreshadows the final words spoken by Paul in Acts to Jews who rejected his teaching: "Let it be known to you then that this salvation of God has been sent to the Gentiles; they will listen" (28:28).

Paul additionally says to his Jewish opponents on his first missionary journey, "For so the Lord has commanded us, 'I have made you a light to the Gentiles, that you may be an instrument of salvation to the ends of the earth'" (Acts 13:47). This ties together the words of Simeon about the infant Jesus (Luke 2:32) and the words of the resurrected Jesus (Acts 1:8) with the rest of the storyline of Acts and Paul's arrival in Rome, the "ends of the earth" (Acts 27–28).

Summary of How Luke Told the Story of the Early Church

Core Concepts

- Acts is not Church history objectively told; Acts is a selective Church history told from the perspective of Luke's beliefs about God's intervention in that history.
- Acts continues the theological aims of Luke's Gospel: to explain and defend the Gentile mission and inclusion into the Church, and to present the innocence of Peter and Paul.

(cont'd.)

(summary of how Luke told the story of the early Church cont'd.)

- The final words of Jesus before his Ascension in Acts 1:8 — "But you will receive power when the holy Spirit comes upon you, and you will be my witnesses in Jerusalem, throughout Judea and Samaria, and to the ends of the earth" — foreshadow the basic storyline of Acts.
- The final words of Paul in Acts 28:28 indicate the Gentile mission is completed and that most Jews have rejected it, thereby losing their place in salvation history.

Supplemental Information

- Luke is the first evangelist to compile an extended narrative of the history of the early Church.
- Luke and Acts share a marked parallel structure; parallel structuring is also repeated within Acts, emphasizing both the united Gentile mission and the innocence of Jesus, Peter, and Paul.
- Speeches comprise nearly a third of Acts.
- The summary statements in Acts provide an idealized portrait of the early Church.
- Luke presents Peter (Acts 1–15) and Paul (Acts 9–28) in the early Church as great apostles who model discipleship.
- The birth of the Church and the mission of the disciples are driven by the descent and presence of the Holy Spirit.
- The Twelve are an important image in Luke's narration of the early Church.
- From Luke 5 to Acts 8, Peter is being readied for the Gentile mission, which he actively supports in Acts 9–15.
- Women are presented favorably and in prominent roles in Acts.
- Acts depicts persecutions of early Christians as stemming from Jews.
- Luke narrates the conversion of Paul three times: 9:1–19; 22:3–16; 26:2–18.
- The story of Paul and the Gentile mission is structured around three missionary journeys: 13:4–14:27; 15:36–18:22; 18:23–21:16.

Questions for Review

1. How is the Acts of the Apostles "Church history"?
2. Why are the prologues to Luke and Acts important to understanding Luke-Acts?
3. How are Luke's Gospel and Acts linked in terms of authorship, date of composition, and intended audience?
4. What sources might Luke have used to compose Acts?
5. What are some of the literary parallel structures between Luke's Gospel and Acts?
6. What is the purpose of the Lukan speeches and summary statements throughout Luke-Acts?
7. Why does Luke narrate the Ascension of Jesus twice, once in his Gospel and once in Acts?
8. How does Luke emphasize women in Acts?
9. Where does Peter exit the storyline of Acts, and why at that point?
10. How does the portrayal of Peter and Paul support Luke's idealized presentation of the early Church?

Questions for Reflection

1. What aspects of Luke's idealized portrait of the early Church do you find most interesting?
2. In your opinion, was Jesus, the deacon Stephen, Polycarp, or someone else the first martyr? Explain. What is the relationship between those who offer a testimony to their faith and those who are killed for having done so?
3. Jesus' final words before his Ascension (Acts 1:8) define the early Church as a "missionary" Church. Do you think all religions should be missionary in nature (that is, seek out others to join their religion)?
4. The Acts of the Apostles ends with the rejection of the message now universally proclaimed (Acts 28:28). What is your reaction to this ending of Acts?

Recommendations for Further Reading

Arlandson, James Malcolm. *Women, Class, and Society in Early Christianity: Models from Luke-Acts*. Peabody, Mass.: Hendrickson, 1997.

Arlandson offers a variety of insights into the social and cultural milieu of women in the Greco-Roman world. Applying these insights to the Gentile Christian community of Luke-Acts, the author provides an intriguing perspective on the social realities of this early Christian community of men and women.

Hengel, Martin. *Acts and the History of Earliest Christianity*. Philadelphia: Fortress, 1979.

A prominent German scholar, Hengel introduces students to many of the historical, theological, and source-critical questions at the core of contemporary studies in Acts. Hengel sees a strong historical basis for Acts of the Apostles.

Powell, Mark Allan. *What Are They Saying about Acts?* Mahwah, N.J.: Paulist, 1991.

This is a companion volume to *What Are They Saying about Luke?* In *What Are They Saying about Acts?* Powell presents current thinking on the composition and theology of Acts, the portrayal of the Church in Acts, and readings of Acts as history and literature.

Talbert, Charles H. *Reading Luke: A Literary and Theological Commentary on the Third Gospel*. New York: Crossroads, 1982. *Reading Acts: A Literary and Theological Commentary on Acts of the Apostles*. New York: Crossroads, 1997.

Talbert's two volumes on Luke and Acts (written fifteen years apart) has become a standard in the field of Luke-Acts studies. Students are exposed to many of the major theological and literary issues that one confronts in reading these two biblical books.

Van Henten, Jan Willem, and Friedrich Avemarie, eds. *Martyrdom and Noble Death: Selected Texts from Graeco-Roman, Jewish, and Christian Antiquity*. London/New York: Routledge, 2002.

The authors present a survey of martyrdoms (noble deaths) from pagan, Jewish, and Christian sources. This sourcebook supplies insights into how the ancient world viewed the deaths of those who died nobly and publicly, especially for a religious, political, or other cause.

See also the recommended reading list from chapter 4, "The Gospel of Luke." Books by Talbert and Tannehill on Luke-Acts are good resources for Acts.

Endnotes

1 Martin Hengel, *Acts and the History of Earliest Christianity* (Philadelphia: Fortress, 1979), 8–9; David Aune, *The New Testament in Its Literary Environment* (Philadelphia: Westminster, 1987), 117; Ben Witherington, *The Acts of the Apostles: A Socio-Rhetorical Commentary* (Grand Rapids, Mich.: William B. Eerdmans, 1998), 4–12.

2 This is the position held by many scholars: e.g., Raymond E. Brown, *An Introduction to the New Testament* (New York and London: Doubleday, 1997), 316.

3 See Jacques Dupont, *The Sources of the Acts: The Present Position* (London: Darton, Longman, 1964), 17–72, for an extended discussion of sources for Acts. Dupont provides a summary position of the three sources for Acts, 71–72. See also Luke Timothy Johnson, *Acts of the Apostles* (SP 5; Collegeville, Minn.: Glazier, 1992), 3–5; Joseph A. Fitzmyer, *The Jerome Biblical Commentary* (Englewood Cliffs, N.J.: Prentice-Hall, 1968), 45–46.

4 Gerd Lüdemann, *Early Christianity According to the Traditions in Acts: A Commentary* (Philadelphia: Fortress, 1989), 7–19, rejects the probability that Luke used Paul's letters as a source for Acts. He thinks it is more plausible "that Luke worked traditions of another kind into his work," 17. See also Ernst Haenchen, *The Acts of the Apostles: A Commentary* (Philadelphia: Westminster, 1971), 81–90.

5 Outside of Luke-Acts the Ascension is mentioned only briefly in Mark 16:19, which is a later addition to Mark's Gospel that may be dependent on Luke-Acts for this formulation. See further: Kelhoffer, *Miracle and Mission*, 111–14.

6 Charles H. Talbert, *Literary Patterns, Theological Themes and the Genre of Luke-Acts* (Missoula, Mont.: Scholars Press, 1974), 15–23, identifies a total of thirty-two parallels between the Gospel and Acts. See also Mark Allan Powell, *Introduction to the Gospels* (Minneapolis: Augsburg Fortress, 1998), 88; Johnson, Acts, 9–10.

7 Talbert, 23–26, identifies a total of sixteen parallels between Acts 1–12 and 13–28. See also Talbert's later work on Acts, *Reading Acts: A Literary and Theological Commentary on the Acts of the Apostles* (New York: Crossroads, 1997), 15–17; cf. Witherington, 72–73.

8 For example, Haenchen, Acts, 90–112, sees the speeches as representing primarily Luke's theology. Lüdemann, *Early Christianity*, offers a more moderate position, arguing that "the speeches in Acts in their present form come from Luke's pen, as redactor. This does not exclude the possibility that the scheme of the speeches . . . and individual elements in them, derive from traditions," 47–48.

The Gospel of John: Jesus as the Word Made Flesh

6

Introduction

Whereas Matthew and Luke expand and revise the story of Jesus as found in Mark, the Gospel of John tells the story of Jesus from a decidedly distinct perspective. How the Johannine presentation differs from that of the Synoptic Gospels will become clear as we focus on the historical setting of John's Gospel and several unique elements that set this evangelist's telling of the Jesus story apart from the rest.

John's Jesus: The Word Made Flesh

Each Gospel has its own slant on Jesus: Mark sees Jesus as the suffering Messiah, Matthew portrays him as the new Moses, Luke presents Jesus as the universal savior, and John speaks of Jesus as the Word made flesh. The emergence of sometimes-disparate oral and written traditions about Jesus teaches us that people have seen and understood Jesus in fundamentally different ways from the very beginning.

Yet, these varied portraits of Jesus retain a basic compatibility. For example, Jesus is the suffering Messiah in all four canonical Gospels. But Matthew and Luke expand and tailor this Markan portrait of

Jesus to fit their own theological assertions, in effect, creating a new portrait drawn from the original suffering Messiah. Likewise, Jesus' suffering and death are integral to John's Gospel, where from early on the idea of Jesus' suffering is linked to the importance of faith in Jesus: "And just as Moses lifted up the serpent in the desert, so must the Son of Man be lifted up (on the cross), so that everyone who believes in him may have eternal life" (John 3:14).

From its opening prologue, however, the Gospel of John also offers its own theological perspective: Jesus as the Word made flesh.

These varied Gospel portraits represent different "streams" of Jesus traditions. The image of streams aptly suggests the movement and fluidity of evolving Jesus traditions over time. The Gospel of John, however, seems to share fewer traditions than do Matthew, Mark, and Luke. For this reason, scholars debate whether John's characterization of Jesus responds to Mark's, let alone Matthew's or Luke's. Some scholars maintain that John's distinctive portrait suggests a parallel stream of oral and written traditions about Jesus as its primary source. While sharing some traditions with the other Gospels (for example, the passion narrative), John is also often independent of those traditions (for example, John's numerous "signs" in Jesus' ministry). Other scholars believe that John's Gospel, especially in a later stage of composition, responded at least in part to the developing and maturing written tradition created by Mark and reinforced by Matthew and Luke.

The Relationship of John to the Synoptic Gospels

The most significant similarity between John and the Synoptics is found in the passion narratives, the sequence of events in Jesus' final days. Recall from chapter 4's discussion of form criticism and the passion narrative that this similarity may stem from each evangelist drawing from a common written tradition circulating in early Christian communities. In all four Gospel traditions, Jesus arrives in Jerusalem for the Jewish feast of Passover, debates with the religious establishment of Jerusalem and the Temple, and is then arrested, tried, and executed by crucifixion. The report of an empty tomb culminates events. There are other points of contact between John and the Synoptics as well, such as the preaching of John the Baptist and the feeding of the five thousand. But on the whole, differences predominate.

We can divide the differences between John and the Synoptics into three categories: materials presented differently in John than in the Synoptics; materials absent from John but present in the Synoptics; and materials unique to John.

Let's begin with materials presented differently in John than in the Synoptics. These are listed as follows:

- Jesus' public ministry lasts for two or three years in John (see the three celebrations of the annual Jewish feast of Passover: 2:13; 6:4; 11:55). In the Synoptics, Jesus celebrates only one Passover feast, implying that his public ministry spans just one year.

- The call of the first disciples in John includes Philip and Nathaniel (1:35–51), while in the Synoptics, the first disciples called are Peter, Andrew, James, and John (for example, see Mark 1:16–20).

- In the Synoptics, the cleansing of the Temple in Jerusalem occurs in the final week of Jesus' life (for example, see Luke 19:45–48). In John, the cleansing of the Temple marks one of the early events in the public ministry of Jesus (John 2:13–22).

- In John's Gospel, there is considerable overlap between the public ministries of Jesus and John the Baptist, with John still baptizing during Jesus' public ministry (see John 3:22–24). But

The Six Jewish Feast Days of John

John 2–12 presents many of Jesus' words and deeds in the context of six Jewish feast days:

- 2:13   Passover
- 5:1   An unnamed festival, presumably either Booths or Dedication
- 6:4   Passover
- 7:12   Booths
- 10:22 Dedication
- 12:1   Passover

Passover celebrates the Hebrews' liberation from slavery in Egypt.

Booths celebrates the forty years that the Israelites wandered in the desert, having fled Egypt in search of the Promised Land.

Dedication celebrates the reconsecration of the Temple in Jerusalem (165 BCE), after the Temple's desecration by Antiochus IV Epiphanes (168 BCE).

In John, the history that each festival celebrates is critical to understanding Jesus' words or deeds.

The Jews celebrated Passover annually; thus, the three Passover celebrations in John suggest that Jesus' public ministry lasted between two and three years.

in the Synoptics, Jesus begins his ministry after John's arrest (for example, see Mark 1:14).

• In the Gospel of John, Jesus dies on a Friday, *before* the Passover meal is to be celebrated that evening (13:1; 18:28). In the Synoptics, Jesus also dies on a Friday, but this is presented as the day *after* the Passover meal, which in the Synoptics takes place on a Thursday evening (Matt 26:17; Mark 14:12; Luke 22:7).

Some material in the Synoptics does not appear in the Gospel of John. Absent from John but present in the Synoptics are the following:

• stories of Jesus' birth, baptism, and temptation, and the passion predictions, all central to the Synoptic Gospels;
• Jesus' parables, the hallmark of his teachings in the Synoptics (in John, Jesus teaches and speaks, at times figuratively and ironically, using long, philosophical discourses);
• exorcisms performed by Jesus;
• Jesus' prediction of the fall of Jerusalem, the so-called eschatological chapters of the Synoptics (Matt 24–25; Mark 13; Luke 21).

The Gospel of John also contains many unique passages and features, including the following:

• the opening Christological prologue (1:1–18), a description of Jesus as the Word made flesh that is, in form and content, a uniquely Johannine image;
• most of the miracles ("signs") that Jesus performs, such as the water turned to wine at the wedding in Cana, healing the man at the pool of Bethesda, healing the man born blind, and raising Lazarus from the dead;
• the abundance of "I am" sayings attributed to Jesus;
• the tradition of Jesus' washing the feet of the disciples (13:1-20) and Jesus' farewell discourse (15–17);
• the Resurrection narratives (20–21), which include appearances to Mary Magdalene, Thomas, and the seven disciples, and also include the dialogue between Jesus and Peter that foreshadows Peter's martyrdom and discusses Jesus' relationship with the beloved disciple.

Outline of the Gospel of John

1:1–18	**Prologue: Jesus as the Word** This Gospel begins with an extended prologue describing Jesus as "the Word" (in Greek, *ho logos*).
1:19–12:50	**Jesus as revealer in the world** The first half of the Gospel of John narrates Jesus' public ministry in Judea and Galilee. Jesus' identity as "the Word" is revealed in the world through the seven signs alternating with extended dialogues. The signs are turning water into wine, healing the royal official's son, healing the paralytic on the Sabbath, feeding the five thousand, walking on the water of the Sea of Galilee, curing the man born blind, and raising Lazarus. Jesus' major dialogues include those with Nicodemus, John the Baptist, the Samaritan woman, the Jews/Judeans, the Pharisees, and crowds.
13:1–20:29	**Jesus as revealer to his own; and Jesus' passion, exaltation, and appearances** The second half of the Gospel of John narrates the final days in Jesus' life, beginning with the farewell discourse where Jesus washes the feet of the disciples, demonstrating the command to love one another. Here Jesus also reveals the coming of "the Advocate" and the prayer to the Father. The passion narrative follows, including Jesus' arrest, his trials before Annas and Pilate, then his torture, crucifixion, death, and burial. The empty tomb is reported along with Jesus' post-Resurrection appearances to Mary Magdalene, the disciples, and Thomas.
20:30–31	**Epilogue** The author concludes by stating that believing motivated his writing of this Gospel and that through believing, "you may have life in his (Jesus') name."
21:1–25	**Resurrection narratives, added later** These narratives include a post-Resurrection appearance of Jesus to seven disciples, an exchange between Jesus and Peter, and the parting words of the beloved disciple.

Part 1: Historical Setting of John's Gospel

As with Matthew, Mark, and Luke, we begin by asking basic historical questions about the Gospel of John. We rely again on the internal evidence from the Gospel of John and the external evidence provided by other New Testament books and the early Church fathers of the second and third centuries.

Authorship

None of the four Gospel writers, including the more self-disclosing author of Luke, leaves behind any clues as to his identity. In John, about the only clue to authorship occurs in a secondary addition to this Gospel:

> It is this disciple who testifies to these things and has written them, and we know that his testimony is true. There are also many other things that Jesus did, but if these were to be described individually, I do not think the whole world would contain the books that would be written.
>
> —John 21:24–25

Because at least this claim to authorship was made, however, a closer look at this secondary ending is warranted. Within the narrative context of John 21, "this disciple" is the figure of the "beloved disciple" who is first introduced into John's Gospel at 13:23 as part of Jesus' farewell discourse.[1] Unfortunately, nowhere does John's Gospel directly identify who the beloved disciple is. Nevertheless, the early Church fathers did attempt to identify this authorial claim.

The Gospel of John and the Johannine Epistles

Many scholars believe that the Johannine Epistles (1, 2, and 3 John) were written by the same author who wrote the Gospel of John. The epistles address the problem of secessionists who left the Johannine community.

The author of the Gospel and the epistles is to be distinguished from the "John" who wrote the New Testament book of Revelation, however.

The characteristics of the Johannine epistles are briefly described as follows:

- 1 John: Anonymous; written to the congregation; ends like a letter, although as a whole this writing lacks many characteristics of an ancient letter

- 2 John: Short letter from "the elder" to the congregation

- 3 John: Short letter from "the elder" to an individual, "the beloved Gaius"

The most common and traditional answer as to the identity of the beloved disciple is that it is John, the son of Zebedee, one of the original Twelve apostles.[2] External evidence from the early Church fathers favors this theory (see Irenaeus, *Against Heresies* 3.1.2; Eusebius, *Church History* 3.13.3 and 4.14.7). But other possibilities include an already established leader within the Johannine community (for example, "the elder" who authored 2 and 3 John) or in the larger Christian community (for example, Paul or John Mark). Some contemporary theories even present the idea that the beloved disciple may be simply a literary device, a kind of ideal disciple intended for the audience to resonate with and aspire to be.

It is worth noting that the author of the Gospel of John, independent of John 21, knew and integrated Jewish details into his narratives (for example, Jewish feast days), which suggests that he was Jewish.

Papyrus Manuscript 52 (P⁵²)

Papyrus P⁵²

Discovered in Oxyrhynchus, Egypt, in 1920, this tiny papyrus manuscript fragment (21 cm x 20 cm) labeled P⁵² is considered by many to hold the distinction of being the earliest manuscript evidence of the New Testament. This double-sided fragment contains John 18:31–33 on one side and John 18:37–38 on the other. This section of John's Gospel depicts Jesus on trial before Pilate (John 18:28–40). P⁵² is commonly dated about 125 CE.

Date of Composition

The date of the Gospel of John is much debated. Though there is some consensus regarding the dates of the Synoptic Gospels (Mark, 70 CE; Matthew and Luke, 80–85 CE), dates suggested for John range from 80–110 CE.[3] A post-70 CE date for John's Gospel is widely accepted due to both internal and external evidence. Internally, John's Gospel speaks of the experience of expulsion from Jewish synagogues (see John 9:22; 12:42; 16:2), which apparently began, or more likely became commonplace, about 85–90 CE. Externally, a fragment of a papyrus manuscript (P^{52}), discovered in Egypt and traditionally dated to the early second century (125 CE), contains verses from John 18. In recent years, some scholars have raised questions about the early dating of this fragmented manuscript, however.[4] If arguments hold for a second-century dating of P^{52}, this would indicate that at least this portion of John's Gospel was being copied and circulated in the early second century and suggests the possibility that the entire Gospel had reached Egypt by this time. Given this internal and external evidence, a time frame of 90–100 CE for the writing of John's Gospel holds the most widespread support among scholars.

Dating the Gospel of John is complicated by the fact that it seems to have been composed and edited in multiple stages. Scholar Raymond Brown contends that John was composed in five stages, a position that has received much scholarly support:[5]

Stage 1 30s CE	Oral traditions of Jesus' words and deeds
Stage 2 30-70 CE	Jesus' preaching and teachings shaped into units
Stage 3 70s CE?	Oral traditions organized into first written draft
Stage 4 80s CE?	First draft of written Gospel revised
Stage 5 90–100 CE	Final editing and addition of John 15–17; 21

As you will recall from chapter 1, all four Gospels went through at least three basic stages of formation. Each of the Gospels is based on the words and deeds of Jesus of Nazareth (the first stage of composition). Each of the Gospels is shaped by a developing oral tradition (the second stage of composition). And each of the Gospels was finally written by an evangelist who shaped and edited these received traditions (the third stage of composition).

The writing of John apparently took place over more stages than did the Synoptics. Literary "seams" or points of incongruity

Are There Two "Farewell Discourses"?

Applying the principle of Johannine literary "seams," scholars argue that John 13:1–17:26 actually contains two farewell discourses. According to this argument, John 13:1–14:31 seems to end the farewell discourse between Jesus and his disciples with Jesus' words, "Get up, let us go" (14:31), after which the reader expects them to depart. But they do not actually depart until John 18:1: "When he had said this, Jesus went out with his disciples across the Kidron valley . . . ," an incongruency indicating a literary "seam." John 15:1–17:26 appears to be a later insertion into an earlier Johannine composition. Some argue this insertion may itself stem from two different sources, because John 15–17 contains not one but two different farewell discourses from Jesus to his disciples (15:1–16:33; 17:1–17:26).

Recent studies have raised serious questions about the case for two farewell discourses, however. John 14:31 may simply be a "false exit," a common feature of drama found in Greco-Roman literature.

within John's narrative point to multiple stages of composition. One example occurs in the narration of the raising of Lazarus from the dead and the anointing at Bethany (11:2 and 12:3–7). John 11:2 refers in the past tense to Lazarus's sister Mary having anointed Jesus for burial. In the final form of this Gospel, however, Mary does not anoint Jesus until John 12:3–7. Another example of a seam occurs at John 8:31 and 8:37b. In John 8:31, Jesus speaks "to the Jews who believed in him." In answering questions from the same group of Jews, Jesus criticizes them, saying, "You are trying to kill me, because my word has no room among you" (8:37b), as though speaking now to skeptics and not "the Jews who believed in him" of 8:31. The existence of such literary seams in John indicates that this Gospel likely went through various stages of composition prior to reaching its final written form.[6]

Sources

Most scholars believe the composition of John's Gospel involved the use of different oral and written sources than those available to the Synoptic authors. However, there is no direct evidence confirming or denying the existence of these sources. Common theories regarding the sources used to write John propose[7]

- the "signs source," used for the construction of John 1–12;
- the "revelatory discourse source," used for Jesus' extensive discourses;
- the "passion source," used for the construction of John 13–19;
- the "beloved disciple" source, used for the collection of the "beloved disciple's" oral teachings.

Where John does resemble one or more of the Synoptics, as in the passion narrative, for example, is it most sensible to suggest the Synoptics as a source?[8] Scholars are divided on this question as well. Evidence that the fourth Gospel used the Synoptics as a source includes the "compositional analogies" between the passion narratives of Mark and John.[9] For instance, Mark's brief report of Jesus on trial before Pilate (15:2–5) is extended and elaborated in John (18:28–19:16a) and forms the central section of the Johannine passion narrative. There are various points of contact between John and Luke as well, for example: the miraculous catch of fish in John 21:1–11 and Luke 5:4–9; Martha and Mary in John 11:1 and Luke 10:38–39; and Jesus sending the Spirit or power from on high in John 14:16 and Luke 24:49. These parallels suggest a Lukan source for John. It is plausible that in one of John's later stages of composition, such as perhaps the stage 4 or stage 5 proposed by Raymond Brown (mentioned above), the editor(s) was responding to the written tradition of the Synoptic Gospels, especially Mark and Luke.

The Hebrew Scriptures provide a source for John, as quotations from them are found throughout John's Gospel (for example, John 1:23/Isa 40:3; John 10:34/Ps 82:6; John 16:21/Isa 26:17–18; John 19:24/Ps 22:19). And although there is no evidence that John had access to or used Paul's authentic letters, numerous agreements between the fourth Gospel and the Pauline letters suggest a connection there as well. For example, John's extensive and integrated use of *believe* (in Greek, *pisteuō*) in his Gospel (98 times) is comparable to Paul's use of *believe* in his letters (54 times). Paul also uses the noun form, *belief* (*pistis*), 142 times. Contrast this with the

Synoptics' use of *believe*: Mark, 14 times; Matthew, 11 times; and Luke, 9 times.

It seems plausible, then, to suggest that the sources used for the final composition of John's Gospel included the Synoptic Gospels (Mark and Luke), the Hebrew Scriptures, and at least some ideas adopted from the Pauline letters.

Intended Audience

The intended audience for John's Gospel is not easily reduced to a single (isolated) community or location, despite the assertions of several influential scholars to this effect.[10] The author's familiarity with things Jewish, such as the five references to annual Jewish feast days, which provide the structure for chapters 5–12, implies a Jewish audience familiar with these feasts. But John's frequent comments clarifying Jewish customs and traditions (for example, 2:6, informing readers that Jewish weddings used large stone water jars for "Jewish ceremonial washings," and 3:1, speaking of Nicodemus and referring to his status as a "Pharisee" and "ruler of the Jews") implies that the intended audience is either a mixed community of Jews and Gentiles, or perhaps even mostly Jews who lived in the Diaspora (outside of Judea and Galilee) and were unaware of the Jewish customs and traditions of Palestinian Jews. Furthermore, the bland and inaccurate references to (all) "the Jews" seen throughout the Gospel of John, without distinguishing between different groups of Jewish leaders or the people as a whole (for instance, 9:22; 13:33), suggest that John's community may have had only a limited or even skewed understanding of first-century Palestinian Judaism.

As is the case with the other Gospels, there is not much internal evidence to suggest a definite place of composition for the Gospel of John. Tradition identifies Ephesus (see, for example, second-century Church father Irenaeus, *Against Heresies* 3.1.2; 2.22.5; 3.3.4, and fourth-century Church historian Eusebius, *Church History* 3.23.3–4).[11] Other possible places of composition offered by scholars include Alexandria, Antioch in Syria, and Palestine.[12] Given that this Gospel apparently enjoyed a complex compositional process with several authors or editors, there may well have been more than one place of composition.

Summary of Historical Setting

Author:	unknown; later Church tradition identifies John, the brother of James (sons of Zebedee), and one of the Twelve apostles
Date of composition:	about 90–100 CE, although likely composed in multiple stages
Sources:	unknown; possibly the Synoptic Gospels (especially Mark and Luke), Hebrew Scriptures, and Pauline letters
Intended audience and place of composition:	mixed audience of Jews and Gentiles, with place of composition unknown

Part 2: How John Told the Story

The opening prologue, the Johannine "signs," the "I am" sayings, and the farewell discourse—these and other prominent themes and passages in the fourth Gospel contribute to John's distinctive way of telling his story of Jesus.

The Prologue: 1:1–18

John begins his Gospel by describing Jesus as "the Word" ("And the Word became flesh and made his dwelling among us," 1:14a) and the Son of God (1:14b). John uses the Greek word *ho logos* ("the Word") to describe Jesus. "The Word" had both a religious and a philosophical meaning in the first-century Mediterranean world. Jewish religion taught that God's "Word" was the creative force that generated everything into being (the book of Genesis) and was personified as God's Wisdom in the world (Wisdom of Solomon 7–8). Greek philosophy taught that *Logos* was the force that governed all intelligible reality. Consequently, people of different backgrounds, both Jews and Gentiles, could derive different meanings from John's identifying Jesus as *ho logos*.

One of John's Key Terms: *Glory*

Throughout the Gospel of John, several key terms and concepts provide insight into Jesus' identity as the Word made flesh: for example, water, eternal life, seeking, love, and John's use of the word *glory*. Beginning in the prologue (John 1:14), the word *glory* carries particular significance throughout John 1 – 17.

1:14	And the Word became flesh and made his dwelling among us, and we saw his *glory*, the *glory* as of the Father's only Son, full of grace and truth.
2:11	Jesus did this as the beginning of his signs in Cana in Galilee and so revealed his *glory*, and his disciples began to believe in him.
7:18	"Whoever speaks on his own seeks his own *glory*, but whoever seeks the *glory* of the one who sent him is truthful, and there is no wrong in him."
8:50	"I do not seek my own *glory*; there is one who seeks it and he is the one who judges."
8:54	Jesus answered, "If I glorify myself, my *glory* is worth nothing; but it is my Father who glorifies me, of whom you say, 'He is our God.'"
11:4	When Jesus heard this he said, "This illness is not to end in death, but is for the *glory* of God, that the Son of God may be glorified through it."
11:40	Jesus said to her, "Did I not tell you that if you believe you will see the *glory* of God?"
12:41	Isaiah said this because he saw his *glory* and spoke about him.
12:43	For they preferred human praise to the *glory* of God.
17:5	"Now glorify me, Father, with you, with the *glory* that I had with you before the world began."
17:22	"And I have given them the *glory* you gave me, so that they may be one, as we are one."
17:24	"Father, they are your gift to me. I wish that where I am they also may be with me, that they may see my *glory* that you gave me, because you loved me before the foundation of the world."

In John's prologue, Jesus, "the Word" and "the Father's only Son," reveals God to all people as the Father. John the Baptist announces the "true light" that has come into the world, but the world rejects Jesus. Those who accept and believe in Jesus as the one who bears testimony to grace and truth become "children of God."

The eighteen-verse prologue alternates between poetic and narrative prose. These microliterary forms may indicate that John (the Gospel evangelist) received a poetic tradition of Jesus as "the Word" and then inserted passages of narrative prose to help clarify the relationship between Jesus and John the Baptist: Jesus is "the Word," the "true light" of the world, and the Baptist is (merely) "a man" sent by God "to testify to the light."

When you read the narrative prose of John's prologue in isolation from the poetic prose, two important points about Jesus become clear. First, Jesus is superior to the Baptist, a point to which the Baptist himself testified (vv. 6–9, 15). In addition, just as the law was given to Moses, so too grace and truth came through Jesus (vv. 16–18). Furthermore, John tells us something about his intentions and his intended audience: he hopes his readers will become "children of God" (v. 12). For John, anyone who comes to believe in Jesus as "the Son of God," whether Jew or Gentile, belongs to the "children of God." The children of God live in the light, "the light (that) shines in the darkness, and the darkness has not overcome it" (John 1:5).

The prologue introduces Jesus in relationship to John the Baptist and Moses and draws upon the ancient concept of a dualism of opposites—light and darkness. These ideas will recur throughout the Gospel of John. The relationship between Jesus and John, and Jesus and Moses, will be developed further in the Gospel dialogues (for example, Jesus and John, 5:31–40; Jesus and Moses, 6:32–40), as will the dualism of light and darkness (for example, light against darkness, 3:19–21).

The Johannine "Signs"

Within the Synoptic tradition, Matthew, Mark, and Luke use the Greek word *dunameis* ("mighty deeds," see Mark 6:2; or "mighty powers," see Matt 14:2) to describe Jesus' miracles and the "mighty powers . . . at work in him." Jesus not only performs many works of power but also bestows *dunameis* onto his disciples, and they too perform mighty deeds (see Mark 6:13; Acts 1:8). Jesus' "mighty deeds" are seen as proof of his authority and of the authority of the disciples to act in Jesus' name.

The Seven Signs of Jesus in John's Gospel

1. Jesus turns water into wine at Cana 2:1–11
2. Jesus cures the royal official's son 4:46–54
3. Jesus cures a paralytic on the Sabbath 5:1–18
4. Jesus feeds the five thousand 6:1–15
5. Jesus walks on the water of the Sea of Galilee 6:16–21
6. Jesus cures the man born blind 9:1–41
7. Jesus raises Lazarus 11:1–44

Only the first two miracles (water turned into wine and the cure of the royal official's son) are explicitly identified as "signs" in John's Gospel. But most scholars conclude that the remaining five are also "signs" because one of the meanings of the number seven in antiquity and in the Hebrew Scriptures (see Gen 2:2) was "complete" or "full." Thus, the total of seven signs may indicate the fullness of Jesus' revelation through these miracles.

In the Gospel of John, the Greek word *sēmeion* (or "signs," see 2:11; 3:2) is used to describe Jesus' miracles. The epilogue of John's Gospel tells us: "Jesus did many other signs (*sēmeia*) in the presence of [his] disciples that are not written in this book" (20:30–31). In John, Jesus' signs or miracles point to his divine glory.

The first half of John's Gospel (1:19–12:50), chronicling Jesus' public ministry in Galilee, Samaria, and Judea, is punctuated with seven signs and numerous dialogues that reveal the identity and meaning of Jesus as the Son of God. The first sign (water turned into wine), for example, reveals the identity of Jesus as the true bridegroom. Furthermore, the first and second signs (the wedding feast at Cana, 2:1–11, and the curing of the royal official's son, 4:46–52) form a symmetrical connection. Both signs are associated with the village of Cana in Galilee. Each sign pulls together two different groups who come to believe in Jesus because of the signs he performs: Jews at the wedding feast ("his disciples began to believe in him," 2:11b) and Gentiles at the home of the royal official ("and he and his whole household came to believe," 4:53b). Each sign is initiated through one person's believing in Jesus: the faith of a Jewish woman (Jesus' mother, Mary) and the faith of a Gentile man (the royal official). The faith of these individuals then leads others to believe in Jesus.

The next three signs (curing a paralytic on the Sabbath, 5:1–18; feeding the five thousand, 6:1–5; walking on water, 6:16–21) are all connected with Jewish feast days. The third sign connects to an unnamed Jewish feast day (presumably Booths or Dedication, 5:1), and the fourth and fifth signs connect to the Jewish feast of Passover (6:4). John connects the feeding of the five thousand and Jesus' walking on water with the Jewish feast of Passover that commemorates the Exodus from Egypt, which included the parting of the Red Sea and the feeding of manna to the Israelites in the desert. Together these signs reveal Jesus as the bread of life and the bread come down from heaven.

The sixth sign, Jesus curing of the man born blind, suggests the blindness of the Jews and the Pharisees to the revelation of Jesus as "the light of the world." Although the man's faith in Jesus (9:38) allows him to see, the Pharisees' lack of faith in Jesus keeps them blind (9:40–41).

The raising of Lazarus (11:1–44), the final sign, shows Jesus'

John's Gospel and the Importance of Believing

The Gospel of John emphasizes the importance of believing in Jesus. In John, Jesus' miracles, or signs, inspire belief in his followers. Yet believing is inspired not only by the signs Jesus performs but also by encounters with him. The Samaritan woman at the well and the other Samaritans (4:4–42), for example, come to believe in Jesus through their encounters with him. Furthermore, one comes to knowledge of the truth through the work of the Paraclete, or Spirit (14:25–26; 15:26; 16:7, 13).

Believing in Jesus is further emphasized in the Resurrection narrative of John 20 (esp. vv. 9, 24–29, 30–31): "Now Jesus did many other signs in the presence of [his] disciples that are not written in this book. But these are written that you may [come to] believe" (John 20:30–31a).

ability to exercise his divine power even over life and death, revealing Jesus as the Resurrection and the life. Unlike in the Synoptics, where the cleansing of the Temple triggers the events that lead to Jesus' execution, in John's Gospel it is Jesus' glorifying God through the resurrection of his friend Lazarus that speedily facilitates his own death by the Sanhedrin (11:45–53).

Jesus' Discourses

In the Synoptic Gospels, Jesus often teaches in parables (for example, the parable of the sower, Matt 13:1–9; Mark 4:1–9; Luke 8:4–8) or with one-liners (for instance, "But many who are first will be last, and the last will be first," Matt 19:30; Mark 10:31; Luke 13:30). Also in the Synoptics, Jesus ranges over various subjects such as the kingdom of God or the Mosaic Law. But in John's Gospel, Jesus teaches primarily through extended discourses in which he himself is often the focal point of the discussion. These discourses often explain aspects of his identity as the Word made flesh. Following are some examples of Jesus' self-revealing discourses:

Jesus as the living water	4:4–42
Jesus as the Son of the Father	5:19–47
Jesus as the bread of life	6:22–71
Jesus as the light of the world	8:12–59
Jesus as the good shepherd	10:1–18

Jesus' discourses are not without controversy. Although some are convinced by Jesus' words, many others find them difficult to accept. In fact, quite often, Jesus' discourses are met with resistance and even hostility (for example, John 5:41–47; 6:60–66; 8:59). John 10:19–22 captures best the pattern of reaction to Jesus' discourses:

> Again there was a division among the Jews because of these words. Many of them said, "He is possessed and out of his mind; why listen to him?" Others said, "These are not words of one possessed; surely a demon cannot open the eyes of the blind, can he?"

Like Jesus' signs, these discourses often lead people to respond by declaring that Jesus is "the savior of the world" (the Samaritans in John 4:42) or the "Holy One of God" (the Twelve in John 6:68–69). Likewise in John 8:28–30, hearing Jesus speak of himself as "the Son of Man," many of the Jews "came to believe in him."

The "I Am" Sayings

At several points in the Gospel of John, Jesus describes himself with the phrase *egō eimi*, "I am" (for example, 4:26; 8:24, 28, 58; 13:19; 18:5, 6, 8).

Jesus uses "I am" sayings as metaphors for his identity. As with the seven "signs" of Jesus, John presents seven metaphorical "I am" sayings indicating the fullness of Jesus' identity as the Word made flesh:

> **Johannine Titles for Jesus**
>
> All of the titles for Jesus used in John's Gospel are presented in the opening chapter. Some of the titles are traditional, while others are uniquely Johannine.
>
> **Titles used in John and elsewhere in the New Testament:**
> Son of God (1:34, 49)
> Son of Man (1:51)
> Messiah (1:41)
> Rabbi (1:38, 49)
>
> **Titles unique to John:**
> The Word (1:1, 14)
> Lamb of God (1:29, 36)
> King of Israel (1:49)

"I am the bread of life" (6:35)
"I am the light of the world" (8:12)
"I am the gate for the sheep" (10:7)
"I am the good shepherd" (10:11)
"I am the resurrection and the life" (11:25)
"I am the way and the truth and the life" (14:6)
"I am the true vine" (15:1)

As part of his extended farewell discourse (John 15:1–17:26), Jesus draws upon the Jewish prophetic tradition and speaks of the image of the vine and the branches: "I am the true vine, and my Father is the vine grower . . . you are the branches" (vv. 1, 5). The three main prophets of Israel (Isaiah, Jeremiah, and Ezekiel) all spoke of Israel metaphorically as a vineyard and a vine (see Isa 5:1–7; Jer 2:21; Ezek 17:5–10). In John, Jesus appropriates this image for himself and his disciples, forewarning of the "pruning" necessary to bear "more fruit." Jesus tells his disciples that the key to bearing fruit rests in a relationship with him: "I am the vine, you are the branches. Whoever remains in me and I in him will bear much fruit, because without me you can do nothing" (15:5). In Jesus speaking of himself as the "true vine," the fullness of his identity as the Word made flesh is made explicit.

Unity of the Father and the Son

The Gospel of John presents a uniquely intimate unity between God the Father and Jesus the Son. The Synoptic Gospels also articulate a unity between Jesus and God as Father and Son. For example, the "voice" from heaven and the clouds at the baptism and the transfiguration speak of Jesus as "my beloved Son" (see Mark 1:11; Matt 3:17; Luke 3:22; and Mark 9:7; Matt 17:5; Luke 9:35—in Luke, "my chosen Son"). But John's Gospel develops more thoroughly the Father-Son relationship.

Beginning already in the Johannine prologue, Jesus is simultaneously presented as both the Word and the Son: "And the Word became flesh and made his dwelling among us, and we saw his glory, the glory as of the Father's only Son, full of grace and truth" (John 1:14). Furthermore, John's Gospel presents this unity between Father and Son in various contexts. For example, in debating with "the Jews" over his messianic identity (10:22–30), Jesus concludes by saying: "The Father and I are one" (v. 30). In his prayer at the farewell discourse (17:1–26), Jesus prays for his future disciples: "I pray . . . so that they may all be one, as you, Father, are in me and I in you, that they also may be in us, that the world may believe that you sent me" (v. 20, 21).

This unity between Father and Son underscores one of John's central theological themes: Jesus as the *incarnation* of God, Jesus as the Word made flesh. For John, this unity between Father and Son is intimately tied to the passion and the cross. This connection is presented in various ways. In his dialogue with Nicodemus, Jesus explains: "And just as Moses lifted up the serpent in the desert, so must the Son of Man be lifted up (on the cross), so that everyone who believes in him may have eternal life. For God so loved the world that he gave his only Son, so that everyone who believes in him might not perish but might have eternal life" (3:14–16). In metaphorical speech, Jesus states: "I am the good shepherd. A good shepherd lays down his life for the sheep" (10:11).

Ultimately, Jesus sees his own coming suffering and death (the cross) as the means by which the Father and Son will be "glorified." The Johannine Jesus speaks of this as his coming "hour" throughout the Gospel and directly with his followers: "The hour has come for the Son of Man to be glorified" (12:23). It is in the cross (as well as the Resurrection and Ascension) that the bond of unity between Father and Son is most visible: "I am troubled now. Yet, what should I say? 'Father, save me from this hour'? But it was for this purpose that I came to this hour. Father, glorify your name" (12:27).

The Coming "Hour"

One of the distinctive ways in which John presents Jesus' impending suffering, death, Resurrection, and Ascension is with the metaphor of the coming "hour." Notice the verb tense changes associated with Jesus' "hour," as the Gospel moves toward the passion narrative.

- In connection with the first sign (turning water into wine, 2:4): "'Woman, how does your concern affect me? My hour has not yet come.'"

- In Jesus' dialogue with the Samaritan woman at the well (4:21): "'Believe me, woman, the hour is coming when you will worship the Father neither on this mountain nor in Jerusalem.'"

- In Jesus' debate with "the Jews" (7:30): "So they tried to arrest him, but no one laid a hand upon him, because his hour had not yet come." (See also 8:20.)

- In Jesus' discussion with his followers (12:23): "'The hour has come for the Son of Man to be glorified.'"

- At the farewell discourse (13:1): "Jesus knew his hour had come to pass from this world to the Father." (See also 16:25.)

- In his prayer to the Father in the farewell discourse (17:1): "'Father, the hour has come. Give glory to your son, so that your son may glorify you.'"

The Kingdom of God in John

A hallmark of Jesus' preaching in the Synoptic Gospels is his reference to the "kingdom of God" and other "kingdom" language (see, for example, Matt 9:35; Mark 1:15; Luke 17:20–21). In fact, the "kingdom of God" emerges in the Synoptics as the cornerstone of Jesus' public ministry. By contrast, "kingdom" and "kingdom of God" language is almost entirely absent from the Gospel of John. The sole reference to the "kingdom of God" occurs in a dialogue between Nicodemus and Jesus early in the Gospel, and it is re-presented in the Johannine language of "being born from above" and "being born of water and Spirit" as in "Jesus answered and said to him, 'Amen, amen, I say to you, no one can see the kingdom of God without being born from above'" and "Jesus answered, 'Amen, Amen, I say to you, no one can enter the kingdom of God without being born of water and Spirit'" (John 3:3, 5).

This de-emphasis on the kingdom of God results from the Gospel of John's focus on the person of Jesus rather than the content of his preaching. In John, Jesus himself is the content of his message. This is most clearly exemplified in the "I am" sayings. This has repercussions for the Johannine eschatology. The Gospel of John is dominated by a present-tense eschatology—salvation is in the here and now: "I am the resurrection and the life; whoever believes in me, even if he dies, will live, and everyone who lives and believes in me will never die" (John 11:25–26). The Synoptic eschatology, although marked by some present tense (see Mark 1:15), is far more future oriented (see Luke 9:27).

Literary Devices: Symbolism, Misunderstanding, and Irony

All of the New Testament Gospel writers use symbolism, irony, and misunderstanding in telling their stories of Jesus. What distinguishes John from the Synoptic Gospels in this regard is John's extensive use of these literary devices.

John is particularly fond of three symbols: bread, water, and light. Symbolic bread and water passages in John include:

Bread—6:5–13, 28–58; 21:9–13
Water—3:5; 4:10–15; 5:2–7; 7:37–39; 9:7; 13:3–10; 19:34

Oftentimes the symbols of bread and water are used in reference to Jesus himself and his identity: "I am the bread of life" (6:35); "whoever drinks the water I shall give will never thirst; the water I shall give will become in him a spring of water welling up to eternal life" (4:14).

The symbol of light often reads as a reference to Jesus himself as well and is frequently presented dualistically with darkness, suggesting a clear choice for the path to eternal life:

> the light shines in the darkness, and the darkness has not overcome it. —1:5

> And this is the verdict, that the light came into the world, but people preferred darkness to light, because their works were evil. —3:19

> Jesus spoke to them again, saying, "I am the light of the world. Whoever follows me will not walk in darkness, but will have the light of life." —8:12

> "I came into the world as light, so that everyone who believes in me might not remain in darkness." —12:46

Misunderstanding about Jesus' true identity and the misinterpretation of Jesus' words often serve as "teachable moments" in John's Gospel. At times, either Jesus or the narrator (John) will offer an explanation clarifying a misunderstanding. For example, when the Jews misunderstand Jesus' reference to the destruction of the Temple (2:19–20), the narrator clarifies what Jesus means (2:21). When Nicodemus misunderstands Jesus' words, "no one can see the kingdom of God without being born from above" (3:3), Jesus explains more directly what he means (3:5–8). When the disciples misunderstand what Jesus meant by "food" (4:31–33), Jesus explains (4:34).

The Gospel of John also makes liberal use of irony. As was the case with misunderstanding, we as readers are likewise able to appreciate the irony, because its intent is to reveal Jesus' true origins as "the Word" from and with God, and his identity as the Son of God. We recognize, for example, the irony in Nathaniel's question to John the Baptist about Jesus' origins: "Can anything good come from Nazareth?" (1:46). We see the irony in the question of the Samaritan woman at the well who challenges Jesus' identity: "Are you greater than our father Jacob?" (4:12). We understand the irony of the Pharisees questioning Jesus in his healing ministry: "Surely we are not also blind, are we?" (9:40). The most significant irony in John's Gospel is the consistent rejection of Jesus as Son of God, as, for example, in the passion narrative, when the crowds shout for Jesus' crucifixion and the chief priests tell Pilate, "We have no king but Caesar," that is, the Roman emperor (19:15).

Jesus' Farewell Discourse

Jesus' farewell discourse plays a prominent role in the Gospel of John. Whereas the Synoptic Gospels devote relatively little narrative space to Jesus' Last Supper (Mark 14:17–31; Matt 26:20–35; Luke 22:14–38), John devotes five chapters and presents a lengthy, two-part discourse between Jesus and his disciples (13:1–17:26) during the last night he spends with them. The section in John begins with Jesus washing the feet of the disciples (13:1–20). This deed of service gives the disciples "a model to follow" (v. 15) and a demonstration of Jesus' "new commandment: love one another" (v. 34). In this first part of the discourse, Jesus also speaks at length about the Paraclete, the "holy Spirit" who comes in his name to guide and instruct the community of believers in Jesus' absence (14:15–31; 16:4–33).

The second part of the discourse includes Jesus' threefold prayer for himself (17:1–5), his disciples (17:6–19), and all future believers

---

The Paraclete in John

In Jesus' first farewell discourse to his disciples, Jesus speaks of *allon paraklēton* ("another Paraclete"), often translated as "Advocate," "Counselor," or "Comforter." In John's Gospel, Jesus was the "first Advocate" sent from the Father in heaven. Jesus now reveals the "second Advocate." The central point seems to be that in Jesus' absence the Paraclete will play an analogous role of guiding the disciples.

In John's Gospel, the Paraclete is "the Spirit of truth" (14:17), the "holy Spirit" (14:26).

The Paraclete comes *only* because the Son has gone back to the Father (16:7). God the Father sends the Paraclete in the name of his Son (14:26a). The Paraclete will always be present to the believing community (14:16). The Paraclete will teach and remind the disciples all that Jesus told them (14:26b).

In the Acts of the Apostles, we see the Holy Spirit is also present to the disciples in a similar way (see Acts 2).

(17:20–26). Jesus' prayer for himself draws upon the notions of Jesus as the source of eternal life and as "the Word," with God before the world began. Jesus' prayer for his disciples is "that they may be one just as we are" (v. 11), that they be kept "from the evil one" (v. 15), and that they be consecrated "in the truth" (v. 17). Jesus' prayer to God for future believers, for "those who will believe in me through their word" (v. 20), is "that they may all be one" (v. 21) and that they may be brought "to perfection as one" (v. 23). The Johannine epistles, which stem from the same Johannine community if not the same author, attest to a divided Christian community whose hope for unity has been dashed (see, for example, 1 John 2:18–23). The divided Johannine community likely took comfort from the idea that Jesus foresaw the potential for disunity, and in fact prayed for the unity of the community.

Discipleship and the Beloved Disciple

The meaning of discipleship and the portrayal of the disciples in the Gospel of John depart in a variety of ways from what we have seen in the Synoptic Gospels. The call of the first disciples in the Synoptics involved Jesus' invitation to a set of brothers (Peter and Andrew, James and John) "to follow" (Mark 1:16–18; Matt 4:18–22; Luke 5:1–1). In John, the first disciples called by Jesus are two of the Baptist's disciples: Andrew and an unnamed disciple (John 1:35–40), as well as Philip and Nathaniel (John 1:43–51). It is Andrew who informs Peter of Jesus, with Peter subsequently following Jesus (John 1:41–42).

Furthermore, whereas in the Synoptics, Jesus selects twelve disciples among his followers and "sends them out" to heal and preach (see Matt 10:1–15; Mark 3:13–19; Luke 6:12–16), there is no such selection of "the Twelve," nor is there any sending-out to heal and preach in John. In fact, the image of "the Twelve" is nearly absent in John, with only two brief references to this group of disciples: 6:67, 70, 71; 20:24. For John, discipleship is not about healing and preaching, or carrying one's cross (see, for example, Mark 8:34); rather, discipleship is about "believing" in Jesus and bringing others to him. In fact, in the dialogue between Jesus and the Samaritan woman at the well, it becomes clear that the woman's belief in Jesus and her ability to bring others to him becomes a model for discipleship (4:4–40).

Perhaps the most distinctive disciple in John is the enigmatic figure of the "beloved disciple," who is first introduced into John's Gospel at Jesus' farewell discourses, where he is presented as "the one whom Jesus loved . . . reclining at Jesus' side" (13:23). At times associated closely with Peter in the second half of John, this beloved disciple:

- 13:24–26   speaks for Peter, asking Jesus who will betray him
- 18:15–16   helps Peter gain access to Pilate's court where Jesus stands trial
- 19:26–27   is entrusted by Jesus as he dies with caring for Jesus' mother, Mary
- 20:4   arrives prior to Peter at the empty tomb
- 20:8   believes in the Resurrection upon seeing the empty tomb

In John 21 (a later addition to John), the author likewise favorably describes this beloved disciple, who identifies the resurrected Christ for Peter (21:7) and is defended by the resurrected Christ from Peter (21:21–23).

Intriguingly, this disciple is never identified by name. It could be that this anonymous "beloved disciple" represents a separate Johannine community that had evolved by the end of the first century and that was considered equally valuable but separate from the Johannine community associated with Peter.

The Johannine Passion Narrative

The sequence of events in the passion narrative of John is consistent with what is presented in the Synoptic Gospels. Yet, though there are many similarities between John and the Synoptics, there are also many differences, which often reflect Johannine rhetorical style and theology. Some of the plot parallels in the passion narratives of John and the Synoptics include the following:

- Judas betrays Jesus.
- Jesus is arrested.
- Peter denies Jesus.
- Jesus is interrogated before Jewish leaders and the Roman official, Pilate.

- Jesus is sentenced to death by crucifixion.
- Jesus dies on the cross.
- Jesus is buried in a tomb.

Features found in John's passion narrative but not in the Synoptics include the following:

- The beloved disciple is present with the women at Jesus' crucifixion.
- Jesus is pierced in his side with a lance while on the cross, and blood and water flow out.
- In his arrest, twice Jesus says, "I AM" (18:5, 8), contrasted with Peter's twice denying Jesus, saying, "I am not" (18:17, 25).
- Peter and the beloved disciple follow Jesus as he is arrested and interrogated.
- The inscription on the cross ("Jesus the Nazorean, the King of the Jews") is written in Hebrew, Latin, and Greek.

Portrayal of "the Jews"

The Gospel of John speaks of "the Jews" and "Jewish leaders" (in Greek *Ioudaios*) as a group far more often than do the Synoptics. The portrayal of the *Ioudaios* is often negative, but not entirely, because Jesus is portrayed as a Jew (4:9), and salvation is said to come from the Jews (4:22). In fact, certain Jewish leaders (Nicodemus, 3:1–21; 7:50–52; 19:39; Joseph of Arimathea, 19:38–42) are portrayed positively. Furthermore, many Jews come to believe in Jesus (see, for example, 8:30–32; 11:45).

However, the *Ioudaios* are often also presented in conflict with Jesus (see, for instance, John 6:41; 8:59) and because of their unbelief in Jesus, characterized as sons of the devil (8:44).

This stereotypical portrayal of a group was also seen in the Synoptics, as in the portrayal of the Pharisees, for example.

- In addition to the women, Peter and the beloved disciple bear witness to the empty tomb.

The similarities in the passion narrative between John and the Synoptics may lie in the evangelists' mutual use of a common written source circulating at an early point in the formation of the Gospel tradition. (Recall the discussion in chapter 4 on form criticism and the interpretation of the passion narrative.) The differences between the Johannine and Synoptic accounts of the passion point more to John's Christology: John's emphasis on blood and water flowing from Jesus' side points symbolically to Jesus as the wellspring of eternal waters.

The Two Endings of John's Gospel

In its final form, the fourth Gospel's original ending (John 20) is supplemented by an additional ending (John 21). These two endings present different encounters between Jesus and his disciples:

20:11–18 Jesus appears to Mary Magdalene	21:1–14 Jesus appears to the disciples
20:19–23 Jesus appears to the disciples	21:15–19 Jesus speaks with Peter
20:24–29 Jesus appears to Thomas	21:20–23 Jesus speaks about the beloved disciple
20:30–31 Concluding remarks	21:24–25 Concluding remarks

Many non-Johannine characteristics in John 21 leave the impression that this chapter is a secondary addition (for example, in John 21:15–17, there is a remarkable variety of synonyms: two different Greek verbs for love; two verbs for *feed/tend*; two nouns for *sheep*; two verbs for *know*). Furthermore, the focus on Peter and the miraculous catch of fish in John 21 has parallels in the Synoptic tradition (see Luke 5:1–11 and Matt 14:28–31), suggesting some type of source dependency.

The concluding remarks in each chapter indicate two different endings; thus, most scholars see John 21 as a secondary addition to the original ending of John 21. Compare the closing comments in these two chapters:

JOHN 20:30–31	JOHN 21:24–25
Now Jesus did many other signs in the presence of [his] disciples that are not written in this book. But these are	It is this disciple who testifies to these things and has written them, and we know that his testimony is true.
	(cont'd.)

(JOHN 20:30–31 cont'd.)	(JOHN 21:24–25 cont'd.)
written that you may [come to] believe that Jesus is the Messiah, the Son of God, and that through this belief you may have life in his name.	There are also many other things that Jesus did, but if these were to be described individually, I do not think the whole world would contain the books that would be written.

Unlike the Gospel of Mark, where early manuscript evidence indicates that Mark 16:9–20 may have been added later to the original ending of Mark 16:1–8, all existing manuscript copies of the Gospel of John contain both chapters 20 and 21. This indicates that John 21 must have been added early, before the widespread publication of the Gospel of John. Because much of the focus of John 21 is on Peter and the beloved disciple, it could be, as suggested earlier, that these two figures represent two different Johannine communities that claimed separate leaders as their founders.

In addition to John 21, the passage about the adulterous woman who was about to be stoned to death for her offense (John 7:53–8:11) is likewise likely a later addition to this Gospel. Along with the use of several sources and the literary "seams" stemming from edited or rearranged passages, John 7:53–8:11 and John 21 highlight this Gospel's complex compositional history and legacy.

Summary of How John Told the Story

Core Concepts
- The Gospel of John presents a parallel stream of Jesus traditions that are similar to, yet largely independent of, the Synoptic Gospels.
- In John's Gospel, Jesus is God's Son in whom all people are called to believe or have faith.
- Jesus' "signs" reveal God's glory at work in Jesus.
- The unity between Father and Son is a major theme in John's Gospel.
- Jesus' "I am" sayings point to his identity as "the Word made flesh."

(cont'd.)

(summary of how John told the story cont'd.)

Supplemental Information

- John's prologue identifies Jesus as "the Word" and the Son of God.
- Unlike in the Synoptics, the Johannine Jesus often speaks in long philosophical discourses, often about his own identity.
- The concept of the kingdom of God plays a minor role in John as compared to the Synoptics.
- Symbolism, irony, and misunderstanding permeate the Gospel of John.
- Discipleship in John is defined as those who bring others to Jesus.
- The image of "the Twelve" apostles is almost absent from John's Gospel.
- The "beloved disciple" makes his first appearance in John's farewell discourses (13:23).
- Jesus introduces the Paraclete to the disciples in his farewell discourses, promising that another "counselor" will guide the believers once Jesus has returned to the Father.
- The passion narratives in John and the Synoptics have both similarities and differences.
- The Resurrection narrative and ending in John 21 is a later addition; John 20 is the original Resurrection narrative and ending.

Questions for Review

1. What evidence is there for multiple authors of the Gospel of John?
2. How does the theory of multiple authors affect questions of date and place of composition for the Gospel of John?
3. Why do we think chapters 20 and 21 are two distinct endings to John's Gospel?
4. What are some of the possible sources used for John's Gospel?
5. Explain Jesus' seven "signs" in connection to the Johannine idea of believing and faith.
6. Name some examples of Johannine literary features and explain their function in the Gospel.

7. When does the "beloved disciple" first appear in the Gospel of John?

8. What is the function of Jesus' "I am" sayings in John's Gospel?

9. Explain the Gospel of John's de-emphasis on the "kingdom of God."

10. How is discipleship defined in the Gospel of John?

Questions for Reflection

1. Why might parallel streams of Jesus traditions have emerged in the first-century world of Christianity?

2. Where in the Gospel of John, outside of the prologue (1:1–18), do you see the theme of Jesus as "the Word made flesh" developed?

3. Do you think John knew of the Synoptic Gospels? Why or why not?

4. Compare Jesus in the Gospel of John with Jesus in the Synoptic Gospels.

Recommendations for Further Reading

Brown, Raymond E. *The Community of the Beloved Disciple: The Life, Loves and Hates of an Individual Church in New Testament Times.* New York: Paulist, 1979.

In what has become a classic study on John, Brown examines the figure of "the beloved disciple" and the evolution of the community that formed around him. Brown investigates the Gospel of John and the three epistles produced by this community (1, 2, and 3 John) in terms of what the literature reveals about them and their community struggles. This is a solid and easy-to-follow historical-critical analysis of the Johannine community.

Culpepper, R. Alan. *Anatomy of the Fourth Gospel: A Study in Literary Design.* Philadelphia: Fortress, 1983.

Anatomy of the Fourth Gospel is one of the earliest and best works exploring the literary features that make the Gospel of John a narrative masterpiece. Culpepper examines the literary design of the fourth Gospel, looking at narrator, point of view, narrative time, plot, characters, irony, symbolism, misunderstanding, implicit commentary, and audience. Very reader-friendly, this book set the benchmark for all subsequent literary studies on the Gospel of John.

Fehribach, Adeline. *The Women in the Life of the Bridegroom: A Feminist Historical-Literary Analysis of the Female Characters of the Fourth Gospel.* Collegeville, Minn.: Liturgical, 1998.

As the title indicates, this study focuses on the major female characters in the Gospel of John. After an introduction to the feminist historical-literary approach and character analysis, Fehribach considers the mother of Jesus at Cana and at the cross, the Samaritan woman, Mary and Martha at Bethany, and Mary Magdalene at the tomb, highlighting how these female characters would have been heard and understood in the first-century world.

Kysar, Robert. *John: The Maverick Gospel.* Rev. ed. Louisville, Ky.: Westminster John Knox Press, 1993.

Kysar revises his original, critically acclaimed study from 1976. Tailored for the beginning student, Kysar begins with an analysis of the historical questions associated with John, including John's relationship to the Synoptic Gospels. The Johannine themes of Christology, dualism, concepts of faith, and eschatology are then developed in some depth. Kysar concludes with a presentation of John as the universal Gospel. Appendixes on the Johannine epistles and women are provided.

Sloyan, Gerard S. *What Are They Saying about John?* Rev. ed. New York: Paulist, 2006.

Revising his original work from 1991, Sloyan tackles the ambitious task of covering some of the best research and scholarship on the Gospel of John from the past forty years, 1965–2005. He begins with a survey of landmark commentaries, starting with the earliest from Heracleon to Origen (second and third centuries CE) and ending with the contributions of the major Johannine scholars of the twentieth century. Sloyan next explores the question of what sources John may have used in writing his Gospel as well as how scholars have examined the Gospel on a literary level. He closes with a survey of Johannine themes.

Endnotes

1 For a discussion on the identity of the author of John, see Raymond E. Brown, *The Gospel According to John I–XII* (AB; New York: Doubleday, 1966), lxxxvii–ciii; D.A. Carson, *The Gospel According to John* (Grand Rapids, Mich.: Eerdmans, 1991), 68–81; Francis J. Moloney, *The Gospel of John* (SP 4; Collegeville, Minn.: Liturgical, 1998), 6–9; D. Moody Smith, *John* (Nashville: Abingdon, 1999), 24–27; George R. Beasley-Murray, *John* (2d ed.; WBC 36; Nashville, Tenn.: Thomas Nelson,

1999), lxvi–lxxv. Moloney well captures the current state of affairs on the authorship of John's Gospel: "It is arrogant to rule out any possibility out of court. It should not worry us that we cannot be sure. The authority of this Gospel flows from the way it tells the story of God and God's Son, Jesus Christ, and its challenge to all who would wish to be his followers," 8–9.

2 See R. Alan Culpepper, *John, the Son of Zebedee: The Life of a Legend* (Columbia, S.C.: University of South Carolina, 1994), 72–83, for a listing and exploration of possible candidates who could fit the identity of the beloved disciple.

3 See Brown, lxxx–lxxxvii, for the earliest and latest plausible dates for the writing of John: "the convergence of probabilities points strongly to a date between 90 and 100." See also Smith, 41–43 (90–110 CE). Carson, 82–87, argues for John being written relatively early: "A date of AD 80–85 for the publication of the Gospel of John seems reasonable." Beasley-Murray, lxxviii: "A date around 80 A.D. would satisfy the evidence, but we admit that to be no more than a plausible guess."

4 See Brent Nongbri, "The Use and Abuse of P [papyrus] 52: Papyrological Pitfalls in the Dating of the Fourth Gospel," *HTR* 98 (2005): 23–48.

5 See Brown, xxiv–xxxix, who argues for five stages of composition behind the canonical Gospel of John. Throughout the twentieth century, many other Johannine scholars have offered their theories on the compositional stages of John's Gospel (for example, Rudolf Bultmann, Oscar Cullmann, and John A.T. Robinson).

6 See the recent study by George Parsenios, *Departure and Consolation: The Johannine Farewell Discourse in Light of Greco-Roman Literature* (SuppNT 117; Leiden: Brill, 2005), which raised serious questions about the common scholarly position that the Johannine farewell discourse offers an example of a literary "seam."

7 Brown, xxviii–xxxii. See also Beasley-Murray, xxxviii–xliii. The signs-source has been developed by Robert T. Fortna, *The Gospel of Signs: A Reconstruction of the Narrative Source Underlying the Fourth Gospel* (SNTSMS 11; Cambridge: Cambridge University Press, 1970). See his further work on this topic, *The Fourth Gospel and Its Predecessor: From Narrative Source to Present Gospel* (Philadelphia: Fortress, 1988). Rudolf Bultmann's thesis of a "revelatory discourse source" is no longer widely accepted by scholars.

8 See Udo Schnelle, *The History and Theology of the New Testament Writings* (transl. M. Eugene Boring; London: SCM, 1998), 496–98,

where he assigns points of agreement between John and the Synoptics to four categories: common narrative texts, agreements in sayings tradition, additional points of contact, and analogical compositions.

9 Ibid., 500–2, for an extended discussion.

10 See Raymond E. Brown, *The Community of the Beloved Disciple: The Life, Loves, and Hates of an Individual Church in New Testament Times* (New York: Paulist, 1979).

11 On matters of setting, see Brown, lxxvii–cv; Carson, 82–87; Moloney, 1–6; Smith, 33–43; Beasley-Murray, lxxv–lxxxi. Within the New Testament itself, we know there was a Christian community established at Ephesus. In Acts 18–19, Luke tells us of Paul's missionary activities there and his ongoing contact with that community (compare 1 Cor 16:8). But Luke never writes of John at Ephesus. He does, however, tell us of John's activities in Jerusalem and Samaria (compare Acts 3:1; 8:14).

12 See Brown, ciii; Beasley-Murray, lxxviii–lxxxi; Carson, 86–87.

7

The Historical Jesus

Introduction

Our discussion of the historical Jesus has been held until now because familiarity with the four New Testament Gospels is a prerequisite to this topic. The Gospels are scholars' main sources for reconstructing the life and person of Jesus. The aim of this chapter is twofold: Part 1 presents three "quests" or attempts by scholars to understand Jesus in his historical context. The resources available for such a quest and the criteria used to establish the authenticity of Jesus' words and deeds are also considered. Part 2 applies these criteria to Jesus' life and teaching and in the process sketches a profile of the historical Jesus.

The Gospels and the Historical Jesus

Roughly a century ago, scholars began questioning if the Jesus of the New Testament Gospels is the "real" Jesus who existed two thousand years ago in the village of Nazareth in lower Galilee. Until then, it had been assumed that the Gospel writers were presenting a straightforward and historically accurate portrait of Jesus. But even a cursory read of the four New Testament Gospels indicates this is unlikely.

Let's consider just one example: the episode in which Jesus overturns the tables and chases the moneychangers from the Temple area. All four New Testament Gospels record this event (Matt 21:12–17; Mark 11:15–19; Luke 19:45–48; John 2:13–17). Whereas Matthew, Mark, and Luke report the incident occurring in the final week of Jesus' public ministry, John situates it near the beginning.

Such discrepancies may have led some second-century Christians to try to harmonize the four Gospels into a single story. Around 170–175 CE, a Syrian Christian named Tatian combined the four New Testament Gospels and at least one other (possibly the *Gospel of Thomas*) into a single story. In its Greek translation, this work became known as the *Diatessaron* ("through the four [Gospels]"). The *Diatessaron* was popular, especially in Syriac-speaking Christian communities, replacing the use of the four Gospels in the early Church for centuries.

Today scholars recognize that though the New Testament Gospels offer much in common about the life of Jesus, each one has a distinct theological perspective and range of sources. Any attempt to harmonize these perspectives into one is viewed as not only historically impossible, because the New Testament Gospels differ on so many irreconcilable details, but also disruptive to the evangelists' theological intentions. In fact, rather than harmonizing the Gospels, today we have works such as *Synopsis of the Four Gospels*, which lays every episode from the four Gospels side by side to preserve the integrity of their storylines and to highlight their similarities and differences.[1]

The Real Jesus, the Historical Jesus, and the Christ of Faith

Attempts by Tatian and others to harmonize the Gospels suggest that early Christians recognized that the four New Testament Gospels each present Jesus' life differently. Early Christians and faithful readers of Scripture do not appear to have questioned the historical reliability of the Gospels. But this sentiment began to change some two hundred years ago, in the wake of the eighteenth-century Age of Enlightenment and Age of Reason in Europe and America. During this period, Western culture began questioning a great many things, including the nature of history and faith itself. The Enlightenment and Age of Reason had a profound impact on the Western intellectual tradition, including its approach to the Bible and to the New Testament Gospels in particular.

During the nineteenth and twentieth centuries, historical-critical and literary-critical methods of interpretation were developed. Applied to the New Testament Gospels, these methods unveil much about the ancient Mediterranean world in which Jesus lived and have yielded what scholars now refer to as the *real Jesus*, the *historical Jesus*, and the *Christ of faith*.

The real Jesus:	The Jewish man from Nazareth who lived from about 4 BCE to 30 CE. No person or methods of historical research can provide direct access to the "real Jesus" (that is, what he looked like, his actual thoughts and feelings, who his friends were, and so on).
The historical Jesus:	The scholarly reconstruction of Jesus of Nazareth's words and deeds using the contemporary methods of historical-critical research.
The Christ of faith:	The Christ that Christians have come to *believe* in through personal reflection on Scripture, tradition, and experience.

Contemporary literary and historical methods of research cannot tell us with certainty what Jesus of Nazareth really did or said two thousand years ago in the villages of lower Galilee or on the streets of Jerusalem. Nor can such methods verify what Christians "believe" about Jesus as the object of their faith.[2]

Part 1: The Search for the Historical Jesus

Modern efforts to find the historical Jesus are commonly referred to as "quests." Since the nineteenth century there have been three distinct quests. First we will consider an overview of these quests and what they reveal about the historical Jesus. Next, we will look at contemporary scholarly reconstructions of Jesus and follow with a look at the Jewish, Roman, and Christian sources pertinent to the historical Jesus and early Christianity. Finally, we will consider the criteria used to determine the authenticity of the reported words and deeds of Jesus.

Quests for the Historical Jesus

Though we cannot pinpoint the exact beginning and ending dates of the three major quests, we can assign to each quest dates associated with their representative scholars.

First quest: David Friedrich Strauss (1835) and Martin Kähler (1896) to Albert Schweitzer (1906)

Second quest: Ernst Käsemann (1953) to Günther Bornkamm (1974)

Third quest: Robert Funk and the Jesus Seminar (1985) to the present

First Quest

The first quest for the historical Jesus began after the Enlightenment, in the nineteenth century. The work of David Friedrich Strauss (1808–1874), author of *The Life of Jesus Critically Examined* (1835), spurred this search.[3] First-questers believed that the Gospel evangelists reported the life of Jesus primarily through the eyes of faith—a lens considered too biased to offer an objective historical report. In other words, Strauss and the first-questers believed the evangelists wrote about the "Christ of faith," not the historical Jesus so many scholars hoped to uncover. A lasting legacy of the first quest was the idea that the "real" Jesus of Nazareth was something other than "the Christ of faith" found in the New Testament Gospels.

Goal of the First Quest

First-questers aimed to develop an unbiased historical approach to the Gospels. These questers believed the faith of the evangelists colored and even distorted their presentations of the life of Jesus. The first quest resulted in the production of dozens of "life of Jesus" studies in the mid-nineteenth and early twentieth centuries. These studies were based partly on harmonized Gospel material judged to be historically accurate and partly on the imaginations of their authors.

Studies by Martin Kähler (1835–1912), *The So-Called Historical Jesus and the Historic Biblical Christ* (1896), and Albert Schweitzer (1875–1965), *The Quest of the Historical Jesus: A Critical Study of Its Progress from Reimarus to Wrede* (1906), are often credited with putting an end to the first quest for the historical Jesus. Kähler convinced many scholars that it is not only impossible but also undesirable to separate the Jesus of history from the Christ of faith. Kähler argued that the Christ of faith, in fact, shaped the history of Christianity. And Schweitzer, critical of the many "life of Jesus" studies, argued they insufficiently accounted for major aspects of Jesus' life, principally Jesus' imminent eschatological hopes and expectations. According to Schweitzer, Jesus' worldview had been shaped by the mistaken belief that the end of the world was near. Schweitzer's research

Albert Schweitzer

The life of Albert Schweitzer was truly remarkable. Specializing in medicine, music, philosophy, and theology, Schweitzer was a medical doctor, prolific writer, and an accomplished musician. (His work on the music of Johann Sebastian Bach produced studies and recordings on Bach still valued today.) Schweitzer's theological training led him to research and publish on the historical Jesus, efforts which gained him widespread respect as a New Testament scholar. Scholars of the historical Jesus today, such as E. P. Sanders and Bart D. Ehrman, are still influenced by Schweitzer's work. Schweitzer shocked the scholarly community in 1905 by leaving his professor's post in Germany to work as a missionary medical doctor in Africa. He was awarded the Nobel Peace Prize in 1952 for his lifetime achievements.

simultaneously silenced the proliferating "life of Jesus" studies and countered their expectation that an historical Jesus could ever be accurately described. A famous line from Schweitzer's 1906 work succinctly captures the end of the first quest: "The historical Jesus will be to our time a stranger and an enigma."[4]

Any new quest for the historical Jesus would have to wait for the next generation of scholars to defy Schweitzer's skepticism about researching "history" with the Gospels.

Second Quest

As the first quest died, historical-critical research continued on the Gospels in the first half of the twentieth century, in particular with the works of Martin Dibelius (1883–1947), *From Tradition to Gospel* (1919), and Rudolf Bultmann (1884–1976), *The History of the Synoptic Tradition* (1921). These scholars pioneered a new method of biblical interpretation called *form criticism*. You will recall from chapter 1 that form critics study how and where specific literary forms or genres developed and circulated in the oral traditions that predate the written Gospels. The form-critical work of Dibelius and Bultmann hardened the conviction that the faith and beliefs of the evangelists and the early Church so permeated the Gospels that the Jesus of history was irretrievable from the Christ of faith. These scholars agreed with the first-questers that the Gospels were largely the *kerygma* (proclamations of faith) of the early Church. Much of the skepticism of disentangling the Jesus of history from the Christ of faith, the hallmark of the first quest, looked as if it would continue in any second quest for the historical Jesus.

> ### Similarities between the First and Second Quests
>
> The first and second quests shared numerous connections:
>
> - Tension between the Jesus of history and the Christ of faith
> - Skepticism about Jesus' miracles
> - Reluctance to explore Jesus' Jewish identity
> - Caution about Jesus' imminent eschatology

Almost fifty years after Schweitzer brought an end to the first quest for the historical Jesus, the second quest stirred with Ernst Käsemann's lecture in 1953, "The Problem of the Historical Jesus." But Käsemann, a doctoral student of Bultmann, was far less skeptical than his mentor that the Jesus of history could be found in the Gospels. With the help of new twentieth-century archeological discoveries (such as the Dead Sea Scrolls and the Nag Hammadi Library, two sets of ancient writings discovered in the 1940s) and refined historical-critical methods for biblical interpretation (such as redaction criticism), scholars of the second quest were able to better differentiate the evangelists' editorial opinions from earlier, more reliable pieces of information about Jesus. Nonetheless, many in the second quest remained convinced that the "Jesus of history" was somehow different than "the Christ of faith" presented by the Gospel writers.

Following Käsemann's lead were two key figures of this renewed pursuit for the historical Jesus: Günther Bornkamm (1905–1990) and Norman Perrin (1920–1976). The works of Bornkamm, *Jesus of Nazareth* (1956), and Perrin, *Rediscovering the Teachings of Jesus* (1967), are often cited as defining the parameters of second-questers. Characteristic of the second quest was its emphasis on Jesus' teachings and sayings over his deeds. Bornkamm and Perrin now spoke of a credible historical core, the "authentic sayings" of Jesus, recorded in the Gospels. Unlike the first quest, the second quest did not attempt to present a chronology of Jesus' life. Instead, by focusing on Jesus' words, the second quest restored a sense that at the core of the "Christ of faith" presented in the Gospels, we could find something of the "Jesus of history," if only some of his authentic sayings and teachings.

What began with Käsemann in the early 1950s as the "new quest" ended in the early 1970s with Perrin's untimely death.

Third Quest

It is difficult to ascertain the beginning of the third quest for the historical Jesus, but it was clearly under way by the early 1980s. The formation of the "Jesus Seminar" in 1985 under the leadership of Robert Funk is one identifiable catalyst for the third quest. Beginning with thirty scholars, the Jesus Seminar has swelled today to more than two hundred scholars specializing in gospel studies. Members of the Jesus Seminar include some of the leading voices of the third quest. They meet twice a year to debate academic papers written by members on the historical Jesus.

The Jesus Seminar is well known for its method of establishing scholarly consensus regarding the authenticity of Jesus' sayings and teachings. Members drop a colored bead into a box to indicate their conviction regarding the degree of authenticity for a particular saying or teaching: red for "certain authenticity," pink for "probable authenticity," gray for "improbable authenticity," and black for "not authentic, later, or a different tradition."

Members of the Jesus Seminar, however, are not the only scholarly voices of the third quest. In fact, one of the main characteristics of this quest is its plurality.[5] As with the second quest, these scholars aim to establish the authenticity of Jesus' sayings and teachings, which they divide into four categories: parables, aphorisms, dialogues, and stories containing words attributed to Jesus. Another defining characteristic of third-questers is their use of material from all surviving gospels from the first three centuries, not just the four canonical Gospels. The gospels outside the New Testament, the so-called extracanonical gospels, will be discussed in more detail in the next chapter.

Third-quest scholars consult ancient sources and apply modern standards to establish the authenticity of Jesus' words and deeds as reported in the gospels. Their research offers a variety of images and insights into what can be known about the historical Jesus. The following chart offers a sample of the broad spectrum of positions in the third quest. Scholars are grouped according to those emphasizing the non-eschatological historical Jesus of the Jesus Seminar (Crossan, Borg, and Mack), the historical Jesus as a marginalized Jew (Meier, Schüssler-Fiorenza), and the eschatological historical Jesus (Sanders, Ehrman).

Scholar	Image of Historical Jesus	Main Conclusion
John Dominic Crossan[6]	Jesus, the Jewish cynic and social reformer	Jesus was a peasant who advocated God's radical social justice against Roman tyranny.
Marcus Borg[7]	Jesus, the Jewish Mystic, "Spirit man"	Jesus' visions and intimacy with God empowered his mission to revitalize Israel with a strong sense of social compassion.
Burton L. Mack[8]	Jesus, the wandering sage	Neither miracle worker nor Son of God, Jesus was simply a wandering philosopher who taught a way of living in the villages of Galilee.

(cont'd.)

(scholar cont'd.)	(image of historical Jesus cont'd.)	(main conclusion cont'd.)
John P. Meier[9]	Jesus, the marginalized Jew	Known as a miracle worker, Jesus chose to live on the margins of society, announcing God's imminent divine intervention.
Elizabeth Schüssler-Fiorenza[10]	Jesus, the sage, teacher of wisdom	Jesus was a teacher of Israel's wisdom traditions, considering himself a prophet of personified wisdom, Israel's "Sophia."
James D. G. Dunn[11]	Jesus, the Jewish Messiah	Jesus saw himself as fulfilling *Jewish* messianic expectations and rejecting the royal (military) claims, thereby refining these expectations in line with his ministry and message.
E. P. Sanders[12]	Jesus, the eschatological prophet	Jesus came as a prophet Jewish Palestinian announcing a new age for Israel in which God was coming to save all, including sinners.
Bart D. Ehrman[13]	Jesus, the apocalyptic prophet	Jesus saw himself as a prophet announcing God's arrival in the world to overthrow the forces of evil.

Sources for the Historical Jesus

Outside of the New Testament, sources telling us about the historical Jesus and early Christianity are few.[14] In addition, with the exception of a single Jewish author, extracanonical sources for the historical Jesus were written in the second century CE, after the four New Testament Gospels, seriously challenging their historical credibility.

Jewish Sources

The most significant non-Christian writer of the first century to mention Jesus is the Jewish historian Flavius Josephus (37–100 CE). Josephus wrote several works, among them *Jewish Antiquities, The Jewish War,* and *Against Apion.* In *Jewish Antiquities,* written near the end of the first century, Josephus makes two references to Jesus that have drawn the attention of historical Jesus scholars. The first reference is particularly valuable:

> At this time there appeared Jesus, a wise man. For he was a doer of startling deeds, a teacher of people who receive the truth with pleasure. And he gained a following both among Jews and among many of Greek origin. And when Pilate, because of an accusation made by the leading men among us, condemned him to the cross, those who loved him previously did not cease to do so. And up until this very day the tribe of Christians (named after him) has not died out.
>
> *Antiquities* 18.3.3[15]

Significantly, Josephus characterizes Jesus as a miracle worker and popular teacher, executed under Pilate, and says that the Jesus movement continued after Jesus' death. Such details, also reported in the New Testament Gospels, are of great interest to those involved in the reconstruction of the historical Jesus.

A passing reference in *Antiquities,* although not particularly informative about Jesus, reports the execution of Jesus' brother, James, the leader of the Church in Jerusalem, in 62 CE.[16]

Roman Sources

Once we leave Josephus, who wrote his *Antiquities* about the same time that Luke wrote Luke-Acts, the major problem with the remaining sources is their second-century origin, which places them at a considerable chronological distance from the historical Jesus of 30 CE. Nonetheless, these sources do mention Jesus and Christianity.

The Roman historian Tacitus (56–117 CE) discusses Roman history from the reign of Augustus in 14 CE to that of Domitian in 96 CE, a time period that overlaps Jesus' public ministry. In *Annals,* Tacitus mentions Christ and Christians in discussing the cruelty that

Emperor Nero inflicted on Christians, and blames them, as did Nero, for setting fire to large sections of Rome in 64 CE:

> Their name (Christian) comes from Christ, who, during the reign of Tiberius, had been executed by the prefect Pontius Pilate. . . . Nero had self-acknowledged Christians arrested. Then, on their information, large numbers of others were condemned. . . . Their deaths were farcical. Dressed in wild animals' skins, they were torn to pieces by wild dogs, or crucified, or made into torches to be ignited after dark as substitutes for daylight. . . . Despite their guilt as Christians and the ruthless punishment it deserved, the victims were pitied, for it was felt that they were being sacrificed to one man's brutality rather than to the national interests.
>
> *Annals* 15.44

Two additional Roman sources offer limited information about the historical Jesus: Roman historian Suetonius and Roman rhetorician and satirist Lucian of Samosata. Suetonius (69 – 130 CE) wrote *Lives of the Twelve Caesars* around 120 CE, in which he tells of Emperor Claudius' expulsion of Jewish-Christians from Rome in 49 CE: "Since the Jews were constantly causing disturbances at the instigation of Chrestus (i.e., Christ), he (Claudius) expelled them from Rome" (*Claudius* 25.4). Lucian of Samosata (120 – 180 CE), writing in the mid-second century, presents a mocking satire of Christians that also includes a passing reference to Christ:

> It was then that he [Peregrinus] learned the wondrous lore of the Christians, by associating with their priests and scribes in Palestine. And — how else could it be? — in a trice he made them all look like children, for he was prophet, cult-leader, head of the synagogue, and everything, all by himself. He interpreted and explained some of their books and even composed many, and they revered him as a god, made use of him as a lawgiver, and set him down as a protector, next after that other, to be sure, whom they still worship, the man who was crucified in Palestine because he introduced this new cult into the world.
>
> *The Passing of Peregrinus*, 11

Most scholars believe the scant details from these Greco-Roman authors confirm Jesus' ministry in Palestine, his execution under Pontius Pilate, and the persecution of his followers. Each of these sources, late as most of them are, are viewed as credible because they were neither invested in promoting Christianity nor otherwise influenced by a "belief" in Jesus.

Christian Sources

The authentic letters of Paul, written from about 50 to 62 CE, predate the writing of the four Gospels and provide a valuable source for the historical Jesus. Although Paul's letters do not offer us many of the words and deeds of Jesus, they do offer early witness to Jesus' death and a belief in the Resurrection. Furthermore, 1 Corinthians contains a pre-Pauline tradition that Paul received from earlier followers of Jesus:

> For I handed on to you as of first importance what I also received: that Christ died for our sins in accordance with the scriptures; that he was buried; that he was raised on the third day in accordance with the scriptures; that he appeared to Cephas, then to the Twelve. After that he appeared to more than five hundred brothers at once, most of whom are still living, though some have fallen asleep. After that he appeared to James, then to all the apostles.
>
> 1 Cor 15:3–7

Paul's Letter to the Philippians 2:6–11 also contains a pre-Pauline formulation about Jesus that likely originated a few years after the death and Resurrection of Jesus:

> Who, though he was in the form of God, did not regard equality with God something to be grasped. Rather, he emptied himself, taking the form of a slave, coming in human likeness; and found human in appearance, he humbled himself, becoming obedient to death, even death on a cross. Because of this, God greatly exalted him, and bestowed on him the name that is above every name, that at the name of Jesus every knee should bend, of those in heaven and on earth and under the earth, and every tongue confess that Jesus Christ is Lord, to the Glory of God the Father.
>
> Phil 2:6–11

These Pauline letters bear the earliest written witness to the life and death of Jesus; namely, that Jesus died by crucifixion and was reportedly seen alive again after his death by some of his followers.

Finally, in terms of Christian sources, we have the New Testament Gospels, dated from 70 to 100 CE, with Mark being the earliest Gospel. No other sources (with the possible exception of the extracanonical *Gospel of Thomas*, see below and chapter 8) provide more historically credible details about the life and death of Jesus than do these four Gospels. Because the New Testament Gospels are the primary sources we have for the historical Jesus, scholars largely focus on these texts.

Criteria of Authenticity for the Historical Jesus

Following are the three main criteria scholars use to assess the authenticity of Jesus' words and deeds as reported in the New Testament Gospels. Applying these criteria does not necessarily verify the authenticity of Jesus' words or deeds or the details of his life, but it increases the likelihood of authenticity—the more criteria that apply to Jesus' life, words, or deeds, the more likely their authenticity. Scholars also apply secondary criteria, but for our introductory purposes, we will focus on the main three.[17]

Criterion of Multiple Attestation

If something about the historical Jesus is found in multiple early sources that are independent of each other, the likelihood of that tradition reaching back to the historical Jesus increases. In order to meet this standard, the multiple sources must be early, distinct, and independent from each other.

Numerous sources meet the standard of multiple attestation: the Gospels of Mark and John; the sources Q, M, and L; the letters of Paul; and the writings of Josephus. The extracanonical *Gospel of Thomas* is often also included, because many scholars date the *Gospel of Thomas* to the first century CE.[18]

Because of the literary dependency of Matthew and Luke on Mark, only those words or deeds attributed to their L-source and M-source qualify as material "independent" of Mark and thus can be used to determine multiple attestation.

Many details about Jesus that are recorded in the New Testament Gospels meet the criterion of multiple attestation. For example, we have Jesus' parables about the kingdom of God, as in the parable of the seed: Mark 4:26–29, Q [Luke 13:18–21; Matt 13:31–33], and *Gospel of Thomas* 9. And for Jesus' use of the metaphor of new wine and old wineskins to suggest the impact of his teachings, we have Mark 2:22 and the *Gospel of Thomas* 47.

Another detail from Jesus' life—that he had brothers, one of whom was named James—is attested to in multiple, early, and independent sources. The following chart illustrates this multiple attestation:

Paul 1 Cor 9:5	Mark 6:3	John 7:5	Josephus *Antiquities* 20.9.1
about 55 CE	about 70 CE	about 90 CE	about 90 CE
Do we not have the right to take along a Christian wife, as do the rest of the apostles, and the *brothers* of the Lord, and Cephas?	Is he not the carpenter, the son of Mary, and the *brother* of James and Joses and Judas and Simon?	For his *brothers* did not believe in him.	. . . so he assembled the Sanhedrin of judges, and brought before them the *brother* of the Lord, who was called Christ, whose name was James . . .

Multiple attestation implies that such details and teachings were widely held in the first century, thus raising their credibility as authentically about Jesus.

Criterion of Dissimilarity

The criterion of dissimilarity contends that sayings or deeds that differ significantly from those of other first-century Jews or from the early Church at the time of the Gospel writers can be more plausibly attributed to the historical Jesus. In other words, words or actions of Jesus falling outside the social norm would have been more easily remembered and therefore more likely preserved.

Source materials meeting this criterion include Jesus' prohibition against all oaths (Matt 5:34, 37), his public association with women (Luke 8:1–3), and his willingness to share table fellowship with tax collectors and sinners (Mark 2:13–17; Luke 19:1–10).

Criterion of Embarrassment

Because New Testament writers were primarily interested in supporting a particular view of Jesus, often in the face of competing views, it would have been natural for them to avoid those aspects of Jesus' life that disagreed with their own views, or even worse, would cause embarrassment. Therefore, when something potentially embarrassing about Jesus is mentioned in the Gospels, it was probably not invented by the early Church or the evangelists and can be judged more authentic.

The strained relationships within Jesus' own family and kinship group certainly might have been embarrassing to the early Church, yet according to all four New Testament Gospels, Jesus was rejected by his kinship group in Nazareth (see Mark 6:1–6; Matt 13:54–58; Luke 4:16–30; John 1:11), and even his own family thought he had gone "out of his mind" (Mark 3:21). Another potentially embarrassing circumstance recorded in the Gospels is that of Jesus being called "a glutton and a drunkard" because of his public association with tax collectors and sinners in table fellowship (Q/Luke 7:33–34). The most embarrassing event associated with Jesus was his crucifixion. As Paul himself wrote, the execution of Jesus as a criminal was "a stumbling block to Jews and foolishness to Gentiles" (1 Cor 1:23).

It should be noted that none of these criteria is foolproof, and that the criteria can at times come into tension with one another, requiring additional arguments and judgments. For example, multiple attestation is no guarantee that something stems from Jesus himself; it only establishes that the tradition stems from a substratum of Synoptic tradition. The criterion of dissimilarity is especially tricky, given that a saying of Jesus, a Jew, must be unlike (yet spoken to!) other Jews in order to be considered genuine.

Summary of the Search for the Historical Jesus

Core Concepts

- The rise of scientific methods for biblical interpretation in the nineteenth century led to three distinct quests for the historical Jesus.
- There are remarkably few Jewish and Roman sources outside the New Testament that discuss Jesus and Christianity. This makes the Christian source (the New Testament) all the more indispensable for reconstructing Jesus' words and deeds.
- Scholars apply specific standards (criteria) to establish whether or not the details of Jesus' life, including his words and deeds, authentically represent the historical Jesus. These standards are multiple attestation, dissimilarity, and embarrassment.

Supplemental Information

- Scholars differentiate between the real Jesus, the historical Jesus, and the Christ of faith.
- Each of the three quests for the historical Jesus in the past two hundred years has a distinct focus and character.

  First quest: Trying to uncover unbiased, objective details about Jesus.

  Second quest: Differentiating the editorial opinions of New Testament evangelists from earlier, more reliable information about Jesus.

  Third quest: Using extracanonical gospels as additional sources about Jesus.

- None of the Jewish or Roman historians who wrote about events in the first century regarded Jesus or Christianity as a particularly noteworthy event.

Part 2: Sketching a Profile of the Historical Jesus

Using the available ancient sources, the criteria of authenticity, and our current knowledge of the historical context and cultural norms of Palestinian Judaism, we can construct the following sketch of the historical Jesus.

The Birth of Jesus

The limited information we have about the birth of Jesus comes from the "infancy narratives" in Matthew and Luke (Matt 1:1–2:23; Luke 1:5–2:52) and a passing reference in Galatians 4:4. Together, these sources (M, L, and Paul) provide multiple attestation for the birth of Jesus.

Galatians, the earliest of the sources, informs us that Jesus was "born of a woman, born under the law" (4:4). This Pauline letter, written about 54 CE, offers the barest of details about Jesus' birth. Matthew and Luke, however, provide more specific information about the date and place of Jesus' birth (Matt 2:1; Luke 1:5, 2:4–7). According to these latter sources, Jesus was born sometime during the reign of Herod the Great (37–4 BCE) in the city of Bethlehem. Scholars believe that Jesus' birth occurred near the end of Herod's reign (6–4 BCE).[19]

Affirming the birthplace of Bethlehem is a little more problematic, because outside the infancy narratives, available sources unanimously refer to Jesus as "Jesus of Nazareth," "Jesus the Nazarene," or "Jesus the Nazorean," implying that Jesus' geographic roots are in the village of Nazareth. Although it is possible that Jesus was born in Bethlehem and raised in Nazareth (as two evangelists indicate: Matt 2:23; Luke 2:39–40), the designation "Jesus of Nazareth" typically would have implied that he was born and raised in Nazareth.

Jesus' "Hidden Years" and Palestinian Village Life in Nazareth

The years between Jesus' birth and the beginning of his public ministry (around 28 CE) are commonly referred to as the "hidden years," because we have no early sources of information for them.[20]

Luke presents one episode from the life of Jesus at age twelve, the story of Jesus in the Temple of Jerusalem (Luke 2:41–51). But this episode appears only in L material. Moreover, the incident lacks the embarrassment factor that might argue for its credibility. Connecting Jesus with the Jerusalem Temple is a prominent theme in Luke, and so for Luke to invent such a detail from Jesus' early life would not be surprising.

If the oral tradition spoke to experiences from Jesus' "hidden years" in Nazareth, other than this Temple episode, such mentions have not been preserved by any New Testament author. Therefore, we must rely on our knowledge of the cultural norms of first-century Palestinian Jewish village life to fill in this gap. What can be said about Jews living in the villages of Palestine under Roman rule can be generalized to the historical Jesus.

Nazareth was a small village nestled in the mountainous region of Galilee. The total geographic area of Galilee was eighty square miles. As a village within Galilee, Nazareth would have been one of several villages clustered around two large cities in southern Galilee, Sepphoris and Tiberius. The Nazarene villagers, and especially Jesus' extended kinship group, would have had a strong sense of collective identity.

As a child growing up in Nazareth, Jesus likely would have learned his father's trade, beginning as early as age five. Joseph was a *tektōn* (in Greek, literally "craftsman," see Mark 6:3; Matt 13:55), a village artisan working with wood, stone, or other materials. Jewish boys of Nazareth, separated from the girls, would have received some kind of instruction, surely in the religious traditions and texts of Judaism in the village synagogue.

Growing up, Jesus also would have been exposed to several spoken languages—Aramaic, Hebrew, Greek, and Latin. We know that Jesus' native spoken language was Aramaic. It is also possible that he could read Hebrew, as the Gospels report. The common language in cities in the eastern parts of the Roman Empire was Greek, so Jesus may have known some Greek, but only enough to meet the needs of his trade. Jesus' own language of Aramaic and the Gospel writers' use of Greek present a complex challenge to scholars trying to trace the evolution of traditions about Jesus from his Aramaic context into the Greek of the Gospels.

Further complicating the issue of language is the use of Latin by the Roman ruling elite. It is doubtful that Jesus knew any Latin, which raises the question of the historicity of the passion narratives, because Latin was the language of the Roman courts and the prefect, Pontius Pilate. It is unlikely that Jesus could have understood, let alone participated in, the proceedings against him.

"Family" for Jesus and his fellow villagers would have entailed not only parents and siblings but also cousins, aunts, uncles, and

Jesus' Brothers and Sisters and the Question of Mary's Perpetual Virginity

The question of Jesus' siblings is raised because the Greek word *adelphos* ("brother") is used by Paul, the evangelists, and Josephus in reference to Jesus. Mark and Matthew also speak of Jesus' *adelphai* ("sisters").

During the formative years of the New Testament period, Jesus' mother, Mary, was not yet the object of extensive theological inquiry; that would begin with Origen of Alexandria in the third century and the Council of Ephesus in the fifth century (431 CE), where Mary was formally and reverently spoken of as *Theotokos*, "the Mother of God." The Gospel writers limit their discussion of Mary to the virginal conception of Jesus and to Mary's presence in Jesus' formative years and public ministry, including at his death.

The first-century New Testament Gospel tradition does seem to imply, however, that Mary had children after Jesus was born (see, for example, Matt 1: 25; 13:55 – 56). Traditional Western/Catholic and Eastern/Orthodox explanations regarding references to Jesus' brothers and sisters involve explaining Jesus' siblings as either his cousins or the children from Joseph's previous marriage. This explanation has no basis in the linguistic or historical evidence available to us, however.

grandparents living in the same house or nearby. There is multiple attestation to Jesus having parents and "brothers" and "sisters" (Mark 3:21, 31–35; 6:1–6 (v. 3); Matt 1:25 with, 13:55–56; 12:46–50; John 7:1–13; Acts 1:14; Gal 1:19; Josephus, *Antiquities* 20.9.1).[21]

In Jesus' day, the central events of a young Jewish man's teenage and early adult years would have been his bar mitzvah and his matching for marriage, as these events marked a boy's transition into manhood both religiously (bar mitzvah) and socially (marriage).[22]

Although celibacy was not unheard of for Jews (see, for example, Paul, who was a celibate Pharisee, or the Essenes, some of whom practiced celibacy),[23] it would have been unusual for a Jewish male in a rural village like Nazareth not to marry. The fact that no New Testament writer speaks of Jesus as married suggests that Jesus never had a family of his own. The silence on this point is probably historically accurate, as given the context of Jesus' day, this detail is so surprising as to make it both believable and likely true.

Jesus' Public Ministry

As we have seen, most of what we know about the "hidden years" of the historical Jesus is known only by inference, because the earliest sources do not discuss the life of Jesus (outside of his birth) prior to his public ministry. The earliest sources focus exclusively on Jesus' ministry as an adult and his final days. As we examine the earliest sources and search for potentially embarrassing words or deeds of Jesus, as well as words or deeds outside the norm of social expectation, we are able to reconstruct a profile of Jesus' public ministry and final days.

Jesus' Association with John the Baptist

All four New Testament Gospels present the activities and preaching of John the Baptist as important to Jesus (Matt 4:13; Mark 1:9; Luke 3:21; John 1:29–34). Jesus was drawn to John and associated with the Baptist movement in the Jordan Valley of Judea, the southern part of Palestine. Outside of the annual Jewish pilgrimages to Jerusalem, it would have been unusual for a Galilean like Jesus to travel so far. Nevertheless, multiple sources indicate that this association marks the beginning of Jesus' public ministry, around 28 CE.

The eschatological (end-time) tone of John's message implies that John and his followers embraced an imminent messianic expectation, insisting that all of Israel repent for the forgiveness of sins in the hope that God would soon act decisively in Israel's history (Matt 3:1–12; Mark 1:2–8; Luke 3:1–20; John 1:19–34). John's preaching may also have influenced Jesus' own messianic expectations and eschatological message. John's preaching ended

Jesus as the Eschatological Son of Man

For Jesus, God's reign was visibly present in his preaching and healing — imminent, in fact (see, for example, Mark 2:1–12). And Jesus' role as Son of God is closely associated with the one title that Jesus gives to himself: "Son of Man" (Mark 2:10; 8:31). Jesus, as Son of Man, was bringing about the presence of God's reign in the here and now as well as in the future (Mark 13:26; 14:62). In this way, there was both an *imminent present* and an *indeterminate future* aspect to God's reign.

abruptly with his arrest, imprisonment, and eventual execution by Herod Antipas (Mark 6:17–29; Luke 3:19–20; Matt 14:3–12; Josephus, *Ant.* 18.5.1–2). According to the Synoptic Gospels, it was John's imprisonment that spurred Jesus to begin his public ministry.

Jesus in the Villages and Countryside of Galilee

The earliest sources present Jesus teaching in the villages and countryside of Galilee (for example, Mark 1:14, 28), often using parables to convey his message. (If Jesus also taught in the cities of Galilee, such as Sepphoris or Tiberius, the earliest written tradition does not report it.) Among these parables, we have the parable of the seed (Mark 4:1–9), the parable of the lost sheep (Q: Luke 15:1–7; Matt 18:12–14), the parable of the laborers in the vineyard (M: Matt 20:1–16), and the parable of the rich man and Lazarus (L: Luke 16:19–31). In

> ### Gospel Formation Beginning in Jesus' Public Ministry
>
> The formation of the Gospel tradition occurred on three levels, as discussed in chapter 1: the ministry of Jesus (28–30 CE), the developing oral tradition (30–70 CE), and the developing written tradition (70–100 CE). The Gospel writers tell us that the people who witnessed Jesus' public ministry created the oral tradition. For example, Mark tells us that after his initial success at calling disciples, teaching, and healing, Jesus' "fame spread everywhere throughout the whole region of Galilee" (Mark 1:28). Those who first spread the word about Jesus we call "human tradents," and in their early evangelization we see the embryonic stages of the formation of the Gospels.
>
> It would take the next generation of Jesus' followers to develop the written tradition of the New Testament Gospels.

Jesus' day, a village craftsman wandering the countryside of Galilee teaching in parables would have been outside the norm of expected social behavior. Thus, Jesus' teaching in parables meets two of our standards for historical credibility: multiple attestation and dissimilarity.

Jesus on the Kingdom of God

A centerpiece of Jesus' preaching, especially in his parables, concerns the kingdom of God. Much of Jesus' message and vision is captured with a phrase attributed to him, *hē basileia tou theou*. Although this phrase is almost universally translated today as "the kingdom of God," in fact, the term *basileia* is more accurately rendered as "reign," "rule," or "kingship." The phrase "the reign (rule) of God" is closer to what scholars think Jesus intended with this phrase and concept, emphasizing the immediacy with which Jesus saw God's interactions with people and with history. Proclaiming the good news of the arrival of God's reign was central to Jesus' eschatological message.

Numerous early and independent sources indicate that the reign of God was central to Jesus' message. It was often the object of his parables, as in the parable of the mustard seed (Mark 4:30–32), the parable of the talents (Q: Matt 25:14–30; Luke 1:11–27), and the parable of the weeds (M: Matt 13:24–30). At other times it was the object of his prayer, as in the Lord's Prayer (Q: Matt 6:9–13; Luke 11:2–4), or the subject of his teaching, as when Jesus blesses the children (Mark-source: Mark 10:13–16) or discusses the role of the law and the prophets (Q: Matt 5:18; 11:13; Luke 16:16–17).

Jesus' preaching and teaching also satisfy the criterion of embarrassment, as Mark preserves the tradition that Jesus' own kin tried "to seize him," saying, "He is out of his mind" (3:21). Mark even reports that Jesus' teaching in the synagogue in Nazareth scandalized his kinship group there (6:3).

Jesus' "Mighty Deeds"

The New Testament Gospel writers report Jesus performing a range of miracles, from exorcisms and healings to raising the dead.[24] In fact, according to the Gospel writers and other early written sources, Jesus gained notoriety and even followers because of his reputation as a popular healer.

Numerous early and independent sources indicate that Jesus performed these "mighty deeds" (*dunameis*), including exorcisms and healings: Mark (1:32–34); Q (Matt 8:5–10, 13; Luke 7:1–10); L (Luke 13:10–17; 14:1–6); John (5:1–9); Josephus (*Ant.* 18.3.3).

The Problem of Miracles for the Modern Historian

Modern historians using the historical-critical method are unable to prove that Jesus performed miracles. At issue is not whether miracles could occur but whether one can prove that they occurred by historical-critical means.

Several of these sources also indicate that Jesus raised the dead: Mark (5:21–24, 35–42); L (Luke 7:11–17); and John (11:1–44).[25]

Thus, these claims meet our criterion of multiple attestation. We have also the utter amazement of those present who believed they had witnessed a miracle (for example, Mark 5:42; Luke 7:16; John 11:45), satisfying our criterion of dissimilarity, because so much of Jesus' popularity and fame (Mark 1:45; Luke 7:17) seems to have been rooted in these "mighty deeds," unexpected from anyone much less a village craftsman from Nazareth.

Jesus' Table Fellowship

The practice of sharing table fellowship was strictly regulated in the first-century world. Social and religious purity laws prevented one from sharing meals with people who were unclean or otherwise deemed unholy and sinful. Multiple sources indicate that Jesus shared table fellowship with a range of people, "clean" and "unclean." For example, Mark 2:13–17 shows Jesus eating with tax collectors and sinners, and Luke 14:1–24 shows Jesus eating with Pharisees. Jesus' willingness to recline at table with tax collectors and sinners would have embarrassed his followers, yet several sources report this behavior. Likewise, the Pharisees' invitation to a village craftsman to dine with them would have been outside the norm of expected social behavior for Pharisees. Thus, Jesus' practice of table fellowship meets all three criteria for authenticity.

Jesus' Final Days

Numerous events in Jesus' final days meet two criteria for authenticity—multiple attestation and embarrassment. Our earliest written sources (Paul, Mark, M, L, John, and Josephus) all speak to the final days of Jesus' life, specifically Jesus' violent death and reported Resurrection. Death by crucifixion in the first-century world was intended as a humiliating, painful, and embarrassing experience for both the victim and his kinship group. This was certainly the case for Jesus, his followers, and kin, given the expectations and hopes that many had placed in Jesus.

A list of events from Jesus' final days that meet the standard for authenticity follows.[26]

The Incident in the Temple

Two early sources, Mark (11:15–19) and John (2:13–22), indicate that Jesus caused a disturbance in the Temple in Jerusalem. This incident was not expected social behavior for a Jewish Galilean craftsman, and the disruptive nature of Jesus' actions would have been an embarrassment to the followers of Jesus and the early Church. Thus, all three criteria of authenticity are met.

Jesus' Final Meal with Followers

In his First Letter to the Corinthians, written in the mid 50s CE, Paul speaks of a tradition handed down to him regarding a final meal that Jesus shared with his followers (11:23–25). Three other early written sources record events associated with this final meal: Mark 14:17–25, John 13–17 (two farewell discourses), and L material (Luke 22:31–32, 35–38).

Arrest and Interrogation by Jewish Authorities

Multiple sources mention Jesus' arrest and interrogation by the Jewish authorities: Mark 14:1–2, 53–65; John 18:12–14, 19–24; and Josephus *Ant.* 18.3.3. Details of this harsh treatment would have been a further source of embarrassment to his followers.

Crucifixion

Multiple sources report the crucifixion of Jesus under the Roman prefect, Pontius Pilate: 1 Cor 15:3–7; Mark 15:1–15; John 18:28–19:16; Josephus *Ant.* 18.3.3. Jesus' shameful treatment by the Roman authorities and his death by crucifixion likewise satisfy the criterion of embarrassment.[27]

Execution by Crucifixion

The Roman Empire practiced crucifixion as its most severe form of capital punishment, reserved for non-Roman citizens including slaves and criminals deemed enemies of Rome.

Death by crucifixion was slow and excruciating. Victims were typically stripped naked, then tied, nailed, or impaled to crosses and left exposed to the elements, slowly

(cont'd.)

(execution by crucifixion cont'd.)

dying over the course of hours or even days, depending upon the strength and physical condition of the prisoner before and during crucifixion. Causes of death ranged from exhaustion and dehydration to exposure and shock. The most common cause of death was asphyxiation.

The scourging of a prisoner before crucifixion could result in considerable blood loss, sending a prisoner into shock. Scourging was meant to hasten the prisoner's death, a bitterly ironic form of mercy.

Death by crucifixion was a mutilating and especially dishonorable form of death. Bodies were typically left to rot on the cross, a futher form of "torture" for the family, because no burial was allowed, accentuating the dishonorable death and intimidating the population into not opposing Rome. As reported in the New Testament Gospels, Jesus' relatively quick death after only a few hours on the cross was probably the result of his scourging, with death likely resulting from blood loss, shock, and ultimately suffocation.

Resurrection

Many of the earliest sources report that Jesus' followers experienced Jesus alive after his death and burial: 1 Cor 15:3–7; John 20–21; M-source (Matt 28:11–20); L-source (Luke 24:13–49). These sources present Jesus' Resurrection as a historical event, as real as any other aspect of his public ministry. Like the "powerful deeds" of Jesus, the Resurrection is beyond historical verification, but claims of Jesus' Resurrection most certainly fall outside the norm of experience at that time—or any other time. To say Jesus' Resurrection meets the criterion of dissimilarity is to state the obvious, and the Resurrection remains the cornerstone of Christian belief.

Criteria for Authenticity

	Multiple Attestation	Dissimilarity	Embarrassment
Birth of Jesus	√		
Jesus' "hidden years"			
Jesus' public ministry:			
• Association with John the Baptist	√		
• Teaching in the villages and countryside of Galilee	√	√	
• Preaching the message of the coming reign of God	√		√
• Performing "mighty deeds" such as healings and exorcisms	√	√	
• Sharing table fellowship with diverse groups	√	√	√
Jesus' final days:			
• Temple incident	√	√	√
• Final meal with followers	√		
• Arrest and interrogation by Jewish authorities	√		√
• Crucifixion	√		√
• Resurrection	√	√	

Summary of Sketching a Profile of the Historical Jesus

Core Concepts

- Any reconstruction of the historical Jesus must include the available ancient sources and is subject to the criteria for authenticity, which include a current knowledge of the historical context and cultural norms of ancient Palestinian Judaism.

Sketch of the Historical Jesus

- Jesus was born about 6–4 BCE, possibly in Bethlehem, and raised in the village of Nazareth in Galilee.

- No early, reliable written sources mention Jesus' "hidden years" after his birth and before the start of his public ministry.

- Jesus was a craftsman who spoke Aramaic and grew up with a kinship group in Nazareth.

- Jesus associated with John the Baptist at the start of his public ministry.

- Jesus preached and taught about "the reign of God" primarily in the villages of Galilee.

- Many of Jesus' followers believed that he performed "mighty deeds" such as healings and exorcisms.

- Jesus shared table fellowship with both "honorable" and "dishonorable" people.

- An incident in the Temple in Jerusalem is associated with Jesus.

- Jesus shared a final meal with his followers before his death.

- Jesus was arrested and interrogated by Jewish authorities, then executed by crucifixion by the Roman prefect Pontius Pilate.

- Jesus' followers reported that they saw Jesus alive again after his death and burial.

Questions for Review

1. How and why do scholars distinguish between the real Jesus, the historical Jesus, and the Christ of faith?

2. Describe the historical and intellectual developments that led to the first quest for the historical Jesus.

3. What surviving Jewish and Roman sources mention Jesus or Christianity?

4. What Christian sources do scholars use in searching for the historical Jesus?

5. Name the three criteria for establishing the authenticity of the historical Jesus. Briefly describe each criterion.

6. What are the main characteristics of the first, second, and third quests for the historical Jesus?

7. What can we say historically about the birth of Jesus?

8. What is meant by Jesus' "hidden years"?

9. Name some of the events in Jesus' public ministry that meet the standard for authenticity.

10. What do scholars know with some certainty about the final days of Jesus?

Questions for Reflection

1. How do differences between the historical Jesus, as reconstructed by scholars, and the Jesus of the Gospels, change or challenge your understanding of Christianity?

2. To what extent do you think that the New Testament Gospels are credible and reliable sources for our reconstruction of the historical Jesus?

3. What aspects of the "historical Jesus" intrigue you, and why?

4. What questions do you have about the historical Jesus?

Recommendations for Further Reading

Dunn, James D.G. *A New Perspective on Jesus: What the Quest for the Historical Jesus Missed.* Grand Rapids, Mich.: Baker Academics, 2005.

This short book (125 pages) is a synopsis of Dunn's larger 893-page book, titled *Jesus Remembered: Christianity in the Making* (Vol. 1; 2003). Dunn summarizes the major points made in *Jesus Remembered*, which include his contention that the oral tradition preceding the Gospels lends much historical credibility and reliability to the New Testament Gospel narratives.

Ehrman, Bart D. *Jesus: Apocalyptic Prophet of a New Millennium.* New York: Oxford University Press, 1999.

Ehrman views the historical Jesus as a first-century Jewish apocalyptic prophet; that is, according to Ehrman, Jesus believed that God was coming to overthrow the forces of evil in the world and, in effect, end history as we know it, creating a new kingdom on earth. Ehrman looks at sources inside and outside the New Testament to help construct his profile of the historical Jesus.

Gowler, David B. *What Are They Saying about the Historical Jesus?* New York: Paulist, 2007.

Typical of the WATSA series, Gowler provides a historical overview of the three quests for the historical Jesus, highlighting their associated scholars and studies. The current quest and the work of the Jesus Seminar are emphasized. Gowler introduces the following third-quest categories and their leading scholars: the eschatological prophet and the restoration of Israel (E.P. Sanders, Paula Fredriksen), the Mediterranean Jewish peasant and the brokerless kingdom (John Dominic Crossan, Jonathan Reed), the Elijah-like eschatological prophet (John P. Meier), and the eschatological prophet of social change (Gerd Theissen, Annette Merz, and William R. Herzog II).

Powell, Mark Allan. *Jesus as a Figure in History: How Modern Historians View the Man from Galilee.* Louisville and London: Westminster John Knox Press, 1998.

Powell offers a range of scholarly opinion on the historical Jesus, including those of John Dominic Crossan, Marcus Borg, E.P. Sanders, John P. Meier, and N.T. Wright. He discusses the quests for the historical Jesus, presents the sources and criteria for judging the authenticity of the historical Jesus, and offers a variety of contemporary images of Jesus. Powell closes with an examination of issues and concerns in the current quest for the historical Jesus.

Sanders, E.P. *The Historical Figure of Jesus.* New York and London: Penguin Books, 1993.

This book provides a political, social, and theological context for understanding the historical figure of Jesus as a miracle worker and eschatological prophet whose message centered on the coming kingdom of God. Sanders examines the available sources outside the New Testament on the historical Jesus, as well as the New Testament Gospels. He then explores specific aspects of the life of the historical Jesus such as the beginning of Jesus' ministry, miracles, the kingdom of God, and the last week of Jesus' life.

Endnotes

1   See Burton H. Throckmorton, Jr., ed., *Gospel Parallels: A Comparison of the Synoptic Gospels* (5th ed.; Nashville: Thomas Nelson, 1992) and Kurt Aland, *Synopsis of the Four Gospels*, Greek-English (8th ed.; Germany: Biblica-Druck Stuttgart, 1987).

2   Recent books on the quests for the historical Jesus include E.P. Sanders, *The Historical Figure of Jesus* (New York and London: Penguin Books, 1993); Bart Ehrman, *Jesus: Apocalyptic Prophet of a New Millennium* (New York: Oxford University Press, 1999); James D.G. Dunn, *A New Perspective on Jesus: What the Quest for the Historical Jesus Missed* (Grand Rapids, Mich.: Baker Academic, 2005). All three books reflect mainstream scholarship on the third quest for the historical Jesus.

3   Other important scholars who are identified as part of the first quest for the historical Jesus include Ernst Renan (1823–1892), *The Life of Jesus* (1863); Martin Kähler (1835–1912), *The So-Called Historical Jesus and the Historic Biblical Christ* (1896) [Kähler is often credited with coining the phrase "the Jesus of history" and "the Christ of faith"]; William Wrede (1859–1906), *The Messianic Secret* (1901); Adolf von Harnack (1851–1930), *What Is Christianity?* (1901); Albert Schweitzer (1875–1965), *The Quest of the Historical Jesus: A Critical Study of Its Progress from Reimarus to Wrede* (1906). It should be noted that many scholars would argue that Hermann Samuel Reimarus (1694–1768) should be credited with the original work in the field of the quest for the historical Jesus because of his unpublished (though known) manuscripts between 1774 and 1778.

4   Schweitzer, 399.

5   In his book on the third quest for the historical Jesus, *The Jesus Quest: The Third Search for the Jew of Nazareth* (Downers Grove, Ill.: Inter-Varsity, 1997), Ben Witherington identifies twenty of today's leading scholars in historical Jesus research: John Dominic Crossan, Burton Mack, F. Gerald Downing, Marcus Borg, Geza Vermes, Graham H. Twelftree, E.P. Sanders, Maurice Casey, Gerd Theissen, Richard A. Horsley, R. David Kaylor, Elisabeth Schüssler Fiorenza, Ben Witherington, John P. Meier, Peter Stuhlmacher, James D.G. Dunn, Marinus de Jonge, Markus Bockmuehl, and N.T. Wright.

6 See John Dominic Crossan, *The Historical Jesus: The Life of a Mediter-ranean Jew* (San Francisco: HarperSanFrancisco, 1991). Crossan is a prolific writer on the historical Jesus. See, for example, *The Cross That Spoke: The Origins of the Passion Narrative* (HarperCollins, 1992) and *Who Killed Jesus? Exposing the Roots of Anti-Semitism in the Gospel Story of the Death of Jesus* (San Francisco: HarperSanFrancisco, 1996).

7 See Marcus J. Borg, *Jesus: A New Vision* (San Francisco: Harper & Row, 1988). For an excellent updated scholarly debate on the historical Jesus, see Borg, *Jesus at 2000* (San Francisco: HarperSanFrancisco, 1996).

8 See Burton L. Mack, *The Myth of Innocence: Mark and Christian Origins* (rev. ed.; Minneapolis, Minn.: Augsburg Fortress, 1998).

9 See John P. Meier, *A Marginal Jew: Rethinking the Historical Jesus* (3 vols.; New York: Doubleday, 1991–2001).

10 See Elizabeth Schüssler-Fiorenza, *Jesus: Miriam's Child and Sophia's Prophet* (New York: Continuum, 1994).

11 See Dunn, *Jesus Remembered: Christianity in the Making* (Grand Rapids, Mich.; Eerdsman, 2003).

12 See E.P. Sanders, *The Historical Figure of Jesus* (New York: Viking, 1994).

13 See Bart D. Ehrman, *Jesus: Apocalyptic Prophet of the Third Millennium* (New York: Oxford University Press, 1999).

14 For an extended discussion on ancient sources for the historical Jesus, see Dunn, 139–72; Meier, volume 1, 56–166. Meier sums it up succinctly: "For all practical purposes, then, our early, independent sources for the historical Jesus boil down to the Four Gospels, a few scattered data elsewhere in the New Testament, and Josephus. . . . For better or for worse, in our quest for the historical Jesus, we are largely confined to the canonical Gospels; the genuine 'corpus' is infuriating in its restrictions," 140.

15 Translation taken from *The Works of Josephus* (trans. William Whiston; Peabody, Mass.: Hendrickson, 1987). See Meier, volume 1, 56–92. This translation of Josephus has edited out what scholars recognize as later Christian interpolations added to Josephus' original words.

16 "Festus was now dead, and Albinus was but upon the road; so he assembled the Sanhedrin of judges, and brought before them the brother of Jesus, who was called Christ, whose name was James, and some others, [or some of his companions]; and when he had formed an accusation against them as breakers of the law, he delivered them to be stoned: but as for those who seemed the most equitable of the citizens, and such as were the most uneasy at the breach of the laws, they disliked what

was done; they also sent to the king [Agrippa], desiring him to send to Ananus that he should act so no more, for that what he had already done was not to be justified; nay, some of them went also to meet Albinus, as he was upon his journey from Alexandria, and informed him that it was not lawful for Ananus to assemble a Sanhedrin without his consent" (*Ant.* 20.9.1). Translation taken from Whiston, *Josephus*. Josephus offers witness to James' martyrdom and refers to James as Jesus' brother. It should be noted that the New Testament Gospels also indicate that Jesus had a "brother" named James (see Mark 6:3 and Matt 13:55). See also Paul's Letter to the Galatians, where Paul too refers to James as "the brother of the Lord" (Gal 1:19). Jesus' "brother(s)" will be discussed in more detail later in this chapter.

17 These are the three main criteria used to establish the authenticity of Jesus' words and deeds. Other criteria do exist, such as the criteria of coherence and the criteria of Palestinian environment. See Meier, volume 1, 167–84, for a list of the primary and secondary criteria.

18 It should be noted that the inclusion of the *Gospel of Thomas* as a source independent from the New Testament Gospels is fiercely debated by scholars.

19 Matt 2:19–20 is the clue: Matthew tells us that Joseph and Mary returned from Egypt after Herod's death and Jesus was still a "little child" (Greek, *paidion*).

20 One extracanonical gospel, the *Infancy Gospel of Thomas* (to be differentiated from the *Gospel of Thomas*, mentioned earlier in this chapter), does narrate the early years of Jesus from ages five through twelve; however, scholars dismiss this second-century gospel as a reflection of the apologetic needs of a later author who possesses no reliable information for Jesus' early years.

21 See Meier, volume 1, 316–32, for an excellent discussion on Jesus' brothers and sisters.

22 Bar mitzvah, usually held around the age of twelve or thirteen, was an important initiation ritual in the life of a Jewish boy; it was a public recognition that he could assume certain adult responsibilities within the life of the village (for example, reading and commenting on Scriptures in the village synagogue). Marriage for Jewish boys in the villages of Galilee would also have been a typical transition following at some point after bar mitzvah. All marriages in Jesus' day and culture were arranged, usually by the fathers or eldest brothers, and the marriages were more of an alignment between families than an alignment between individuals. The aligning of families through marriage was an important social and

economic event that ensured the survival and interconnectedness of village life.

23 The Dead Sea Scrolls preserved by the community at Qumran point to a celibate community, but other scrolls and archeological evidence point to a mixed community that included men, women, and children (i.e., families).

24 Meier, volume 2, 509–1038, has an extended discussion on Jesus' miracles. Meier's extensive work here needs to be carefully read before anyone too easily dismisses the historical grounding of Jesus' miracles.

25 Dunn, by comparison, in *Jesus Remembered*, spends very little time discussing Jesus' miracles aside from a brief history of the scholarly debate, 29–34.

26 Meier, volume 3, chapter 23, "The So-Called Nature Miracles," 874–1038, argues that most of the so-called nature miracles "appear to have been created by the early Church to serve various theological reasons," 970. Meier sees a valid historical grounding for many of the miracles involving exorcism, healing, and raising of the dead.

27 An excellent resource discussing the historical-critical questions associated with the death of Jesus, according to the four New Testament Gospel traditions, is Raymond E. Brown, *The Death of the Messiah: From Gethsemane to the Grave, A Commentary on the Passion Narratives in the Four Gospels* (2 vols.; New York: Doubleday, 1994).

Other Early Christian Gospels

8

Introduction

The early centuries of Christianity produced numerous gospels in addition to the four we find in the Bible. In fact, many of these gospels were embraced as Scripture just like the four Gospels eventually incorporated into the New Testament. Some have dubbed these "other" gospels the "*apocryphal* gospels," a somewhat misleading name because apocryphal means "hidden, concealed, secret" and these other early Christian gospels were none of these. Many scholars prefer the term *extracanonical*, because these additional gospels do not appear in the canon of the New Testament. These extracanonical gospels are important sources of information about early Christian theology and provide a more complete witness to early Christian understandings of Jesus, his life, and his teaching.

We begin here with the relationship of the extracanonical gospels to the canonical Gospels. Then we will discuss the early Church witness to the existence of these Gospels and their discoveries in modern times, followed by a consideration of the gospels' authorship, dates of composition, and audiences. Last, we will look at the content of several of these extracanonical gospels, which are commonly divided into the Judaic-Christian gospels, the narrative gospels, and the sayings gospels.

What Are the Other Early Christian Gospels?

Matthew, Mark, Luke, and John are called the "canonical Gospels" because these four Gospels eventually came to be included in the canon of the New Testament. The process of forming the New Testament canon actually took centuries and was complex and often disputed. Other gospels produced in the first few centuries of the Christian era, although not ultimately accepted as part of the canon, were widely circulated among early Christian congregations and read during worship. Thus, the terms used today to differentiate these gospels as *canonical* and *extracanonical* would not have made sense to early Christians, because the New Testament canon was not set until centuries after all of the gospels had been written.

Various factors motivated the writing of the extracanonical gospels.[1] Jewish-Christian authors wrote some of the gospels, debating their own theological understanding of Jesus (for example, the *Gospel of the Ebionites* denies the virgin birth of Jesus). Other gospels were the work of Gentile-Christian authors who were filling in "gaps" left by the New Testament Gospels (for example, the *Infancy Gospel of Thomas*, which presents Jesus as a mischievous little boy from ages

How Was the New Testament Canon Chosen?

The process of "canonization" took centuries to accomplish. The twenty-seven writings that eventually made it into the New Testament had to pass certain criteria considered integral by the early Church to granting any writing the authority of canonical status. Some of the key criteria included

- *Apostolic origin* (rooted in the period of the original apostles),
- *Normative ideas* (articulated a theology that resembled and supported current theological trends),
- *Universal appeal* (accepted by the majority of Christians at that time).

Although other criteria may also have been used, there is no evidence to suggest that the early Church included "divine inspiration" (the belief that the biblical authors were inspired in their writing by the Holy Spirit) as one of their criterion for canonicity.

five to twelve). Still other gospels reflect 'Gnostic' influence (for a discussion of *Gnostic* and *Gnosticism*, see sidebar). The *Gospel of Philip*, for example, presents a 'Gnostic' Christian instruction on the sacraments.

'Gnosticism' and 'Gnostic' Christians

In recent decades, the early religious movement known as 'Gnosticism' has received much scholarly attention. But the plurality of definitions for *Gnosticism* indicates a lack of scholarly consensus on the nature of this movement. In fact, many scholars contend that the terms *Gnosticism* and *Gnostic* should be discarded, because they imply a monolithic religious movement, which can be misleading. Two important points have emerged from this discussion: people with 'Gnostic' beliefs did not refer to *themselves* as 'Gnostics', and those who embraced 'Gnostic' beliefs could be Jewish, Christian, or polytheist. Therefore, an uncritical use of the term *Gnosticism* risks oversimplifying what was a complex religious phenomenon.

The writings found at Nag Hammadi in Egypt provide us with many insights into the various new religious movements that were active in the Roman Empire as early as the second century CE. It is becoming increasingly clear to scholars that categorizing all of these complex and diverse movements as 'Gnosticism' is insufficient; a better definition and description are needed.

For example, Michael A. Williams, a leading scholar in this area, maintains that these ancient religious movements would be better called "biblical demiurgical traditions" and that the term *Gnosticism* for such movements should be discarded. Williams' category highlights one of the few characteristics these diverse religious movements shared: the belief that the known universe was created and is managed by lower god(s) or demiurges (from the Greek *demiurgos*, meaning "fashioner, creator"), as distinct from the most transcendent God. 'Gnostic' Christians believed that the Jewish Scriptures revealed this lower god(s); thus the term, *demiurgical*. Some scholars have criticized Williams, however, for using a different term in reference to a group of writers that overlaps substantially with what scholars of an earlier generation referred to as 'Gnostic' literature. In recognition of this continuing debate among scholars, in this chapter the terms *Gnostic* and *Gnosticism* occur within single quotation marks. See the recommendations for further reading at the end of this chapter for more information on this topic.

Why Did the Early Church Produce So Many Gospels?

The first centuries of Christianity produced a remarkable number of gospels. As we have seen, most scholars date the composition of the four New Testament Gospels within the second-half of the first century CE, ranging from about 70 to 100 CE. To these first-century gospels, we would add Q and possibly the *Gospel of Thomas* and the *Gospel of Peter*, gospels that some scholars believe preserve traditions from the first century CE. Most of the extracanonical gospels, however, are products of the mid- to late second century CE. These gospels (at least two dozen) represent the diverse portraits of Jesus articulated by different Christian groups.

Even at the end of the second century CE, it is too early to speak of an "orthodoxy" (correct teaching) of Christian beliefs as established by the four canonical written Gospels.[2] In fact, what we do know about the four New Testament Gospels in the second century is rather murky. For example, the manuscript copies of these four Gospels were quite unstable, and they were far from universally distributed to other Christian communities.[3] Furthermore, we know that Christian communities at times used one or more of the New Testament Gospels alongside one or more of the extracanonical gospels. While there may be a literary dependency between some of the canonical and extracanonical gospels (later in this chapter, we will look at a possible relationship between the Gospel of Luke and the *Infancy Gospel of Thomas*), for the most part, all of these first- and second-century gospels circulated independently in the early Church and were used by believing communities as a means of expressing their beliefs, diverse as these beliefs were.

Part 1: Witnesses to and Discoveries of the Extracanonical Gospels

Scholars have discovered extracanonical gospels in several ways. Some of these gospels we know of only through the early Church fathers, who cite the gospels, oftentimes critically. These references are found in the surviving fragments of ancient manuscripts. Other extracanonical gospels have been discovered in major and minor archeological finds.

The Early Church Witness

Before the discovery of several of these gospels, scholars only knew of their existence from the witness of the early Church fathers, such as Irenaeus, Clement of Alexandria, Origen, Eusebius, Epiphanius, and Jerome. These second- through fifth-century Church fathers were acquainted with some of these gospels. For example, Irenaeus (late second century) speaks of the *Gospel of Judas* in his attack on second-century heresies.[4] In his commentary on the Gospel of Matthew, Origen (early third century), tells of his knowledge of the *Book of James* (also known as the *Infancy Gospel of James*).[5] And Epiphanius (mid-third century) writes about the *Gospel of the Hebrews* used by the Ebionites.[6] These three Church fathers witness to three early extracanonical gospels. Two of these gospels (the *Gospel of Judas* and the *Infancy Gospel of James*) were subsequently discovered in the modern period, while one (*Gospel of the Hebrews*) remains lost and must therefore be reconstructed from the citations of Church fathers.

Archeological Gold Mines

Numerous extracanonical gospels, letters, apocalypses, and other writings were discovered in a major archeological find in 1945. A peasant living in the village of Nag Hammadi in southern Egypt discovered the remains of a collection of ancient written materials dating back to the fourth century CE. Known today as the Nag Hammadi Library,[7] this collection contains forty-five different works.

In addition to the gospels found at Nag Hammadi, other gospels that for centuries were unknown to scholars have been found in poorly preserved manuscripts. For example, fragments of the *Gospel of Peter* were discovered in Akhmim, Egypt, in 1886–1887, along with two other important writings (the *Apocalypse of Peter* and the composite apocalypse known as *1 Enoch*). More recently, in the 1970s, the *Gospel of Judas* was discovered in Beni Masah, Egypt. Most of these gospels were discovered in the last century or so, with Egypt, because of its arid climate and distance from Rome (where Church authorities tried to destroy such "heretical" literature), being the "gold mine" for these discoveries.

This mix of scholarly reconstruction and modern discovery of extracanonical gospels helps us piece together the history of the gospel tradition, which extended into the first few centuries of Christianity. It should be noted, however, that just knowing the title of a work does not necessarily mean the Church fathers knew "our" work by the same title. For example, they may have had access to an oral form or a different written version of the work, or perhaps more than one work by the same (or a similar) title may have existed.

Authors, Audiences, Dates, and Places of Composition

As with the New Testament Gospels, there is often little or no internal or external evidence that can shed light on the authors of extracanonical gospels. Also like the four New Testament Gospels, many extracanonical gospels are associated with figures from the apostolic period (for example, the *Gospel of Peter* and the *Gospel of Thomas*). This link to the apostles' names provided extracanonical gospels with a level of authority necessary for them to be taken seriously in the early centuries.[8]

Who the intended audiences were for these extracanonical gospels is no clearer than the identity of their authors. In some cases, these gospels are obviously 'Gnostic' in theology and orientation (for example, the *Gospel of Philip* and the *Dialogue of the Savior*), whereas in others, the extracanonical gospels are Jewish in nature (for example, the *Gospel of the Hebrews*). In places like Egypt, where many of these gospels were discovered, boundaries between Jews, proto-Orthodox Christians, and 'Gnostic' Christian circles were rather fluid. (This lack of fixed boundaries applied likewise to Jewish, Christian, and polytheist 'Gnostics.') All of this makes the identification of the intended audiences and places of composition of these extracanonical gospels quite uncertain.

Finally, most of the extracanonical gospels appear to be products of the second and third century CE, with the gospels presented in this chapter all dating to the second century CE.

Summary of Witnesses to and Discoveries of the Extracanonical Gospels

Core Concepts

- We know of these extracanonical gospels through the early Church fathers and recent archeological discoveries.
- Most extracanonical gospels date to the second century CE.

Supplemental Information

- Second- through fifth-century Church fathers were familiar with some of the extracanonical gospels.
- The 1945 discovery of writings in Nag Hammadi, Egypt, proved to be an archeological gold mine for extracanonical gospels.
- Some extracanonical gospels have been discovered in minor archeological finds.
- Like the New Testament Gospels, we know little about the authors, intended audiences, and places of composition of the extracanonical gospels.

Part 2: Introducing the Extracanonical Gospels

Following are brief introductions to several extracanonical gospels. They are classified by either content (for example, narrative gospels about Jesus' infancy) or theological character (for example, Judaic-Christian gospels).

Judaic-Christian Gospels

Three gospels commonly clustered under the heading of Judaic-Christian are the *Gospel of the Nazareans*, the *Gospel of the Hebrews*, and the *Gospel of the Ebionites*. All three exist only in fragmented manuscripts. Much of what we know about them comes from the testimony of the early Church fathers.

Gospel of the Nazareans

Church fathers such as Jerome claimed that some Judaic Christians, whom he called the "Nazareans" (possibly an anti-heretical label), had their own Aramaic translation of the Greek Gospel of Matthew. The Nazareans' translation of Matthew did not include the infancy narrative (Matt 1–2 mentions a miraculous virgin birth, which these followers of Jesus denied) but added other materials (for example, additional sayings of Jesus). It is plausible that Aramaic-speaking Jews from the Nazareth area would have wanted a version of Matthew's Gospel in their own language. The omission of Matthew 1–2 also makes sense given that Jews would have been less inclined than Greeks to believe in the virgin birth of Jesus. (Nowhere in the Hebrew Scriptures is there precedent for a virgin birth.)

> **Where to Begin Reading the Extracanonical Gospels?**
>
> You are encouraged to read one or more of the extracanonical gospels. You can find English translations listed in the recommended readings at the end of this chapter. A starting point could be the *Gospel of Thomas*, because this gospel has received much scholarly attention. Also, with the recent discovery and published English translation of the *Gospel of Judas*, much public interest has been generated in this gospel. For an extracanonical gospel that presents a rather humorous view of the boy Jesus, read the *Infancy Gospel of Thomas*.

We do not possess a full manuscript copy of the *Gospel of the Nazareans*, although more of it has survived than the handful of fragments that remain of the *Gospel of the Hebrews* and the *Gospel of the Ebionites*. The sparseness of these gospel materials, preserved and labeled by Church fathers hostile to their contents, has led some scholars to ask whether in fact they stem originally not from three different gospels but from perhaps one or two gospels.[9] It could be that the Church fathers, in their opposition to these gospels, have misrepresented the historical record.

Gospel of the Ebionites

All seven fragments that remain of the *Gospel of the Ebionites* come from the fourth-century Church father Epiphanius. According to Epiphanius, a Judaic-Christian sect known as the

Ebionites produced this gospel, which may have been one of the earliest attempts to harmonize the three Synoptic Gospels into one. This sect, widespread in Palestine during the second through fourth centuries, both denied Jesus' divinity and argued that Jesus' sacrifice on the cross atoned for the sins of the world, thereby rendering all future (Jewish) sacrifice unnecessary.

The word *ebion* is thought to be based on the Aramaic word for "poor," thus identifying the gospel with Jesus' poverty. One fragment drawing scholarly attention explains how John the Baptist ate honey and manna (not locusts!, compare Matt 3:4), which could correspond to the vegetarian practices of the Ebionites (locusts are meat).[10]

Gospel of the Hebrews

Although only seven fragments of the *Gospel of the Hebrews* survive, numerous Church fathers attest to the existence of a gospel by this title (Clement of Alexandria, Origen, Didymus the Blind, and Jerome). The theology contained in these fragments appears to be based on Jewish Wisdom thinking; for example, Clement of Alexandria wrote,

> As it is written in the Gospel of the Hebrews, "He who wonders shall reign, and he who reigns shall rest."
>
> — *Stromata* 2.9.45[11]

This gospel had as part of its focus James, the brother of Jesus and head of the Church in Jerusalem. (See references to this James in Mark 6:3 and Gal 1:19; 2:9.) One surviving fragment refers to the resurrected Christ, who appears to James and speaks to him. The *Gospel of the Hebrews* likely contained stories of Jesus' public ministry, including his baptism, temptation, and Resurrection, given that the other Judaic-Christian gospels show an interest in the key events in the life of Jesus.

Other Narrative Gospels

Early Christians produced other narrative gospels that focused on various aspects of the life of Jesus. These gospels range in topic from the childhoods of Jesus and Mary, mother of Jesus, to the details of Jesus' betrayal and passion. We will focus on the *Infancy Gospel of*

Thomas and the *Infancy Gospel of James*, as well as the *Gospel of Peter* and the *Gospel of Judas*, because they address the infancy and the passion of Jesus.

Infancy Gospel of Thomas

The *Infancy Gospel of Thomas* narrates the adventures of the boy Jesus from age five through age twelve. This gospel fills in some of the gaps left by the infancy narrative in the Gospel of Luke, which as you will recall is the only New Testament Gospel to mention Jesus at twelve years old in the Jerusalem Temple.[12] Thought to have been composed in the first half of the second century CE, the large volume of surviving manuscripts suggests this gospel enjoyed some degree of popularity among Christians in the early centuries.

One episode from this gospel foreshadows details of Jesus' adult public ministry. In it, we find a young Jesus breaking Sabbath law and amazing witnesses:

> When the child Jesus was five years old, he was playing by the ford of a stream; and he gathered the flowing waters into pools and made them immediately pure. These things he ordered simply by speaking a word. He then made some soft mud and fashioned twelve sparrows from it. It was the Sabbath when he did this. A number of other children were also playing with him. But when a certain Jew saw what Jesus had done while playing on the Sabbath, he left right away and reported to his father, Joseph, "Look, your child at the stream has taken mud and formed twelve sparrows. He has profaned the Sabbath!" When Joseph came to the place and saw what had happened, he cried out to him, "Why are you doing what is forbidden on the Sabbath?" But Jesus clapped his hands and cried to the sparrows, "Be gone!" And the sparrows took flight and went off, chirping. When the Jews saw this they were amazed; and they went away and reported to their leaders what they had seen Jesus do.
>
> —*Inf. Gos. Thom.* 2:1–5[13]

Some scholars see significance in this gospel's portrayal of the boy Jesus as a miracle worker. Ancient critics of Christianity sometimes charged that Jesus' miracles were not unique. For example, a second-century skeptic named Celsus (about 170 CE) charged that as an adult, Jesus learned to practice magic when he traveled to Egypt (see Matt 2:13–15). Early Christians could use the *Infancy Gospel of Thomas* to affirm that Jesus was always able to work miracles.

Infancy Gospel of James

Known also as the *Book of James* or the *Protevangelium of James* (to be distinguished from the New Testament Epistle of James), the *Infancy Gospel of James* narrates Jesus' birth but focuses mostly on events that took place prior to his birth, especially the childhood of Mary. The author may well have known the infancy narratives of the Gospels of Matthew and Luke, because parts of this gospel develop further details from Matthew 1–2 and Luke 1–2. For example, *Protevangelium of James* 11:1–9 tells of Mary being told by an angel of her miraculous pregnancy (compare Luke 1:26–38).

This infancy gospel enjoyed enormous popularity in subsequent centuries, preserving details about the life of Mary that many Christians believe to this day, such as the names of Mary's parents (Anna and Joachim, *Prot. Jas.* 4:1–2) or the notion that Joseph was considerably older than Mary. The *Infancy Gospel of James* also reports that Joseph had children from an earlier marriage (*Prot. Jas.* 9:2) and includes the tradition that Mary was sixteen when she gave birth to Jesus:

> And she remained three months with Elizabeth. Day by day her womb grew, and Mary was afraid and went into her house and hid herself from the children of Israel. And Mary was sixteen years old when all these mysterious things happened.
>
> —*Prot. Jas.* 12:3[14]

Protevangelium of James 16:1–2 records the rather remarkable story of the high priest's accusation that Joseph impregnated Mary before their marriage. In this passage, Joseph and Mary are made "to drink the water of the conviction of the Lord" (*Prot. Jas.* 16:1). According to Numbers 5:11–31 in the Hebrew Scriptures, the priest is to give a woman suspected of adultery the water of testing. If she is guilty, the water will cause a brutal hysterectomy. Conversely, if this water does her no harm she will be exonerated. In *Protevangelium of James* 16:1–2, this passage about the "water of the conviction" demonstrates to all, including the Jewish high priest, that Mary was indeed a virgin when Jesus was conceived. This text may again be in response to the critic Celsus, who charged that Jesus' father was not Joseph, but rather a Roman soldier named Panertha. In Greek, the term *parthenos* means "virgin," and the name may be a play on words by the author of *Protevangelium of James*.

We turn next to two extracanonical narrative gospels that focus on Jesus' passion: the *Gospel of Peter* and the *Gospel of Judas*.

Gospel of Peter

The *Gospel of Peter* exists today in only one fragmentary manuscript found in the tomb of a Christian monk buried in Egypt in the late nineteenth century. The fragments contain the passion and Resurrection narrative, beginning with the story of Pilate washing his hands at Jesus' trial and concluding with events associated with Jesus' Resurrection. It is possible that the original *Gospel of Peter* contained the public ministry of Jesus as well, because what we have of this partial manuscript seems to begin in the middle of a longer narrative and then closely follows the passion narrative as found in the New Testament Gospels, especially Matthew.

Although the *Gospel of Peter* overlaps at numerous points with the passion narratives of the New Testament Gospels, it also contains several distinctive depictions of Jesus' passion. For example, this extracanonical gospel narrates Jesus' emergence from the tomb, a detail not found in the four New Testament Gospels, and presents the cross of Jesus speaking:

> When the soldiers saw these things, they woke up the centurion and the elders—for they were also there on guard. As they were explaining what they had seen, they saw three men emerge from the tomb, two of the men supporting the other, with a cross following behind them. The heads of the two reached up to the sky, but the head of the one they were leading went up above the skies. And they heard a voice from the skies, "Have you preached to those who are asleep?" And a reply came from the cross, "Yes."
>
> — *Gos. Pet.* 38–42[15]

Some scholars have argued that the *Gospel of Peter*, a gospel focused on the passion of Jesus, may have been one source that Matthew, Mark, and Luke shared in common in writing their passion narratives.[16]

Gospel of Judas

Recently, the 'Gnostic' *Gospel of Judas* has gained widespread attention.[17] Although the *Gospel of Judas* is mentioned by some of the early Church fathers, no extant copies of the manuscript were thought to exist until 1983, when the gospel came to light among a group of Greek and Coptic (the Egyptian language of the second century CE) manuscripts.[18] Some scholars see a strikingly different picture of Judas than that found in the New Testament Gospels.[19] Rather than characterizing Judas as willingly betraying Jesus, this gospel presents a reluctant Judas whom Jesus must convince to betray him. The betrayal of Jesus is necessary, according to the *Gospel of Judas*, for Jesus to return to his heavenly father. According to this gospel, this infamous disciple is actually a reluctant hero:

> Judas said to Jesus, "Look, what will those who have been baptized in your name do?" Jesus said, "Truly I say to you, this baptism [. . .] my name [. . . about nine lines missing] to me. Truly I say to you Judas [those who] offer sacrifices to Saklas [. . .] God [. . . three lines missing] everything that is evil. But you will exceed all of them. For you will sacrifice the man that clothes me."

> — *Gos. Jud.* 56

Other scholars see a more traditional portrayal of Judas in the *Gospel of Judas*—one that presents Judas as the disciple who willingly betrays Jesus.[20] These strikingly different scholarly interpretations—a good Judas or a bad Judas—often come down to how scholars translate specific Greek words.[21] For example, the Greek word *daimōn* in *Gospel of Judas* 44. Whereas some scholars translate *daimōn* as "spirit," others translate it as "demon." Thus two different translations are rendered:

> "O thirteenth spirit, why do you try so hard?"[22]
> "O thirteenth demon, why do you try so hard?"[23]

Translating *daimōn* as "demon" presents Judas in the more traditional role of bad Judas.

A possible apologetic intent of the *Gospel of Judas* might be to explain how it was Jesus was betrayed by one of his own followers, an apology likewise taken up in the New Testament Gospel of Luke. For his part, Luke explains Judas' treacherous behavior by saying, "Satan entered into Judas" (see Luke 22:3–4).

Sayings Gospels

Found in the Nag Hammadi writings, the "sayings gospels" present sayings of Jesus without any narrative framework or plot. That is to say, in these gospels we read only Jesus' words and nothing about his deeds. Each of these sayings gospels represents various aspects of the theology of 'Gnostic' Christianity.[24]

Gospel of Thomas

Of all the extracanonical gospels, the *Gospel of Thomas* has commanded the most attention in recent scholarship. This gospel deserves special attention because of its possibly early composition, its resemblance to the hypothesized "sayings source" Q for Matthew and Luke, and its parallels with the Synoptics.

The *Gospel of Thomas* is comprised entirely of 114 sayings, mostly attributed to Jesus. Unlike the other extracanonical gospels discovered to date, the *Gospel of Thomas* has many parallels in Matthew, Mark, and Luke.[25] This has led scholars to ask about a possible direct literary relationship between *Thomas* and the Synoptics. To this day, scholars are divided over whether *Thomas* borrows from and rewrites Synoptic materials or preserves earlier and independent versions of the Synoptics. We need not assume, however, that all sayings in the Coptic translation of *Thomas* are either pre-Synoptic or post-Synoptic. Some scholars maintain that the question of literary relationship should be posed for each individual saying in the *Gospel of Thomas*, leaving open the possibility that the Coptic version of this gospel preserves an eclectic mix of sayings from the first, second, and even third centuries.

Evidence of the *Gospel of Thomas* was first discovered in 1899 in Oxyrhynchus, Egypt, where three Greek fragments of the gospel were unearthed. In 1945, a much fuller version of the *Gospel of Thomas*, written in Coptic, was found among the Nag Hammadi writings. Scholars were intrigued that the Coptic translation of *Thomas* included sayings preserved in the three Greek-language papyrus fragments found at Oxyrhynchus. This correlation prompted the since hotly debated question of how much of the fuller Coptic version of the *Gospel of Thomas* existed in Greek in the second or possibly even the first century.

The sayings throughout the *Gospel of Thomas*—with their alternately Synoptic and 'Gnostic' parallels—may in fact point to a complicated redaction history behind this gospel. Indeed, it is possible that the Coptic version of the *Gospel of Thomas* found at Nag Hammadi is the third-century 'Gnostic' result of a transformed original Christian gospel from the late first or second century CE.

The *Gospel of Thomas* also intrigues scholars because it bears a striking resemblance to Q—the list of Jesus' sayings that Matthew and Luke used as a source to compose their Gospels. Some scholars speculate that both Q and *Thomas* were, therefore, precursors to the narrative gospels of the New Testament.

Some of the sayings in the *Gospel of Thomas* have clear 'Gnostic' overtones with their emphasis on knowledge and negative view of the created world. For example, saying 56:

> Jesus said, "He who has come to understand the world has found a corpse, and the world is not worthy of him who has found a corpse."

Still other sayings of Jesus as recorded in *Thomas* seem to have parallels in the Synoptic Gospels. Consider the following:

Thomas 20	Matt 13:31–32	Mark 4:30–32	Luke 13:18–19
The disciples said to Jesus, "Tell us what is the kingdom of heaven like." He said to them, "It is like a grain of mustard	He proposed another parable to them. "The kingdom of heaven is like a mustard seed	He said, "To what shall we compare the kingdom of God, or what parable can we use for it? It is	Then he said, "What is the kingdom of God like? To what can I compare it? It is like a mustard

(cont'd.)

(*Thomas* 20 cont'd.)	(Matt 13:31–32 cont'd.)	(Mark 4:30–32 cont'd.)	(Luke 13:18–19 cont'd.)
seed, smaller than all seeds. But when it falls on cultivated ground, the soil puts forth a large branch and provides a shelter for the birds of heaven."	that a person took and sowed in a field. It is the smallest of all seeds, yet when full-grown it is the largest of plants. It becomes a large bush, and the 'birds of the sky come and dwell in its branches.'"	like a mustard seed that, when it is sown in the ground, is the smallest of all the seeds on the earth. But once it is sown, it springs up and becomes the largest of plants and puts forth large branches, so that the birds of the sky can dwell in its shade."	seed that a person took and planted in the garden. When it was fully grown, it became a large bush and 'the birds of the sky dwelt in its branches.'"

Observations like these have led scholars to postulate that *Thomas* may, in fact, preserve both very early (possibly original?) versions of Jesus' sayings as well as more theologically developed and later 'Gnostic' sayings. In other words, the Coptic version of *Thomas* discovered at Nag Hammadi may be a significantly more developed and expanded version than the very early Greek text upon which the three Oxyrhynchus papyri were based. Such a composite text layered with sayings attributed to Jesus could range in date of composition from the mid-first century to the second or even third century CE. In recent decades, a minority of scholars have even argued that some or all of the *Gospel of Thomas* is rooted in the first century CE, perhaps as early as the 50s CE.

Gospel of Mary

Half of the manuscript containing the *Gospel of Mary* found at Nag Hammadi is missing. Although two Greek manuscripts of this gospel also exist, dating to the third century CE, these, too, are fragmented. Consequently, the *Gospel of Mary*, like so many other extracanonical gospels, is only partially known.

Although the surviving manuscripts do not list a title for this work, scholars have dubbed it the *Gospel of Mary* because Mary Magdalene is the gospel's subject, and in it she is accorded a high status among the other apostles. In this gospel, Jesus reveals to Mary the true ('Gnostic') nature of reality. This, in turn, creates a special relationship between Mary and Jesus that is not shared with the other apostles. For example, at one point Peter says to Mary:

> "Sister, we know that the Savior loved you more than the rest of the women. Tell us the words of the Savior which you remember—which you know (but) we do not, nor have we heard them." Mary answered and said, "What is hidden from you I will proclaim to you."
>
> —*Gos. Mary* 10[26]

Typical of the gospels discovered at Nag Hammadi (the *Gospel of Mary*, the *Gospel of Philip*, and *Dialogue of the Savior*), the dialogue between Mary and Jesus and the apostles occurs in a post-Easter context: it is the resurrected Christ with whom Mary, Philip, and the other apostles interact. Insider "knowledge" (from the Greek, *gnōsis*) is often passed on from the resurrected Christ and then shared among the apostles.

Gospel of Philip

The *Gospel of Philip* may be one of the most difficult extracanonical gospels to understand. Thoroughly 'Gnostic' in orientation, it is actually less a sayings gospel and more a random collection of mystical reflections on the sacramental theology of the group or the individual behind this gospel. *Philip* includes reflections on baptism, anointing, Eucharist, salvation, and the "bridal chamber." Scholars do, however, consider *Philip* a "gospel," because it presents the words of the resurrected Christ to his followers.

The *Gospel of Philip* provides little context for understanding the specifics of its 'Gnostic' sacramentals. The bridal chamber in particular has caught the attention of scholars, who search for the meaning of this image and sacrament within the complex and diverse movement of 'Gnosticism.'

One of the more intriguing texts preserved in *Philip* speaks of the relationship between Jesus and three women named Mary.

> Three women always used to walk with the Lord: Mary his mother, his sister, and the Magdalene, who is called his companion. For "Mary" is the name of his sister and his mother, and it is the name of his partner.
>
> — *Gos. Phil.* 28[27]

The New Testament Gospels speak of Mary, Jesus' mother, and Mary Magdalene. They also speak of Jesus' having sisters (see Mark 6:3; Matt 13:54), but do not mention any of them by name. *Philip*'s reference to Mary Magdalene as Jesus' "companion" is another distinctive characterization that has recently been popularized in Dan Brown's best-selling novel, *The Da Vinci Code*. Brown uses this gospel as a source for his plot and interprets "companion" to mean "spouse" of Jesus. Some English translations use the word "lover." In the New Testament Gospels, Mary Magdalene is never portrayed this way, although she is presented in close association with Jesus and the Twelve (see Luke 8:1–3). This New Testament association may be all that the *Gospel of Philip* implies as well.

Dialogue of the Savior

Dialogue of the Savior is another fragmented gospel. As with many extracanonical gospels, no Church fathers, or other ancient sources, indicate any awareness of this gospel. However, *Dialogue of the Savior* has close parallels to the New Testament Gospels, especially the Gospels of Matthew, Luke, and John, as well as another extracanonical gospel, the *Gospel of Thomas*. For example, both the *Gospel of Thomas* and *Dialogue of the Savior* (like the New Testament Gospels) speak of an eschatology ("end-time") with present and future dimensions:[28]

Jesus said, "Let him who seeks continue seeking until he finds. When he finds, he will become troubled. When he becomes troubled, he will be astonished, and he will rule over the all." —*Gos. Thom.* 2	The Savior said to his disciples, "Already the time has come, brothers, for us to abandon our labor and stand at rest. For whoever stands at rest will rest 'forever.'" —*Dial. Sav.* 1

What remains of this fragmented gospel appears mostly to be a dialogue between the "Savior" or the "Lord" and three named disciples: Judas, Mary, and Matthew. Some of the dialogue between Jesus and these disciples is 'Gnostic' in tone, articulating a negative view of material things:

> The Lord said, "Brother [Matthew], you will not be able to see it [as long as you are] carrying flesh around."
>
> — *Dial. Sav.* 28

Other dialogue material seems to elaborate traditional sayings found in the New Testament Gospels, such as the prologue to the Gospel of John 1:1–18, where Jesus is spoken of as "the Word":

> He [said] to them, "That which supports [the earth] is that which supports heaven. When a Word comes forth from the Greatness, it will come on what supports the heaven and the earth. For the earth does not move. Were it to move, it would fall. But it neither moves nor falls, in order that the First Word might not fail. For it was that which established the cosmos and inhabited it and inhaled fragrance from it."
>
> — *Dial. Sav.* 34

The dialogue shared between Jesus and the three disciples has led scholars to conclude that *Dialogue of the Savior* is the author's attempt to reinterpret the sayings of Jesus in light of 'Gnostic' theology.

Summary of Interpreting the Gospels

Core Concepts

- The extracanonical gospels exemplify how traditions about Jesus continued to flourish and evolve during the second and later centuries.
- These gospels offer a more complete witness to early Christian understandings of Jesus and a more complete view of the sources for early Christian theology.

(cont'd.)

(summary of interpreting the gospels cont'd.)

Supplemental Information

- The extracanonical gospels can be divided into sayings gospels, Judaic-Christian gospels, and narrative gospels.
- The *Gospel of Thomas* has received much scholarly attention owing to its parallels to the New Testament Gospels and Q.
- Some extracanonical gospels focus on Jesus' infancy (the *Infancy Gospel of Thomas* and *Infancy Gospel of James*), while others focus on Jesus' passion (the gospels of *Peter* and *Judas*).
- Several of the gospels discovered at Nag Hammadi provide evidence of the complex system of 'Gnosticism.'

Overview of the Extracanonical Gospels[29]

Gospel	Attribution	Date and Place of Composition	Surviving Witnesses and Discovery
Gospel of the Nazareans	unknown, no attribution	approximately 125–150 CE, perhaps in Beroea	fragmented references, early Church fathers
Gospel of the Hebrews	unknown, no attribution	approximately 125 CE, perhaps in Alexandria, Egypt	fragmented references, early Church fathers
Gospel of the Ebionites	unknown, no attribution	approximately 125–150 CE, perhaps in the Transjordan	fragmented references, early Church fathers

(cont'd.)

(overview of the extracanonical gospels cont'd.)

Gospel	Attribution	Date and Place of Composition	Surviving Witnesses and Discovery
Infancy Gospel of Thomas	unknown, attributed to "Thomas the Israelite"	approximately 125–150 CE, unknown place of composition	as early as sixth century CE, many manuscripts, languages
Infancy Gospel of James	unknown, attributed to James, "brother of the Lord"	approximately 150–180 CE, unknown place of composition	as early as third century CE, many manuscripts, languages
Gospel of Peter	unknown, attributed to Peter, apostle	approximately 150 CE, perhaps in Syria	1886–87 in three fragments
Gospel of Judas	unknown, no attribution	approximately 150–180 CE, perhaps in Beni Masah, Egypt	1970s, in one manuscript
Gospel of Thomas	unknown, attributed to "Didymus Judas Thomas"	approximately 140 CE, perhaps in Syria	1945, part of the Nag Hammadi Library, also Greek fragments
Gospel of Mary	unknown, no attribution	approximately 150–180 CE, unknown place of composition	1945, part of the Nag Hammadi Library, fragmented copy; also Greek fragments
Gospel of Philip	unknown, no attribution	approximately 150–180 CE, in Syria	1945, part of the Nag Hammadi Library
Dialogue of the Savior	unknown, no attribution	approximately 150 CE, unknown place of composition	1945, part of the Nag Hammadi Library, fragmented copy

Questions for Review

1. How do we know about the Judaic-Christian gospels of the *Hebrews*, the *Ebionites*, and the *Nazareans*?

2. What is the focus of both the *Infancy Gospel of Thomas* and the *Infancy Gospel of James*? In what ways do these gospels respond to second-century critics like Celsus?

3. What was the significance of the archeological discovery at Nag Hammadi in 1945?

4. Why does this chapter devote special attention to the *Gospel of Thomas*?

5. What is the difference between a narrative gospel and a sayings gospel?

6. How have some of these extracanonical gospels been discovered?

7. In what context did the early Church fathers discuss some of these extracanonical gospels?

8. Why do many of the extracanonical gospels have apostles' names attributed to them?

9. When do scholars think most of the extracanonical gospels were written?

10. What do we know of the intended audiences of the extracanonical gospels?

Questions for Reflection

1. Explain what is meant by *extracanonical* and *canonical* and distinguish between the two.

2. Do the extracanonical gospels have merit today? Explain your response.

3. Why do you think the early Christians stopped writing gospels about Jesus?

4. The extracanonical gospels have been viewed as both a threat and an opportunity to further reflect on Jesus' life and significance. Explain this mixed response.

Recommendations for Further Reading

Ehrman, Bart D. *Lost Scriptures: Books That Did Not Make It into the New Testament.* New York: Oxford University Press, 2003.

As his subtitle indicates, Ehrman provides a collection of early Christian writings that were not included in the canon of the New Testament. These writings, which reveal the diverse voices of early Christianity, are divided into fifteen gospels, five acts of the apostles, thirteen epistles and related writings, as well as several apocalypses and revelatory treatises. Ehrman includes a brief introduction to each writing.

Elliott, J.K. *The Apocryphal New Testament: A Collection of Apocryphal Christian Literature in an English Translation.* Oxford: Clarendon, 1993.

Similar to Ehrman but with more technical information, Elliott provides in one volume a collection of early Christian extracanonical gospels, acts, epistles, and apocalypses. Elliott offers a more extended introduction to these writings than does Ehrman, and also supplies patristic citations, extant editions, and a list of modern translations.

Klauck, Hans-Josef. *Apocryphal Gospels: An Introduction.* London and New York: T & T International, 2003.

An excellent introduction to the extracanonical gospels, *Apocryphal Gospels* begins by placing the modern study of these gospels in context. Klauck divides the gospels into groups, including fragments, infancy gospels, gospels about Jesus' death and Resurrection, and gospels from Nag Hammadi. He then summarizes the gospels and reflects on their significance.

Robinson, James M., ed. *The Nag Hammadi Library.* 3d ed. San Francisco: Harper and Row, 1988.

Robinson provides translations of the forty-five documents discovered at Nag Hammadi, including the extracanonical gospels. After an extended introduction, in which Robinson describes the discovery of these gospels, he notes the assorted literature found at Nag Hammadi and discusses important developments in the study of 'Gnosticism' in the 1970s and 1980s. Various scholars then introduce and translate each Nag Hammadi text. This is one of the best single-volume resources available for the documents of the Nag Hammadi Library.

Williams, Michael Allen. *Rethinking "Gnosticism": An Argument for Dismantling a Dubious Category.* Princeton, N.J.: Princeton University Press, 1996.

Williams provides a first-rate contemporary discussion of the complex, ancient religious movement that scholars for centuries have called 'Gnosticism.' As the title indicates, the author argues that the work of even twentieth-century scholars has contributed to an uncertain and misleading representation of this religious movement; therefore, some "rethinking" about what we call 'Gnosticism' is in order. 'Gnosticism' is far more complex and diverse than previously imagined, and according to Williams, we should no longer use the term *Gnostic* to describe this diverse phenomenon.

Endnotes

1 See John P. Meier, *A Marginal Jew: The Roots of the Problem and the Person* (vol. 1; New York and London: Doubleday, 1991), 140, where he highlights three basic points. Meier discusses the extracanonical gospels as potential sources for the historical Jesus, 112–66. He sees these gospels as secondary to, and often derivative of, the canonical gospels, and therefore not helpful in the quest for the historical Jesus.

2 See James A. Kelhoffer, "'How Soon a Book' Revisited: EUAGGE-LION as a Reference to 'Gospel' Materials in the First Half of the Second Century," *Zeitschrift für die neutestamentliche Wissenschaft und die Kunde der älteren Kirche*, 95/1–2 (2004): 1–34. Kelhoffer questions when the term *gospel*, used by early Christian writers, would have referred to the written gospels of the New Testament. He argues for an early date, between the composition of the Gospel of Matthew and the writing of the *Didache*.

3 See William L. Pederson, "Textual Traditions Examined: What the Text of the Apostolic Fathers Tells Us about the Text of the New Testament in the Second Century," in *The Reception of the New Testament in the Apostolic Fathers* (ed. Andrew Gregory and Christopher Tuckett; Oxford: Oxford University Press, 2005), 29–46, where Pedersen describes the New Testament Gospels in the second century as neither stable nor established.

4 See Irenaeus, *Against Heresies*, 1.31.1: "Others again declare that Cain derived his being from the Power above, and acknowledge that Esau, Korah, the Sodomites, and all such persons, are related to themselves. On this account, they add, they have been assailed by the Creator, yet no one of them has suffered injury. For Sophia was in the habit of carrying off that which belonged to her from them to herself. They declare that Judas the traitor was thoroughly acquainted with these things, and that he alone, knowing the truth as no others did, accomplished the mystery of the betrayal; by him all things, both earthly and heavenly, were thus thrown into confusion. They produce a fictitious history of this kind, which they style the Gospel of Judas."

5 See Origen, *On Matthew*, 10.17: "They thought, then, that He (Jesus) was the son of Joseph and Mary. But some say, basing it on a tradition in the Gospel according to Peter, as it is entitled, or 'The Book of James,' that the brethren of Jesus were sons of Joseph by a former wife, whom he married before Mary."

6 See Epiphanius, *Against Heresies*, 30.13: "In the Gospel of Matthew used by them—not in a perfect but in a mutilated and castrated form—called the Gospel of the Hebrews, it is recorded: 'And there was a man named Jesus, and he was about thirty years old; he has chosen us and he came into Capernaum and entered into the house of Simon, sur-named Peter, and he opened his mouth and said, "As I walked by the sea of Tiberius, I chose John and James, the sons of Zebedee, and Simon and Andrew and Thaddaeus and Simon Zelotes, and Judas Iscariot; you also, Matthew, when you were sitting at the receipt of custom, did I call you and you followed me. According to my intention you shall be twelve apostles for a testimony to Israel."'" This quote of Epiphanius is taken from Elliott, 14–15.

7 See Robinson, *The Nag Hammadi Library*, for an English translation of all the Nag Hammadi texts, along with brief introductions.

8 See Hans-Josef Klauck, *Apocryphal Gospels: An Introduction* (London and New York: T & T International, 2003), which includes a discussion of the titles associated with these extracanonical gospels.

9 See Klauck, 36–37, for a discussion on whether these three Judaic-Christian gospels were originally one, two, or three gospels.

10 For a translation of the seven fragments, see J.K. Elliott, *The Apocry-phal New Testament: A Collection of Apocryphal Christian Literature in an English Translation* (Oxford: Clarendon, 1993), 14–16.

11 This quote of Clement of Alexandria is taken from a translation by Elliott, 9.

12 The final episode of this gospel (*Inf. Gos. Thom* 19) parallels Luke 2:41–52: both speak of Jesus at age twelve, lost and found by his parents in the Temple in Jerusalem.

13 This translation of the *Infancy Gospel of Thomas* 19:1–13 is taken from the translation of Elliott, 81.

14 This translation of *Protevangelium of James* 12.3 is taken from the translation of Elliott, 62.

15 This translation of the *Gospel of Peter* 38–42 is taken from the transla-tion of Elliott, 156–57.

16 For an early, influential study on the *Gospel of Peter* and its relationship to the New Testament Gospels, particularly the passion narrative, see John Dominic Crossan, *The Cross That Spoke: The Origins of the Passion Narrative* (San Francisco: HarperCollins, 1992).

17 For an excellent overview and discussion of this gospel, see Bart D. Ehrman, *The Lost Gospel of Judas Iscariot: A New Look at Betrayer and Betrayed* (New York: Oxford University Press, 2006). See also Rodolphe Kasser, Marvin Meyer, and Gregor Wurst, eds., *The Gospel of Judas from Codex Tchacos* (Washington, DC: National Geographic, 2006); Herbert Krisney, *The Lost Gospel: The Quest for the Gospel of Judas Iscariot* (Washington, DC: National Geographic, 2006). See also April D. DeConick, *The Thirteenth Apostle: What the Gospel of Judas Really Says* (New York and London: Continuum, 2007), 45 – 94, who challenges the translation of the *Gospel of Judas* offered by Meyer and Ehrman, as well as their presentation of Judas as reluctantly betraying Jesus.

18 Much mystery still surrounds the complicated history of transmission of this fragmented manuscript, but it is thought to have first been discovered in the 1970s by an Egyptian treasure hunter near the village of Beni Masah, Egypt.

19 See Ehrman and Meyer.

20 See DeConick.

21 For a discussion on the scholarly debate between translations of the *Gospel of Judas* and the presentation of Judas as either good or bad, see Thomas Bartlett, "The Betrayal of Judas: Did a 'Dream Team' of Biblical Scholars Mislead Millions?" *The Chronicle Review* (May 30, 2008): 6 – 10.

22 Meyer's translation.

23 DeConick's translation.

24 For background reading on 'Gnosticism,' see Kurt Rudolph, *Gnosis: The Nature and History of 'Gnosticism'* (San Francisco: Harper and Row, 1977) and Bentley Layton, *The 'Gnostic' Scriptures* (Garden City, N.Y.: Doubleday, 1987). For an updated discussion on 'Gnosticism,' see Michael Allen Williams, *Rethinking "Gnosticism": An Argument for Dismantling a Dubious Category* (New Jersey: Princeton University Press, 1996). Information for the sidebar "'Gnosticism' and 'Gnostic' Christians" is taken from the excellent work of Williams, *Rethinking "Gnosticism."*

25 See Elliott, 133 – 35, for a list of New Testament parallels (mostly Matthew, Mark, and Luke) to the *Gospel of Thomas.*

26 This translation of the *Gospel of Mary* 10 is taken from the translation of MacRae and Wilson, in James M. Robinson, ed., *The Nag Hammadi Library: The Definitive New Translation of the 'Gnostic' Scriptures, Complete in One Volume* (3d ed.; San Francisco: Harper and Row, 1988), 525.

27 This translation of the *Gospel of Philip* 28 comes from Bentley Layton, *The Gnostic Scriptures* (Garden City, N.Y.: Doubleday, 1987), 335.

28 Translation of the *Dialogue of the Savior* and the *Gospel of Thomas* is taken from the English translation in Robinson, *The Nag Hammadi Library*.

29 The data for this overview chart is taken from numerous secondary sources: Bart D. Ehrman, *Lost Scriptures: Books That Did Not Make It into the New Testament* (New York: Oxford University Press, 2003); Wilhelm Schneemelcher, *New Testament Apocrypha: Gospels and Related Writings* (vol. 1; Louisville, Ky.: Westminster John Knox Press, 1991); Robert J. Miller, ed., *The Complete Gospels* (Santa Rosa, Calif.: Polebridge, 1994); Robinson, *The Nag Hammadi Library*; Elliott, *The Apocryphal New Testament*.

Index